Accountability in Reading Instruction

The Charles E. Merrill
COMPREHENSIVE READING PROGRAM

Arthur W. Heilman
Consulting Editor

Accountability in Reading Instruction

Lucille B. Strain
Northeast Louisiana University

Charles E. Merrill Publishing Company
A Bell & Howell Company
Columbus, Ohio

Published by
Charles E. Merrill Publishing Company
A Bell & Howell Company
Columbus, Ohio   43216

This book was set in *Bodoni Book* and *Optima*.
The Production Editor was Susan Sylvester-Glick.
The cover was designed by Will Chenoweth.

Library of Congress Cat. Card No 75–11323
International Standard Book No. 0–675–08680–9

Printed in the United States of America
1 2 3 4 5 6 7 8 — 80 79 78 77 76

Preface

The demand for educational accountability, compelling and pervasive at all levels of education and in all areas of the curriculum, is particularly relevant in reading instruction. The crux of accountability is whether results accruing from education become definite, identifiable, and measurable. Similarly, effectiveness of reading instruction can be claimed only to the extent to which it produces in learners specific, observable evidence of competencies in reading.

This book focuses on establishing accountability in basic procedures essential for improving reading instruction. Accountability is achievable in education only if its principles are understood and implemented by classroom teachers themselves. Only through informed and dedicated efforts by teachers can the concept of accountability be realized in education.

The concept of accountability can be applied most directly to development of behaviors that are highly tangible in nature. Applications that are less direct, but just as important, can be made to promote the less tangible behaviors sought as a result of humanistic education. Both reading achievement and reading instruction require balanced emphasis on both cognitive and affective behaviors.

This book is addressed, primarily, to persons who are or will be teaching reading. It seeks to assist users in developing a perspective toward the total process of reading instruction and its relation to educational accountability. Accountability in reading instruction requires more of the teacher than knowledge of skills and concepts related to the process of reading. Effective results of reading instruction must be sought through knowledge of the learners' needs, determination of appropriate objectives, individualization of instruction, humanistic values, and careful evaluation. This book emphasizes these aspects of reading instruction, although the subject matter of reading is not ignored. To foster accountability, each chapter begins with statements of general and specific behavioral objectives which the chapter then focuses on. Teacher competencies related to the aspect of instruction discussed in the chapter are presented in each chapter and questions keyed to the behavioral objectives conclude each chapter.

The content of the book is presented in three major parts: Part I, a description of major aspects of accountability and their application to reading instruction; Part II, basic procedures in reading instruction; and Part III, an overview of concepts and skills in reading. Appendixes include (1) a glossary of terms used in discussions of educational accountability and (2) sample plans for reading instruction including objectives and criterion-referenced measures.

I extend my appreciation for the direct and indirect ways by which I have been influenced by several persons in development of this book. These persons include students to whom I have attempted to be accountable in my classes at Sacramento State University, The University of Miami, Coral Gables, Florida, Kent State University, The American University, and Howard University. Included, also, are Dr. Lowry W. Harding, Professor of Education at The Ohio State University, and members of my family, each of whom inspired and encouraged me in unique and valuable ways. Numerous administrators and teachers throughout the state of California enriched my understanding as I worked with them in the quest for educational accountability in their school districts and schools. Finally, thanks are extended to Mr. Fred Kinne and Ms. Susan Glick of Charles E. Merrill Publishing Company for their editorial reviews and comments.

Lucille B. Strain
Chevy Chase, Maryland

Contents

Page

PART I   **Introduction: Accountability in Reading Instruction**

   1   **Accountability in Reading Instruction**   **1**

Behavioral Objectives, 1
The Nature of Educational Accountability, 3
Factors Influencing the Movement Toward
   Educational Accountability, 5
The Teacher and Educational Accountability, 6
Accountability and Reading Instruction, 7
Constraints on a Teacher's
   Potential for Accountability, 8
To Whom Are Teachers Accountable? 9
Accountability and Humanistic Education, 10
For What Should Reading Teachers
   Be Accountable? 12
Summary, 15
Review Questions, 16
Selected References, 17

PART II   **Basic Procedures in Reading Instruction**

   2   **Assessing Learners' Needs in Reading**   **21**

Behavioral Objectives, 21

Page

Importance of Need Assessment in Reading
Instruction, 23
Meaning of Need Assessment in Reading
Instruction, 25
Procedures and Materials Used in Need
Assessment, 26
Planning for Need Assessment in the Classroom, 28
Assessing Needs Related to Reading Readiness, 29
Tests of Reading Readiness, 32
Individual Tests in Specific Areas of Reading
Readiness, 33
Formal Procedures and Materials for Assessing
General Needs in Reading, 34
Survey Tests for Assessing Specific Reading
Abilities and Skills, 37
More Precise Formal Measures of
Reading Abilities, 38
Oral Reading Tests, 41
Assessing Needs of Learners Through Informal
Procedures, 42
Materials for Informal Assessment of Reading
Skills and Abilities, 43
Need Assessment, Diagnosis, and Evaluation, 47
Problems in Need Assessment, 48
Competencies Required of Teachers, 49
Summary, 49
Review Questions, 50
Selected References, 52

3   Objectives For Reading Instruction   54

Behavioral Objectives, 55
The Nature of Objectives, 56
Roles of Objectives in Reading Instruction, 59
Sources of Objectives in Reading Instruction, 61
Considerations in Determination of Objectives, 65
Problems Related to Stating Objectives, 67
How to State Objectives in Reading Instruction, 68
Stating Objectives in the Cognitive Domain, 71
Stating Objectives in the Affective Domain, 71
Competencies Required of Teachers, 74
Summary, 75
Review Questions, 76
Selected References, 78

4   Individualizing Reading Instruction   80

Behavioral Objectives, 81

Page

The Necessity for Individualizing Instruction, 82
The Meaning of Individualized Reading, 86
Conventional Approaches to Individualizing
    Reading Instruction, 90
Planning for Individualizing Instruction, 93
Strategies and Materials for Individualizing
    Instruction, 97
Approaches to Reading as Means for
    Individualizing Instruction, 104
Helping Learners Develop Independence in
    Reading, 106
Competencies for Individualizing Reading
    Instruction, 109
Summary, 110
Review Questions, 110
Selected References, 112

5   Developing Interests and Attitudes in Reading   115

Behavioral Objectives, 115
Humanistic Concerns in Reading Instruction, 117
Readiness in Development of Interests and
    Attitudes, 121
Improving the Experiential Backgrounds of
    Learners, 123
Relating Reading to Other Activities
    In and Out of School, 125
Influence of the Teacher's Attitudes and
    Interests, 128
Specific Activities and Techniques for Stimulating
    Reading Interest, 130
Competencies Required of Teachers, 132
Summary, 133
Review Questions, 133
Selected References, 135

6   Evaluation of Achievement in Reading   137

Behavioral Objectives, 137
Meaning of Evaluation in Reading Instruction, 138
The Role of Measurement in Accountability, 141
Major Tests Used in Measurement of Reading
    Achievement, 144
Criteria for Selection of Standardized Tests, 145
Sources of Test Information, 149
Observational Techniques and Accountability
    in Reading Instruction, 151
Competencies Required of Teachers, 157

Page

Summary, 158
Review Questions, 158
Selected References, 159

PART III   Basic Skills and Concepts in Reading

7   Developing Skills in Word Recognition   **163**

Behavioral Objectives, 163
The Nature of Reading, 165
Readiness for Initial Reading Instruction, 168
Factors Related to Reading Readiness, 170
Typical Activities Used In
   Development of Initial Reading Readiness, 174
Developmental Readiness for Reading, 177
Emphasis in Initial Development of Word-
   Recognition Skills, 179
Approaches to Initial Reading Instruction, 184
The Developmental Nature of Reading Skills, 185
Linguistics' Influences on Development of Skills
   in Word Recognition, 195
Competencies Required of Teachers, 197
Summary, 198
Review Questions, 199
Selected References, 201

8   Skills and Abilities in Reading Comprehension   **203**

Behavioral Objectives, 203
The Nature of Reading Comprehension, 204
Factors Related to Reading Comprehension, 207
Levels of Comprehension, 212
Specific Skills in Reading Comprehension, 214
Instructional Procedures for Development of
   Reading Comprehension, 217
Skills Indirectly Influential on Reading
   Comprehension, 221
Competencies Required of Teachers, 223
Summary, 223
Review Questions, 224
Selected References, 226

Appendixes   **229**

Appendix A Glossary   231
Appendix B Instructional Units in
   Reading   237
Index   277

PART

I

Introduction: Accountability in Reading Instruction

1 Accountability in Reading Instruction

A relatively new but potent idea—at once profound, promising, complex, and even controversial—educational accountability is affecting practices and trends in all areas of the curriculum and at all levels of education. Implication of basic operations implied in the concept of educational accountability portend increased effectiveness in the results of education. Reading instruction by its very nature and reading by its uses in the curriculum and even in life are not only particularly amenable to applications of the basic tenets of accountability, but particularly in need of them for improved effectiveness. How these tenets can be applied to improve the results of reading instruction is an appropriate concern of all teachers involved in helping individuals learn to read.

Behavioral Objectives

The content of Chapter 1 is presented in such a way that after reading it, an individual

1.0 Knows basic concepts related to educational accountability

    1.1 Defines the term "educational accountability"

    1.2 Identifies the crucial focus of educational accountability

    1.3 Describes the relationship between responsibility and educational accountability

    1.4 Indicates various perspectives from which educational accountability may be viewed

    1.5 Identifies the role in instruction played by each of the following elements stressed in the concept of educational accountability:

        1.5.1 Objectives

        1.5.2 Instructional strategies

1.5.3 Instructional materials

1.5.4 Evaluation

2.0 Recognizes significant factors in the movement toward educational accountability

2.1 Identifies factors in theoretical development which support the concept of educational accountability

2.2 Describes major studies that have stimulated interest in educational accountability

2.3 Describes the role of the federal government in educational accountability

3.0 Understands the effect of accountability on the role of the teacher

3.1 Compares past and present conceptions of the teacher's role in instruction

3.2 Explains how educational accountability affects the teacher's role in relation to each of the following:

3.2.1 Planning for instruction

3.2.2 Selecting learning experiences

3.3.3 Evaluating results of instruction

4.0 Understands limitations within which a teacher can be held accountable

4.1 Explains how each of the following may operate as a constraint upon a teacher's potential for accountability:

4.1.1 Nature of learners

4.1.2 Learners' background experiences

4.1.3 Nature of the school

4.1.4 The teacher's understandings, skills, and attitudes

5.0 Knows individuals or groups to whom teachers may be considered to be accountable

5.1 Lists individuals or groups to whom teachers may be accountable

5.2 Identifies ways in which teachers can show accountability

5.3 States problems involved in determining persons to whom teachers may be accountable

6.0 Understands the relationship between accountability and humanistic education

6.1 Describes how educational accountability may influence development of humanistic education in a classroom

6.2 Explains some implications of educational accountability for humanistic education

6.3 Defines some problems that may arise when educational accountability and humanistic education are sought simultaneously

7.0 Recognizes aspects of reading instruction for which a teacher should be held accountable

7.1 States a rationale for holding the teacher of reading accountable for each of the following:

7.1.1 Assessing the needs of learners

7.1.2 Establishing objectives for reading instruction in the classroom

7.1.3 Individualizing instruction to the highest extent possible in a given situation

7.1.4 Establishing conditions for learning that have a positive effect on development of learners' attitudes and interests in reading

7.1.5 Using strategies of teaching to achieve objectives in all domains of learning

7.1.6 Utilizing effective and efficient means of evaluation

7.1.7 Possessing knowledge, understanding, and skills related to the content of reading instruction

The Nature of Educational Accountability

Shorn of specifications attributed to it by its linkage to education, accountability as a concept is not new. The term "accountability" has been used with somewhat the same meaning as the term "responsibility." Traditionally, so far as educators have been concerned, accountability has meant fulfillment of overt or tacit promises to conduct effectiveness educational programs for learners in the schools. Dictionary definitions of accountability are adequate to the extent that synonyms can be used to define such a concept. Words such as "reporting," "exploration," "justification," and "responsibility"[1] can only introduce key ideas in various interpretations currently offered for educational accountability. Emphasis in educational accountability is on identification and production of specific results ("end products") from education. If specific, identifiable results are expected to accrue from educational efforts, it follows that these can be "reported," "explained," and "justified." It should be noted, however, that reporting the results of education does not necessarily imply that the exact nature of results or the time of their occurrence can be guaranteed.

The concept of responsibility is also included in the meaning of educational accountability. Responsibility as required of educators, however, is not met satisfactorily by merely conducting programs for the general educational progress of learners. Responsibility in educational accountability focuses directly on specific, identifiable achievements by learners. According to Leon Lessinger, "the concept rests on three fundamental bases: student accomplishment, independent review of student accomplishment, and a public report relating dollars spent to student accomplishment."[2] From the standpoint of the teacher, accountability means that learners will be helped to develop behaviors that are specific, measurable, and reportable. A more detailed examination of the nature of educational accountability, however, reveals several different perspectives from which it may be perceived.

Educational Accountability as an Attitude

Viewed from one perspective, educational accountability can be described as an attitude that should characterize persons involved in various phases of the educational process in the schools. This attitude is marked by commitment to the idea that education should make a significant difference in the behaviors of learners to whom it is directed and it is expressed in serious concern that pointless educational practices are replaced by practices that lead to the achievement of recognizable objectives productive for, and relevant to the needs of, the particular learners involved in a program. Accountability as an attitude is re-

---

[1] *The Random House Dictionary of the English Language*, unabridged edition (N. Y.: Random House, 1966), p. 10, "accountability."

[2] L. M. Lessinger, "The Powerful Notion of Accountability in Education" (paper presented at the Academy on Educational Engineering, Oregon State Department of Public Instruction, Werme, Oregon, August, 1970).

flected in respect shown for the potentialities and personality of each learner subject to the demands of education. It is an attitude that recognizes the right of each person to know what is expected of him and to participate, actively, in achieving those expectations.

Educational accountability as an attitude should be embraced by educators at all levels of the educational system. For instance, among classroom teachers' attitudes should be willingness to assess the needs of individuals and use results of the assessment as one basis for instructional objectives. Teachers should select strategies for instruction and use these in light of their objectives. Further, attitudes held by administrators should reflect willingness to establish the kinds of conditions favorable for effective instruction. Favorable conditions include classes of sizes appropriate for the faculty and staff available. Included also are essential materials and other resources for teaching and learning. In general, administrators should give priority to facilitating the teacher's work. All educators should embrace attitudes that regard the individual as the central concern in education.

Educational Accountability Linked with a System Approach to Education

From another perspective, educational accountability can be viewed as a concomitant of a system approach to education. Several models have been suggested in educational literature as system approaches that can be applied to various aspects of education, including instruction.[3] Use of several clearly defined steps characterizes most of these "systems." Steps generally recommended include (1) a comprehensive assessment of the needs of learners involved in a program, (2) determination of objectives that mark the direction learning will take, (3) selection and use of strategies and materials to facilitate achievement of the objectives, and (4) use of evaluation as a continuous, comprehensive, and cooperative process focused on objectives and other aspects of the instructional process.

Educational accountability as concomitant with a system approach is not restricted to use of one or more specified systems of instruction. Rather, the steps indicated here suggest an organizational framework for instruction. It is reasonable that learners should be taught those things that they do not know and need to know. In order to determine what these things are, it is essential to engage in a process of inquiry—need assessment. Largely on the basis of the results of need assessment, objectives can be determined to establish the direction that instruction will take. Evaluation is needed to give both the teacher and the learner knowledge of continuing needs and progress and to provide guideposts for further learning or modification of instructional processes. All of these functions are required in effective instruction and learning regardless of the nature of the instructional system.

Educational Accountability as Cost Effectiveness

In yet another sense, educational accountability can be viewed as achievement of desired results when products of education are ana-

---

[3] L. F. Carter, *The Systems Approach to Education: The Mystique and the Reality* (System Development Corporation, SP-3291, January, 1969).

R.A. Kaufman, "A System Approach to Education: Derivation and Definition," *A. V. Communication Review* (Winter 1968).

lyzed according to their costs. This aspect of accountability involves examination of financial investments made in education in relation to the end results or products resultant from education. The term *cost effectiveness* refers to the results of comparing units of achievement based on objectives with unit costs.[4] Although classroom teachers need to be aware of this aspect of educational accountability, details involved in cost analysis are not within the range of responsibilities that can reasonably be expected of them. Cost effectiveness, however, does rest largely on effectiveness of instructional efforts by teachers. Instructional concerns are the chief priorities of teachers. Accounting for the dollars and cents value of a unit of achievement lies outside the range of priorities with which a teacher is normally faced. Details of the process involved in determining cost effectiveness must remain the responsibility of persons other than those charged with instruction in the classroom. The teacher's energies and concerns must be focused on learners and their learning rather than upon the costs of instruction.

Factors Influencing the Movement Toward Educational Accountability

Several factors and conditions in society, generally, and in education, particularly, are influencing the intensity of the movement toward educational accountability. Outstanding among these factors are (1) the rapidly increasing costs of education, (2) a growing surplus of teachers in many areas of the curriculum, (3) the state of the national economy, (4) taxpayers' concerns about school tax issues, (5) the effects of racial integration in the schools, and (6) a seriously large number of learners deficient in basic academic skills.[5] The most immediate factor emphasizing the urgency of accountability, from the standpoint of the teacher in the classroom, is the large number of learners who continue to lack mastery of basic skills after typical instructional processes have been applied.

The movement for national assessment of education is another factor that has had a significant impact upon development of the concept of educational accountability. The National Assessment of Educational Progress has been called the "most extensive assessment project ever initiated in the United States."[6] The purpose of this project was to gather data which would indicate whether or not financial investments in education were justified in terms of student achievement. In other words, data from the National Assessment of Educational Progress were designed to offer the public a clear statement regarding effectiveness of the billions of dollars spent each year for education in the United States. Similarly, the crucial point of educa-

---

[4] Robert B. Thompson, *A Systems Approach to Instruction* (Hamden, Conn.: Shoe String Press, 1971), pp. 71-74.

[5] Frank J. Sciara and Richard K. Jantz, *Accountability in American Education* (Boston: Allyn and Bacon, 1972), p. 229.

[6] William A. Mehrens, "National Assessment for Educational Progress," *Childhood Education*, 46, No. 8 (May, 1970).

tional accountability is to permit educators and the general public to discover what is actually being accomplished in education. This assessment is vital and basic if effectiveness of education is to be improved. It is unfortunate but true that many teachers can speak only in general and vague terms regarding the nature of learners' achievements in the classrooms. In a larger sense, the results of education traditionally have been, to a large extent, obscure both to the general public and to educators at various levels in the hierarchy of professional education.

Participation by the federal government in education also has been highly influential in stimulating the movement toward educational accountability. Many of the requirements set forth for programs and projects to be funded under various Titles supported by the United States Office of Education have exemplified procedures applicable to the effectiveness of educational programs in general. For instance, need assessment, statement of precise objectives, and careful evaluation, as required in projects for which funding was sought, are recognized as basic and valid in the pursuit of educational accountability.

Perhaps the most compelling factor that has given impetus to educational accountability is that the general public and persons engaged professionally in education have grown increasingly concerned about the extent and quality of results achieved through education. This concern has been reflected in publications ranging from articles of news and opinions about educational problems in newspapers to articles and research reports in professional journals and periodicals. Several books, such as Silberman's *Crisis in the Classroom*,[7] Barr's *Who Pushed Humpty Dumpty?*,[8] and Illich's *Deschooling Society*,[9] have focused on the unsatisfactory nature of education as it has been carried out traditionally. This concern is reflected as well in increased efforts to meet the needs of diverse school populations, to accommodate various learning styles, and to make use of modern materials and technological aids to increase the effectiveness of education.

The Teacher and Educational Accountability

As is true of many broad and complex concepts in education, the concept of educational accountability has particular significance in particular positions. The teacher's position in education, for example, differs from that of the school administrator or school supervisor of instruction. Therefore, implications of the concept of educational accountability for the teacher in the classroom differ from those pertinent to people in other positions in education. It must be stressed that the differences in implications relate to implementation rather than to importance. Bowers has observed that the most profound influence of the

---

[7] Charles E. Silberman, *Crisis in the Classroom* (N. Y.: Random House, 1970).
[8] Donald Barr, *Who Pushed Humpty Dumpty?* (N. Y.: Atheneum Press, 1971).
[9] Ivan Illich, *Deschooling Society* (N. Y.: Harper and Row, 1971).

concept of educational accountability lies, perhaps, in its potential for classroom use.[10] The concept of educational accountability helps to clarify and give structure to the teacher's role in instruction. Instructional efforts, in the light of accountability, become purposeful rather than vague. A clear concept of the nature of results expected of instruction provides guidance for all other phases of the instructional process. Strategies and materials of instruction can be selected so that these are meaningful to the learners in the situation at hand. This is in contrast to the way the teacher's responsibilities in instruction often have been perceived in the past.

Traditionally, parents, school officials, and even teachers themselves have expected instruction to produce learning. This general expectation gave little, if any, direction either for instruction or for learning. Likewise, evidence that learning had resulted from teachers' efforts often tended to be vague. Results of learning have been believed to be somewhat intangible and long-range in occurring. "Having classes" or "keeping school" have too often been used as descriptions of the instructional process and its results. Implications of the concept of educational accountability add to the professional dimensions of the teacher's role in instruction.

Accountability and Reading Instruction

Implications of the concept of educational accountability are most easily implemented in those areas of the curriculum in which objectives of instruction are most tangible. Objectives at the levels of basic skill development and knowledge have been categorized as being highly tangible and measurable.[11] Somewhat less tangible, yet still capable of being measured to a relatively high degree of precision, are objectives related to basic understanding and even higher levels of thinking.[12] Since many important aspects of reading instruction are directed toward achievement of such highly tangible objectives, accountability becomes a practical pursuit. It is true that a learner's ability to decode a printed or written selection becomes highly visible in his performance. Likewise, his responses to carefully formulated questions serve to make his comprehension abilities largely apparent. In both word recognition skills and comprehension abilities, achievement can be measured to a relatively high degree of precision and objectivity.

Furthermore, the principle of accountability that stresses importance of need assessment can be applied readily in the area of reading instruction. Often a learner's needs and abilities in reading are observable even without the aid of

---

[10] C. C. Bowers, "Accountability From a Humanist Point of View," *The Educational Forum*, 35 (May, 1971), pp. 470-86.

[11] Raymond Gerberich, *Specimen Objective Test Items: A Guide to Achievement Test Construction* (N. Y.: Longman's Green, 1956), Chapters 3 and 4.

[12] Norman E. Gronlund, *Measurement and Evaluation in Teaching*, Second edition (N. Y.: Macmillan, 1971), p. 31.

sophisticated instruments and techniques of measurement. Yet, numerous types of instruments and assessment procedures are available for determining those needs in reading that cannot be observed informally.

Individualization of instruction becomes increasingly important in the face of educational accountability. Learning to read is an individual matter, and effectiveness in reading instruction demands that a high degree of individualization be achieved in each classroom situation. Recognition of the need for individualization in reading instruction is reflected in several texts in reading education.* Achieving effectiveness in helping each learner develop appropriate competencies in reading and achieving accountability in reading instruction are essentially the same concerns.

Constraints on a Teacher's Potential for Accountability

If the concept of educational accountability is to make a significant contribution to improvement of reading instruction, its implications must be perceived, realistically, from the standpoint of the teacher's power and influence. There are many variables in any learning situation that must be recognized as constraints on what the teacher is able to accomplish. Among these constraints are factors stemming from the nature of learners, the nature of their background experiences, the nature of the school in which instruction is given, and the nature of the teacher's own skills, understandings, and attitudes.

The Nature of the Learners

Many factors pertaining to the nature of the learners in a classroom are beyond the power of the teacher to affect to any significant degree. Individual differences related to ability to learn and capacity for learning, for example, are realities in any classroom group of learners regardless of the basis used for forming the group. Establishment of objectives, beyond the simplest and most basic types, with expectations that these will be achieved equally by all children in a class is an unrealistic approach to accountability. The nature of learners' background experiences functions to increase their differences and to strengthen the idea that uniform expectations for all learners are not feasible. Learners' differences must be taken into consideration in determining the teacher's potential for accountability. Clearly, the teacher's accountability cannot be based on uniform achievement for all learners in a group.

The teacher's potential for accountability is also affected by various emotional, physical, and social characteristics of learners. Problems of social or emotional

---

*For example, individualization of reading instruction is discussed at length in the following texts designed for the preparation of teachers in reading:

Walter B. Barbe, *Educator's Guide to Personalized Reading Instruction* (Englewood Cliffs, N. J.: Prentice-Hall, 1961.

Jeannette Veatch, *Individualizing Your Reading Program* (N. Y.: G. P. Putnam's Sons, 1959).

adjustments and attitudes and interests held by the learners can have either an inhibiting or expanding effect on the teacher's potential for accountability.

To be considered, as well, is the level of competency achieved by each learner prior to contact with a given teacher in a given situation. The level of competency will affect the nature and number of behavioral changes that will be developed by the learners during a period of time. Each learner must be taken on the basis of his development regardless of grade level or other designations. Level and type of achievement anticipated for any learner at any future time must depend, to an extent, upon the level of his achievement when instruction was begun. The teacher's potential for accountability must be determined within these limits.

The Nature of the School

Within any school there are conditions that inhere regardless of a teacher's influence. These, too, affect his potential for accountability. The kind of administrative control and support, the physical setting that characterizes the classroom, the size of the class, and the system of evaluating and reporting achievement of learners are examples of factors within the school that can increase or decrease the teacher's potential for accountability.

Constraints Within the Teacher

Understandings, skills, attitudes, and interests held by the teacher are possible constraints upon personal potential for accountability. Proficiency in knowledge and understanding of the content and skills of the subject involved and of the nature of human development and learning are basic in guiding instruction effectively. Skills in human relations and in methods of instruction are essential elements in the performance of the professional teacher. So, also, are his attitudes and interests related both to the area of the curriculum in which he is performing and to the learners whom he instructs. All of these can exert positive or negative influences on the degree of accountability realized.

Understandings, skills, attitudes, and interests held by the teacher are constraints on his potential for accountability over which he has a large measure of control. Acceptance of professional responsibility for instruction makes the teacher liable for his continued professional growth and development. Effective instruction of a given group of individuals in a given situation becomes a highly personal matter for the teacher. Many attributes and competencies needed for effective instruction in a situation must be determined by the teacher in the context of the particular situation.

To Whom Are Teachers Accountable?

The idea that one is accountable for something implies that there exists some person or persons to whom accounting is to be made. The concept of accountability implies that an account is made regarding the nature of the educational product. Because of the unique and complex nature of education, it is difficult to determine the specific person or persons to whom teachers are accountable.

From a practical standpoint, it is generally accepted that teachers are legally responsible to the local administration under which they work. The local administrator is answerable to the authority of state codes and governing boards. According to Stoops and Marks, "teachers are accountable in a number of ways to school authorities to whom they are responsibile."[13] This opinion is supported by other authorities in the fields of administration and supervision who have indicated that "all institutions, whether private or public, are controlled by the governing boards to which the chief executive is directly responsible."[14] In turn, "these boards are by rules and laws held responsible by their public for the overall operation of the institution."[15]

Accountability required legally of teachers can be traced immediately to the local administrator and ultimately to society represented in the governing boards of the schools. In the past, teachers' accountability to society has been of a general nature and manifest in ways other than that of detailed evidence of effectiveness as exemplified in specific behavioral changes of learners. Teachers' agreement with policies, statutes, and programs adopted by the agents of the state has been considered satisfactory evidence of their accountability.

I propose here that teachers should consider themselves accountable, not only to administrators and governing boards, but also to their clients. In all cases, this includes learners and, in many cases, their parents or guardians. Acceptance of the responsibility of classroom instruction implies acceptance of the responsibility for facilitating learning for the learners involved. Fulfillment of this responsibility, to the highest degree possible, is in the primary interest of learners, their parents or guardians, and of the teacher.

Teachers should be accountable to themselves and to their profession. In this way, interests of both teachers and learners are served. It is reasonable to expect that each and every child should have an adequate education. Teachers who are accountable to themselves and to their profession undertake to make as great a contribution as possible to the adequate education of each learner for whom they are responsible. This is the essence of professionalism in education and also of accountability.

Accountability and Humanistic Education

An area of major concern related to educational accountability involves its effect on development of those qualities and attributes

---

[13] Emery Stoops and James R. Marks, *Elementary School Supervision* (Boston: Allyn and Bacon, 1965), p. 25.

[14] Donald P. Cottrell, editor, *Teacher Education for a Free People* (Oneonta, N. Y.: The American Association of Colleges for Teacher Education, 1956), p. 361.

[15] Cottrell, *Teacher Education for a Free People*, p. 361.

sought through humanistic education. It is chiefly in relation to this concern that educational accountability is frequently attacked by its critics. Arthur W. Combs called attention to this concern when he stated

> The humane qualities we seek in education, such as positive self-concepts, feelings of identification, responsibility, openness to experience, adaptability, creativity, effective human relationships are, like any other behavior, outcomes of personal meaning; and it is here that we need to look for answers to our problems of accountability.[16]

Several formal operations stressed in the pursuit of accountability are doubtlessly responsible for the concern that their use may result in mechanization or dehumanization of education. Need assessment, use of precise and specific objectives, and application of exacting procedures for evaluation suggest to some persons that educational accountability constitutes an impersonal approach to education that may cause neglect of desirable humanistic concerns. Use of modularization, computerization, and cost effectiveness often serve to accentuate this concern.

Humanistic education focuses on development of attitudes, interests, values, and other human qualities believed to be essential and desirable in members of a democratic society. In humanistic education, emphasis is on development of the individual as a human being. Qualities such as a sense of personal worth and meaning, self-actualization, and a sense of community are paramount concerns. All of these qualities and many related ones are widely recognized goals of American education. Educational accountability, in and of itself, does not necessitate neglect of these goals of humanistic education.

Educational accountability is a complex and many-sided concept. To view it simply in terms of certain operations required in its implementation is to view it in a very limited sense. In its broad perspective, educational accountability offers a positive approach to achievement of objectives related to humanistic education. One major reason for this is that many objectives of an affective nature do not lend themselves to direct teaching. Instead of being taught directly, these must be sought as an outgrowth of the prevailing intellectual and social climates in a classroom. Intellectual and social climates are generally improved when learners become involved in their own learning through recognition and acceptance of clearly determined objectives and as they cultivate habits and skills related to independent learning.

On the other hand, it should be realized that the concept of educational accountability is not a panacea for problems in education. Implementation of the concept of educational accountability cannot apply, equally, to all areas of teaching and learning in the schools; however, many direct benefits for producing identifiable behavioral changes can accrue if accountability is sought in those areas in which objectives are primarily tangible in nature. Because of the nature of affective

---

[16] Arthur W. Combs, *Educational Accountability: Beyond Behavioral Objectives* (Washington, D. C.: Association for Supervision and Curriculum Development, 1972), p. 25.

objectives, application of accountability techniques may be expected to be more difficult and less productive of definite results.

Importance of the concept of educational accountability is not decreased, however, by recognition of its limitations. The fact that it cannot be extended with the same degree of precision to all areas of learning in the schools does not mean that its values should be abandoned. It is the teacher's responsibility to distinguish between those objectives that lend themselves to quantification and those that do not. Instruments and procedures are not yet available for yielding unquestionably accurate and precise measurement for all human qualities desirable as a result of education. In areas where the objectives are least tangible, benefits forthcoming from accountability are only incidental concomitants. Such benefits do not constitute appropriate bases for determining the value of educational accountability.

For What Should Reading Teachers Be Accountable?

Several authorities in education have proposed that all teachers, regardless of the curriculum areas in which they perform, be held accountable (1) for certain facets of learners' development and behavior, (2) for knowledge of their subject areas, (3) for purposes they attempt to carry out, and (4) for the methods they use in the attempt to meet their purposes.[17]

The question of what teachers should be held accountable for is currently a topic for debate. Many voices are discussing various philosophical and legal issues related to the matter. While larger issues remain to be resolved, this discussion will propose that teachers engaged in reading instruction be held accountable for several specific, interrelated instructional functions, all of which portend achievement of a high degree of educational accountability.

Assessment of Learners' Needs in Reading

Accountability in reading instruction begins with assessment of the needs of the learners who are to be instructed in reading. Needs of learners are related to their abilities, interests, attitudes, experiential backgrounds, and the demands of school and society. Teachers of reading should be held accountable for acquiring as thorough an acquaintance and understanding of each learner's needs as time, facilities, and other resources permit. Knowledge of essential principles involved in need assessment, and development of the required skills are important competencies for the teacher of reading. Instructional processes in classrooms should be characterized by diagnostic approaches.[18] The emphasis in

---

[17] Combs, *Educational Accountability: Beyond Behavioral Objectives*, pp. 36-37.

Henry S. Dyer, "Toward Objective Criteria of Professional Accountability in the Schools of New York City," *Phi Delta Kappan*, 52 (December, 1970), pp. 206-11.

[18] Larry A. Harris and Carl B. Smith, *Reading Instruction through Diagnostic Teaching* (N. Y.: Holt, Rinehart and Winston, 1972), p. 8.

Chapter 2 of this book is upon need assessment and use of diagnostic procedures in reading instruction.

Determination of Objectives for Reading Instruction

Teachers of reading should be held accountable for determining the objectives to give direction to the process of instruction and to the efforts of each learner. Objectives constitute a crucial basis for accountability. In the absence of definite, specified objectives, no basis exists for measurement or evaluation, and there is thus no basis for accountability. To be useful, objectives must be determined, to a major extent, in the light of the needs of each learner. Once determined, objectives provide direction for all other phases of the instructional process. These instructional concerns include selection and use of pertinent strategies and materials as well as evaluation. In short, objectives mark the beginning of and a tentative conclusion to an instructional cycle. Accountability in reading instruction requires use of objectives whose meanings are precise and whose nature will not permit varied and inaccurate interpretations. The importance, roles, and construction of objectives for reading instruction are discussed in Chapter 3.

Individualization of Reading Instruction

Obviously the degree of individualization in reading instruction that can be realized must be determined within constraints imposed by each teaching-learning situation. As a minimum, however, teachers should be held accountable for recognizing the uniqueness of each individual in a class, and for making provisions for this uniqueness to the highest degree possible. Individual uniqueness is revealed in all major characteristics of learners including their abilities, interests, learning styles, and the like. In light of what is known about individual differences, major goals of reading instruction can be achieved more certainly through use of instructional approaches that accommodate the uniqueness of individuals.

Strategies, techniques, and materials can be used to help meet individual differences in ways that are practical in most classroom situations. Major concerns in Chapter 4 involve the nature and use of these to improve individualization of reading instruction.

Humanistic Education: Development of Attitudes and Interests in Reading

Those persons directly involved in teaching learners how to read should be held accountable for simultaneously promoting development of humanistic education. In its simplest aspects, humanistic education can be interpreted as embracing learners' attitudes, interest, habits, appreciations, and the like. Strategies for instruction in how to read should be selected and used according to their potential for helping learners want to read and use reading. At the same time, the act of reading should be conducive to broadening and strengthening those humanistic attributes of individuals that make them better human beings. Although objectives related to development of humanistic attributes are difficult to specify, and even more difficult to measure or evaluate, conscious efforts should be directed to these ends.

All objectives sought through reading instruction, regardless of their categorization, are interrelated and interdependent. Effectiveness in achieving one or the other types of objectives must be sought simultaneously. Strategies used in developing skills in reading can help or hinder development of desirable attitudes and interests. Similarly, the nature of the intellectual and social climates fostered in the classroom contributes importantly to achievement of all objectives. These, and other concerns related to humanistic education and its implications for reading instruction, are discussed in Chapter 5.

Evaluation of Processes and Products of Reading Instruction

Teachers of reading should be held accountable for utilizing effective and efficient means of evaluation in every aspect of reading instruction. The meaning of evaluation should be conceived of as inclusive of both quantitative and qualitative approaches to determining the degree to which all objectives sought are achieved. Evaluation should be regarded, also, as a process that should accompany every important step in the instructional system. The concept of accountability embraces evaluation and is dependent on it to a large extent in instruction and reporting.

Appropriateness of objectives, learning experiences, and materials for individuals' use and instruction, for example, can be determined only through the process of evaluation. Likewise, evaluation is essential for determining effectiveness of those strategies used in reading instruction. Progress made by individuals toward objectives presently sought and their needs for future objectives are determined, as well, through the process of evaluation. Implications of principles of evaluation that stipulate continuity, comprehensiveness, and cooperation in the process should be recognized and implemented by teachers in undergirding practices of evaluation. In Chapter 6, attention is given to concerns related to evaluation in reading instruction.

Knowledge, Understandings, and Skills Related to Reading

Teachers should be held accountable for possessing knowledge, understandings, and skills related to what they attempt to teach. In other words, teachers must know what a learner must know and what skills he must possess in order to read effectively. A body of information related to reading as an area of the curriculum comprises some of this content. Although concepts and skills related directly to the area of reading do not all stem from textual materials, these constitute an important part of the reading teacher's background knowledge.

Many educational leaders have indicated that effective teaching in the elementary schools requires substantial knowledge of subject matter. This is true regardless of the area of the curriculum under consideration. Indicating that teachers must know not only how to teach, but what to teach, Gilbert Highet stated:

> First and most necessary of all, he (the teacher) must know the subject. He must know what he teaches. This

> sounds obvious, yet it is not always practiced.... One
> cannot understand even the rudiments of a subject
> without knowing its higher levels, at least not well enough
> to teach it....[19]

Esther G. Swenson concurs with this point of view:

> If the teacher is not thoroughly grounded in areas of the
> subject matter his students need to learn, he may not be
> effective in dealing with differences among learners. Suc-
> cess in introducing the amount of flexibility required to
> meet the needs of students possessing different goals,
> abilities, and backgrounds is dependent to a large degree
> on the security of the teacher in his field of study.[20]

Accountability in reading instruction accentuates the importance of the teacher's knowledge of content in helping learners achieve successful performance in
reading. Identification of the needs of learners, determination of objectives, and
individualization of reading instruction are among operations that are effectuated
through the teacher's ability to deal with fundamentals in reading. Furthermore,
knowledge of fundamentals in reading is essential for selection of content appropriate for learners in a particular situation. No exact blueprint exists regarding
precise concepts and skills that learners in particular situations should be helped
to develop. Chapters 7 and 8 are devoted to content considered to be basic in
reading instruction.

SUMMARY

The concept of educational accountability emphasizes
the responsibility of educators to help learners achieve specified and identifiable
results of an educational endeavor. Acceptance of responsibility merely for conducting educational programs in the traditional manner is no longer tenable when
educational accountability is expected.

Educational accountability has direct implications for improving instruction in
areas of the curriculum where objectives are highly tangible. Reading instruction,
which includes among its concerns achievement of many highly tangible behaviors,
is especially suitable for application of the tenets of accountability. Furthermore,
effectiveness in achieving results of reading instruction depends on implementation
of major operations implied in educational accountability.

The question of whom teachers should be accountable to can be answered, in a
practical sense, if teachers consider themselves primarily accountable to their
immediate clients—learners under their guidance—to themselves, and to their
profession. In this way, accountability to others involved in the educational enter-
prise can be achieved indirectly.

Many controversial issues related to educational accountability and its effect
on development of humanistic attributes can be resolved by viewing these concerns
in proper perspective. Educational accountability and humanistic education are not

---

[19] Gilbert Highet, *The Art of Teaching* (N. Y.: Vintage Books, 1959), pp. 12-14.

[20] Esther J. Swenson, "Teacher Preparation" in NSSE, *Individualizing Instruction*, 61st Yearbook (Chicago: University of Chicago Press, 1962), p. 291.

opposing concerns in education. Production of identifiable results of instruction does not, in and of itself, limit achievement of humanistic values. Interests, attitudes, habits, tastes, and appreciations that comprise humanistic concerns in education are encouraged by the nature of instructional strategies used and by the intellectual and social climates fostered in the classroom. An appropriate approach to the achievement of educational accountability and humanistic education accommodates both thrusts simultaneously.

Several factors must be recognized as constraints on the teacher's potential for educational accountability. Some of these factors are the nature of learners, their background experiences, their previously achieved levels of competencies, the nature of the school, and the competencies, interests and attitudes possessed by the teacher.

Teachers involved in reading instruction should be held accountable for implementing several basic operations in their approaches to instruction. These interrelated operations believed to be paramount in achieving educational accountability are also essential to effective reading instruction. These include (1) assessment of the needs of learners, (2) use of precise objectives based largely on the needs of learners to give direction both to instruction and to learning, (3) use of instructional strategies and materials to facilitate achievement of objectives, (4) individualization of instruction, and (5) evaluation of products and processes of instruction in accordance with the principles of comprehensiveness, continuity, and cooperation.

Review Questions

1. How does educational accountability differ from responsibility as traditionally expected of educators? **(1.1)***

2. What is the focal concern in educational accountability? **(1.2)**

3. Is there a difference between responsibility for general progress of learners and educational accountability? If so, explain the difference. **(1.3)**

4. In what ways might educational accountability be perceived differently from the perspective of persons with each of the following concerns in education? **(1.4)**
   a. School administration
   b. Supervision of instruction
   c. Classroom instruction

5. What role is played in education by each of the following factors stressed in the concept of educational accountability? **(1.5)**
   a. Need assessment
   b. Objectives
   c. Individualization of instruction
   d. Instructional strategies and materials
   e. Evaluation

6. What factors, in a major sense, seem to be responsible for giving impetus to the movement toward educational accountability? Do you agree that the factors mentioned in

---

*Boldface numbers in parentheses refer to the numbered behavioral objectives at the beginning of the chapter.

this chapter are major factors stimulating the movement toward accountability? What other factors do you believe have influenced this movement? (**2.1**)

7. What procedures and results from the national assessment of educational progress may have had some bearing on increasing the demand for educational accountability? (**2.2**)

8. How has participation by the federal government in education affected the movement toward educational accountability? (**2.3**)

9. In what ways has the concept of educational accountability contributed to changed perceptions of the teacher's role in instruction? (**3.1**)

10. Give examples of the effect of educational accountability on the following instructional activities:
    a. Planning for instruction (**3.2.1**)
    b. Selecting learning activities (**3.2.2**)
    c. Evaluating results of instruction (**3.2.3**)

11. How might the nature of each of the following factors influence the teacher's potential for accountability?
    a. Learners (**4.1.1**)
    b. Learner's background experiences (**4.1.2**)
    c. The school (**4.1.3**)

12. What individuals or groups might teachers be held accountable to? State a rationale for your selections. (**5.1**)

13. Describe ways in which the teacher can establish accountability for instruction. (**5.2**)

14. Discuss some of the problems involved in attempting to determine individuals or groups to whom teachers are accountable. (**5.3**)

15. What is humanistic education? What factors seem to foster humanistic education? (**6.1**)

16. Explain how implications of the concept of educational accountability might influence development of humanistic attributes. (**6.2**)

17. What advantages and disadvantages seem to be implied in seeking educational accountability and humanistic education simultaneously? (**6.3**)

18. Discuss aspects of reading instruction for which teachers should be held accountable. (**7.0**)

Selected References

1. Barro, Stephen M., "An Approach to Developing Accountability Measures for the Public Schools," *Phi Delta Kappan*, 52, No. 4 (December, 1970), 196–205.
2. Bishop, Lloyd K., *Individualizing Educational Systems.* N. Y.: Harper and Row, 1971.
3. Bowers, C. A., "Accountability from a Humanistic Point of View," *The Educational Forum*, 35 (May, 1971), 470–86.
4. Briner, Conrad, "Administrators and Accountability," *Theory Into Practice*, 8 (October, 1969), 203–6.
5. Carlson, Thorsten R., editor, *Administrators and Reading.* N. Y.: Harcourt Brace Jovanovich, 1972.

6. Combs, Arthur W., *Educational Accountability: Beyond Behavioral Objectives.* Washington, D. C.: Association for Supervision and Curriculum Development, 1972.

7. Cottrell, Donald P., editor, *Teacher Education for a Free People.* Oneonta, N. Y.: American Association of Colleges for Teacher Education, 1956.

8. Dyer, Henry S., "Toward Objective Criteria of Professional Accountability in the Schools of New York City," *Phi Delta Kappan,* 52, No. 4 (December, 1970), 206–11.

9. Frymier, Jack R., *The Nature of Educational Method.* Columbus, Ohio: Charles E. Merrill, 1965.

10. Harris, Larry A., and Carl B. Smith, *Reading Instruction Through Diagnostic Teaching.* N. Y.: Holt, Rinehart and Winston, 1972.

11. Heilman, Arthur W., *Principles and Practices of Teaching Reading.* Columbus, Ohio: Charles E. Merrill, 1967.

12. Houston, W. Robert, and Robert B. Howsam, *Competency-Based Teacher Education.* Chicago: Science Research Associates, 1972.

13. Gerberich, Raymond, *Specimen Objective Test Items: A Guide to Achievement Test Construction.* N. Y.: Longmans, Green, 1956.

14. Gronlund, Norman E., *Measurement and Evaluation in Teaching.* N. Y.: Macmillan, 1971.

15. Lessinger, Leon, "Engineering Accountability for Results in Public Education," *Phi Delta Kappan,* 52, No. 4 (December, 1970), 217–25.

16. _____, *Every Kid a Winner: Accountability in Education.* Palo Alto, Ca.: Science Research Associates. 1970.

17. Lieberman, Myron, "An Overview of Accountability," *Phi Delta Kappan,* 52, No. 4 (December, 1970), 194–95.

18. Mehrens, William A., "National Assessment for Educational Progress," *Childhood Education,* 51, No. 3 (December, 1969), 215–17.

19. Morris, John E., "Accountability: Watchword for the 70's," *The Clearing House,* 45 (February, 1971), 323-27.

20. Raths, Louis E., Merrill Harmin, and Sidney B. Simon, *Values and Teaching: Working With Values in the Classroom.* Columbus, Ohio: Charles E. Merrill, 1966.

21. Robinson, Donald W., "Accountability for Whom? for What?," *Phi Delta Kappan,* 52, No. 4 (December, 1970), 193.

22. Sciara, Frank J., and Richard K. Jantz, *Accountability in American Education.* Boston: Allyn and Bacon, 1972.

23. Silberman, Charles E., *Crisis in the Classroom.* N. Y.: Random House, 1970.

24. Stoops, Emery, and James R. Marks, *Elementary School Supervision.* Boston: Allyn and Bacon, 1965.

25. Thompson, Robert B., *A Systems Approach to Instruction.* Hamden, Conn.: Shoe String Press, 1971.

26. Wallen, Carl J., *Competency in Teaching Reading.* Chicago: Science Research Associates, 1972.

27. Wick, John W., and Donald L. Beggs, *Evaluation for Decision-Making in the Schools.* Boston: Houghton-Mifflin, 1971.

28. Wildavsky, Aaron, "A Program of Accountability for Elementary Schools," *Phi Delta Kappan,* 52, No. 4 (December, 1970), 212–16.

PART

II

Basic Procedures in Reading Instruction

2 Assessing Learners' Needs in Reading

The goal of accountability in reading instruction is the establishment of definite, specifiable changes in the behaviors of learners as a result of instruction. One way to assure that desirable changes in behavior of learners are sought and achieved is to make sure that instructional efforts are focused upon the needs of learners.

Behavioral Objectives

The content of Chapter 2 is presented in such a way that after reading it, an individual

1.0 Understands the importance of assessing the needs of learners

    1.1 Explains why a teacher should be aware of learners' strengths and weaknesses in reading

    1.2 Interprets the role of need assessment in the total process of reading instruction

    1.3 Identifies the relationship between need assessment and accountability in reading instruction

    1.4 Explains the relationship between need assessment and individualization of instruction

2.0 Understands the meaning of need assessment in reading instruction

    2.1 Explains the meaning of need assessment in reading instruction

    2.2 Describes the nature of a need in reading

    2.3 Identifies factors influential in the teacher's interpretation of a need in reading

3.0 Knows procedures and materials used in need assessment

    3.1 Explains why several types of procedures and materials are essential in an adequate assessment of learners' needs in reading

    3.2 Distinguishes between procedures and materials used in need assessment

3.3   Identifies categories of procedures and materials used in need assessment
3.4   Identifies the basis upon which selection of procedures and materials to be used in need assessment should depend
3.5   States a point of view for guiding assessment of learners' needs in a classroom situation
4.0   Knows how to plan for need assessment in a classroom situation
4.1   Identifies factors in a classroom situation that tend to complicate the task of need assessment
4.2   Suggests an overall plan for assessing needs of learners in a classroom situation
4.3   Lists types of procedures and materials available for assessing the needs of learners in a classroom
5.0   Understands how to assess needs related to reading readiness
5.1   Explains the meaning of "reading readiness"
5.2   Identifies factors related to initial reading readiness
5.3   Lists formal tests of reading readiness
5.4   Describes types of skills and abilities usually measured by reading readiness tests
5.5   Details procedures for determining the nature of a test of reading readiness
5.6   Describes general characteristics of tests of reading readiness
6.0   Knows types of tests available for assessing needs related to reading readiness
6.1   Gives examples of group tests of reading readiness
6.2   Gives examples of individual tests of special abilities
7.0   Understands how to assess needs related to skills and abilities in reading
7.1   Distinguishes between formal and informal methods of assessment
7.2   Identifies areas in reading to which needs may relate
7.3   Identifies survey tests in reading
7.4   Describes tests that are useful for assessing specific needs of individuals
7.4   Distinguishes between purposes of survey tests and those of more precise measures of specific reading abilities
8.0   Understands the importance of informal procedures and materials in need assessment
8.1   Explains why affective behaviors should be assessed in determination of learners' needs in reading
8.2   Describes procedures and materials appropriate for informal assessment of needs
8.3   Identifies techniques for recording the results of observation
8.4   Describes characteristics of an informal reading inventory
8.5   Explains uses of an informal reading inventory
8.6   Describes the "Cloze" procedure
8.7   Explains uses of the cloze procedure
9.0   Recognizes relationships among the processes of need assessment, diagnosis, and evaluation
9.1   Compares characteristics of the processes of need assessment and diagnosis
9.2   Compares characteristics of the processes of need assessment and evaluation of achievement
10.0   Recognizes problems that may accompany the process of need assessment
10.1   Explains the tentative nature of the results of need assessment
10.2   Identifies sources of problems related to need assessment
11.0   Recognizes competencies required of teachers for assessing needs of learners in reading

Importance of Need Assessment in Reading Instruction

Instructional procedures should be directed toward those areas of human development and reading abilities that reflect the needs of specific learners. Accountability cannot be sought effectively by focusing on areas in which learners have already achieved competence. Nor can accountability be achieved by attempting to teach learners material that is irrelevant in terms of their personal or societal needs. Perhaps of most importance, accountability for results of learning cannot be achieved by attempting to teach all learners in a classroom group the same thing at the same time.

Unquestionably, there should be a close relationship between instruction and the needs of the learners under consideration. The degree of closeness in this relationship will depend, to a large extent, on the degree to which conscious, deliberate, and continuing efforts are made to assess the needs of learners as an integral part of the instructional program in reading. Such need assessment is a primary as well as a continuing task in reading instruction. Its results are basic in making individualization of instruction possible. Results of need assessment serve as a major determinant of the nature of all subsequent steps to be taken in the total instructional process.

A Primary and Recurrent Task

Where does the process of reading instruction begin? What are the initial crucial tasks that must be performed by teachers in order to establish a reliable basis for effective instruction? What materials should be selected and used to initiate a period of instruction? What are the most effective teaching strategies that should be used? What differences among individuals must be provided for? These are some of the questions often raised by inexperienced teachers and prospective teachers anticipating actual instructional performance in classrooms. Answers to all of these questions and to many related ones depend on what is known, or becomes known, about the needs of the individuals who comprise a given classroom group. Becoming acquainted with the needs of learners for whom instruction is anticipated is the primary task of the teacher involved in reading instruction.

Seldom can needs of learners be determined by means other than direct assessment by the teacher. Assumptions sometimes are made that information about needs of learners becomes obvious as a result of the way classroom units are formed. Classroom units often are assigned, administratively, on bases such as learners' age, grade, or achievement levels. Despite these assignments, differences among individuals invariably remain. Consequently, need assessment is still an important task.

Furthermore, the responsibility of the teacher for assessing needs of individuals in a particular classroom group cannot be effectively discharged solely through perusal of information found recorded in various types of school records. Even when properly recorded and interpreted, information from these sources generally must be verified and supplemented by that available only through use of first-hand assessment procedures.

Since results of need assessment are required as a basis for determining the nature of subsequent instructional tasks, need assessment is the first concern in instruction. This is the case whether an entire program of instruction or recurrent cycles of it are in question. Since needs of learners continually change (with time, growth, and experiences), assessment is not only an initial task of reading instruction, but also a recurrent one. The purpose of initial need assessment is to locate strengths and weaknesses of learners in order to determine appropriate starting points of instruction. As instruction proceeds, need assessment is essential for determining important next steps.

A Basis for Individualizing Instruction

Effective individualization of instruction requires knowledge of each learner's characteristics. These characteristics include factors such as the learner's favored style of learning, conceptual ability, level of competence in reading, interests, attitudes, and the like. Attempts to individualize instruction without this kind of knowledge generally are futile. Individualization of instruction does not mean merely permitting learners to work separately and singly. Individualization of instruction means that the needs of each learner are ascertained and met to the highest degree possible in a particular situation. Strategies used to help meet the needs of each individual may include individual work or group work.

A Determinant of Subsequent
Instructional Procedures

Teachers must make decisions regarding the nature of instructional procedures that will be most worthwhile for learners. Decisions that are made regarding procedures to be used during instruction should be based on and proceed from results of need assessment. Instructional procedures are worthwhile in proportion to the degree to which they relate to the results of need assessment. Some of these procedures include: (1) determination of appropriate instructional objectives, (2) selection and use of instructional strategies and materials, and (3) evaluation of achievement.

One major purpose of objectives is to provide direction for instruction and learning. Objectives are not all that are needed, however, to insure appropriateness of direction for particular learners in particular situations. Needs of the particular learners under consideration provide the basis for determining whether or not direction indicated by general objectives is appropriate.

Quality of strategies and materials used in the program of instruction cannot be determined apart from the usefulness these serve in accommodating characteristics of learners. Adequate need assessment reveals the nature of these characteristics that in turn suggest the nature of strategies and materials needed in the program.

Results of need assessment are vital in order that valid decisions can be made regarding either relative or absolute progress that a learner makes as a result of instruction. Therefore, if adequate evaluation of achievement is to be made, the beginning status of a learner's needs must be known. Without this knowledge, it is impossible to establish accountability for achievement resulting from instruction.

Meaning of Need Assessment in Reading Instruction

Need assessment has been defined in several ways. Henderson and Lanier have defined it as a systematic process involving examination of the behaviors shown by learners and the factors that are influential in development of those behaviors.[1] Applied to reading instruction, in a literal sense, this view of need assessment would require examination of all behaviors manifest by learners in relation to the reading process. It would require, also, examination of those factors, both in and out of school, that contribute to development of reading ability. Considering the complex nature of the reading process and the numerous influences, biologically and environmentally, that bear upon an individual's ability to read, implementation of this definition would be a formidable—if not impossible —task, for the teacher in the typical classroom situation. The competencies of many teachers and the resources available to them for assessing needs of learners would be insufficient for the task.

In simple terms, need assessment can be called a process whereby information about learners' strengths and weaknesses in reading is obtained. The process includes the steps of (1) deciding the types of information needed, (2) using procedures and materials essential for gathering the information, (3) gathering the information, (4) interpreting the information, and (5) using the information to improve instruction. These steps can be implemented, to an appreciable degree, in most classroom situations.

Determining a Need in Reading

A "need" has been defined as "a problem which exists because of a discrepancy that should be zero . . . . the discrepancy can be between two states, the 'actual' state and the 'desired' state."[2] In order to determine whether a learner has a need related to reading, two kinds of information are needed. One kind of information reveals the present status of the learner in relation to factors involved in effective reading. The other kind describes a level of reading ability that is desirable for the particular learner. Various measures can be applied to gather the first kind of information. The teacher's concepts of reading will affect his or her interpretation of what constitutes a desired state for a certain reader.

---

[1]Judith E. Henderson and Perry E. Lanier, "What Teachers Need to Know . . . ," *The Journal of Teacher Education*, 24, No. 1 (Spring, 1973), pp. 4–16.

[2]John Mordechai Gottman and Robert Earl Clasen, *Evaluation in Education, A Practitioner's Guide* (Itasca, Ill.: F. E. Peacock Publishers, 1972), p. 46.

These include the teacher's biases regarding the nature of reading, the nature of maturity in reading, and levels of competency desirable for a learner at a particular point in development.

In order to clarify this personal conception of the nature of reading, the teacher should be acquainted with descriptions of reading that have been offered by various authorities. Nevertheless, it is the teacher's concept of the nature of reading,* in the final analysis, that will be influential in determining a learner's needs in reading. To the degree that the teacher's concept of the nature of reading reflects the best that is known on the subject, his or her determination of a learner's needs in reading has potential for accuracy.

The teacher's concept of maturity in reading also affects interpretation of a learner's needs in reading. The mature adult reader has been identified as one who has mastery of essential skills related to basic and higher competencies in all aspects of reading. At the same time, the mature reader has extensive and varied interests in reading and regards it as a desirable means for enhancing personal, social, and utilitarian aspects of life.[3]

Maturity in reading can be viewed as a continuum running the gamut from characteristics desirable for a beginning reader through those that should be expected of a mature adult reader. Maturity in reading is certainly not the same for all persons. It must be measured on the basis of a number of individually determined factors. A person's reading needs should be assessed in light of the level of maturity that reasonably can be expected of him.

A learner's needs are influenced, also, by the level of his or her reading that is under consideration. Several levels that may be found in the total complex of an individual's ability to read have been identified.[4] These include the level at which an individual can function independently in reading, the level at which he can be instructed profitably, his frustration level and the level at which he is capable only of understanding the meaning of a selection if it is read to him. Knowledge of what may be expected of a learner's performance at each of these levels can help in assessing needs more precisely and accurately.

Procedures and Materials Used in Need Assessment

Several different types of procedures and materials are required in gathering information essential for determining reading needs. The various types of characteristics that must be examined necessitate variety in procedures and materials.

---

*The nature of reading and importance of the teacher's concept of reading are discussed in Chapter 7 of this text.

[3]Miles A. Tinker and Constance McCullough, *Teaching Elementary Reading* (N. Y.: Appleton-Century-Crofts, 1968), pp. 5–6.

[4]E. A. Betts, *Foundations of Reading Instruction* (N. Y.: American Book Co., 1946), Chapter 21.

Procedures of need assessment can be distinguished from materials used in the assessment, although both of these can be similarly categorized. Procedures include the mode of conduct, course of action, techniques or plans implemented in the process of assessment. Materials are the things, objects, or apparatus used or consumed in the process. Procedures and materials used in assessing needs of learners can be categorized several ways, including formal or informal approaches, quantitative or qualitative measures, or testing and observational techniques.

Procedures and materials used in need assessment can be categorized as formal or informal depending on the degree to which they conform to rigid standards, rules, or conventions. Their results usually can be distinguished on the basis of the extent to which they are valid, reliable, and objective.

"Quantitative" and "qualitative" are terms generally indicative of the nature of results produced by various types of procedures and materials of assessment. Quantitative results generally accrue from procedures and materials designed to measure or test behavior or performance. These generally are represented by test scores of various types. Qualitative results generally are those resultant from use of observational techniques.

Regardless of ways in which procedures and materials may be categorized, and dependent on the purposes of assessment, all types of results are potentially valuable for contributing the kinds of information useful for determining needs of learners. Procedures and materials should be selected and used according to the purposes they are suited for serving.

Procedures and materials capable of producing quantitative results are useful for gathering information related directly to skills in reading. Qualitative results frequently must be relied upon in assessment of interests, attitudes, appreciations, and other affective behaviors. Information about factors such as experiential backgrounds, nature of concepts, and linguistic abilities can be gathered indirectly through interpretation of test scores, or directly through use of observational techniques.

A Point of View Regarding Need Assessment in the Classroom

Realization of several practical considerations of need assessment in classroom situations helps to keep the task in perspective for the teacher and to facilitate its implementation. Need assessment in a classroom situation will not be, nor need to be, so thorough as types of diagnosis generally accomplished in clinical situations. A large number of learners will have needs that tend to be similar and, thus, can be ascertained through group procedures of assessment. Many needs of learners will become apparent without the necessity of detailed or prolonged probing.

Efforts made by a classroom teacher toward need assessment can be supplemented, in many instances, by the help of specialists who may be available in the setting. Needs of some learners cannot be adequately assessed by means generally available to the classroom teacher.

The entire process of need assessment, even that which is done during the initial stages of instruction, is not one for which immediate completion should be expected.

Need assessment can be a gradual approach that requires a considerable amount of time before information about the needs of the learners can be acquired.

Need assessment is not of value in and of iteslf. Its value lies in what it contributes to the effectiveness of instruction and learning for the learners under consideration in a particular situation. The task should be approached as efficiently as possible. Only as many procedures and materials as are essential in gathering the information sought should be used in the process.

Planning for Need Assessment in the Classroom

Gathering information essential for assessing the needs of all learners in a classroom situation can seem to be a formidable task. The task is complicated not only by the complex nature of reading, but also by the requirement that information be gathered about not just one but all learners in the situation. Making the task even more difficult, assessment of needs of learners in a classroom generally must be undertaken simultaneously with other important ongoing activities. A task of these large dimensions requires a feasible plan of operation.

A plan for need assessment that can be placed into operation in a typical classroom situation should provide for several different levels of assessment.[5] It is recommended that appropriate measures first be used to provide information about gross needs of the entire class. This level of assessment is then followed by use of measures that permit collection of more specific information about special cases. Still more precise measures might be used in those cases where the assessment at either of the first two levels was not adequate.

As a minimum, the plan for assessing needs of learners as a class group should provide sufficient information for meeting initial instructional tasks. These tasks include organizational and instructional strategies for getting the program started. Information gained at the initial stage of assessment should be regarded as tentative. Any strategies based upon this information should be regarded chiefly as sources of further information that will indicate learners' strengths and weaknesses in reading more dependably as time proceeds.

Generally, several options are available to the classroom teacher for gathering information at the outset of the instructional program. Any one or several of the following procedures and types of materials may be used:
1. Administration of a standardized test or tests of general academic achievement to the entire class
2. Administration of a reading survey test or tests to the entire class
3. Administration of a reading survey test or tests to selected members of the class whose results on previous measures failed to supply the information needed

---

[5]Larry A. Harris and Carl B. Smith, *Reading Instruction Through Diagnostic Teaching* (N. Y.: Holt, Rinehart and Winston, 1972), pp. 107–16.

Robert M. Wilson, *Diagnostic and Remedial Reading for Classroom and Clinic* (Columbus, Oh.: Charles E. Merrill, 1972), pp. 86–108.

4. Administration of a more precise measure — such as a diagnostic test in reading or a detailed inventory — to individuals for whom further information is still needed
5. Administration of a test or tests of specific abilities to learners for whom it is necessary
6. Referral of special cases, for whom adequate assessment is beyond the means of the classroom teacher, to specialists that may be available for the task
7. Application of informal, observational techniques appropriate for assessing the nature of pertinent affective behaviors of all members of the class
8. Validation of any results acquired from use of formal procedures and materials with the results of observation techniques

A general plan for assessment of learners' needs in reading, involving procedures such as mentioned above, can be adapted to apply to reading instruction at any level. If learners are at the level of initial reading readiness, for example, tests of general academic achievement or survey tests in reading would be replaced by tests of reading readiness or other appropriate tests. Specific tests selected for subsequent levels of assessment would pertain to specific areas of readiness about which information should be sought.

Assessing Needs Related to Reading Readiness

Procedures and materials useful in assessing needs related to initial reading readiness require special attention. Readiness, even at subsequent levels of developmental reading, must be a continuing concern in any effective program of reading instruction. Special attention, however, usually must be given to a learner's readiness for reading prior to, and at inception of, a formal program of instruction in reading.

Being ready to learn any skill facilitates that learning for a human being of any age. Readiness means, generally, that all major factors relating to an individual in terms of that learning are in an "optimal state favoring learning."[6]

Authorities are in general agreement regarding the nature of factors that influence an individual's readiness to read. According to Gertrude Hildreth, these factors include (1) mental maturity, (2) perceptual maturity, (3) experiential background, (4) linguistic maturity, (5) sensory acuity, (6) social adjustment, and (7) emotional adjustment.[7] Using different terms, but referring to the same factors, essentially, Spache and Spache cite these as (1) intelligence, (2) mental age, (3) language facility, (4) auditory and visual factors, (4) preschool learning, and (5) emotional adjustment.[8] While there is much agreement among authorities regarding the nature of factors influential in reading readiness, many questions related to the degree to which each factor influences an individual's total readiness remain unanswered.

---

[6]William H. Burton, *Reading in Child Development* (Indianapolis, Ind.: Bobbs-Merrill, 1959), p. 194.

[7]Gertrude Hildreth, *Teaching Reading* (N. Y.: Holt, Rinehart, and Winston, 1958), pp. 165–66.

[8]George D. Spache and Evelyn B. Spache, *Reading in the Elementary School* (Boston: Allyn Allyn and Bacon, 1973), pp. 53–84.

Need assessment in modern programs of initial reading readiness attempts to answer two important questions. One of these is "In what ways is this person ready to read?"; the other, "In what ways does this individual need to develop strengths required for formal reading instruction?" Answers to these questions are found by examining an individual's strengths and weaknesses in those aspects of development that relate closely to the skills and attributes required in reading.

A variety of procedures and materials can be used to estimate the nature of a learner's strengths and weaknesses in regard to each and all the major factors believed to influence readiness for reading. These procedures and materials include (1) intelligence tests, (2) formal tests of reading readiness, and (3) observational techniques.

Tests of intelligence* have been omitted from discussion here for several reasons. Group tests of intelligence for young children have several important limitations. Their results often lack the degree of validity and reliability essential as a basis for crucial decisions that must be made about learners. Individual tests of intelligence, on the other hand, are seldom administered and interpreted by classroom teachers. In many school districts and in many schools, group tests of intelligence are not used. Finally, formal tests of reading readiness measure characteristics that are highly similar to those measured by group intelligence tests.

Formal Tests of Reading Readiness

Formal tests of reading readiness are administered, in many schools, to children during the latter part of the kindergarten year or during the early part of first grade. Results of these tests serve several purposes. One of these purposes, often, is to identify learners who need to develop strengths in certain areas of development before they are subjected to formal reading instruction. Another important purpose is to identify learners whose strengths and weaknesses are somewhat similar. Both of these purposes are important in helping teachers make valid decisions related to organizational and instructional strategies that will be most effective in the program.

Information gathered as a result of using formal tests of reading readiness, or by any other formal means, should be examined in light of evidence gathered from the use of other techniques of assessment.

Usefulness that test results are expected to serve in an instructional situation should be decided prior to administration of the tests. Many important decisions must be based on the purpose of the test. For instance, selection of an appropriate test or tests greatly depends on the purpose or purposes that are expected to be served. In need assessment, the major purpose of test results generally is to indicate strengths and weaknesses learners show in relation to several skills and abilities required in reading.

---

*For a discussion of measures frequently used in assessment of intelligence, see "Assessment of Pre-Reading Skills: A Review of Frequently Employed Measures" by John J. Pikulski in *Reading World*, 13, No. 3 (March, 1974), pp. 171–97.

Skills and Abilities Measured by Many Formal Tests of Reading Readiness

While choices must be made among the large variety of reading readiness tests available for use, many tests are highly similar in terms of the specific abilities and skills they are designed to measure. Some of the skills and abilities for which measures are provided by many widely used tests include the following:

1. Listening comprehension
2. Auditory discrimination
3. Visual discrimination
4. Following directions
5. Recognition of letters of the alphabet
6. Visual-motor coordination
7. Word-recognition
8. Recognition of numerals
9. Using symbols
10. Using the context
11. Using context and auditory clues
12. Nature of concepts
13. Recognition of similarities and differences in beginning sounds of words
14. Recognition and interpretation of pictures
15. Visual perception

Although most of these characteristics are common to many tests of reading readiness, the teacher still should examine a proposed test in terms of its usefulness in a particular situation. It is usually necessary to analyze specific items provided in the subtests of a reading readiness test in order to determine if the test measures what it claims to measure. Careful examination of the accompanying manual is also necessary. The teacher should check information regarding claims for reliability and validity of test results. The nature of norms provided and the nature of the norming population are of great importance here.

General Characteristics of Reading Readiness Tests

Certain general characteristics common to most widely used tests of reading readiness include the following:

1. Tests of reading readiness usually include a variety of subtests designed for assessing strengths and weaknesses believed to be related to success in beginning reading.
2. Most tests of reading readiness contain measures of visual and auditory discrimination.
3. Certain behaviors are required of learners in responding to tests of reading readiness. Generally, the learner must be able to understand and follow directions and make the indicated response.
4. Several measures of language understanding are included in leading tests of reading readiness.
5. Results of tests of reading readiness should not be taken as absolute and exact indicators of a learner's total readiness for reading.

6. It is the task of the teacher to determine how well a test discriminates among skills for which a measure is sought and whether the test measures what it is claimed to measure.

7. Total scores from tests of reading readiness are generally less valuable in determining strengths and weaknesses than are the scores from the subtests included in the tests.

Tests of
Reading Readiness

Many formal tests of reading readiness are in wide use throughout the elementary schools in the United States. Some of these tests were developed, originally, several decades ago during a period when many concepts viewed as important for reading readiness were different from those currently accepted. Most of these tests were later revised in light of newer conceptions of factors pertinent in reading readiness. (See the footnotes to the following tests for the most recent revision.) Descriptions of some widely used tests of reading readiness are the following:

Gates-MacGinitie Reading Tests:
Readiness Skills[9]

Recommended for administration at the end of kindergarten or at the beginning of first grade, the Gates-MacGinitie Readiness Skills Test includes eight subtests. The subtests are measures of (1) listening comprehension, (2) auditory discrimination, (3) visual discrimination, (4) following directions, (5) letter recognition, (6) visual-motor coordination, (7) auditory blending, and (8) word recognition.

Harrison-Stroud Reading Readiness Profiles[10]

Six subtests designed to measure skills essential in several areas of beginning reading are included in the Harrison-Stroud Reading Readiness Profiles. Five of the subtests can be administered as group tests. These include (1) using symbols, (2) making visual discriminations, (3) using the context, (4) making auditory discriminations, and (5) using context and auditory clues. The sixth subtest, giving the names of the letters, must be administered on an individual basis. The test is available in one form and is recommended for use with children in kindergarten or first grade.

Lee-Clark Reading Readiness Test[11]

The Lee-Clark Reading Readiness Test consists of one form and can be administered in approximately twenty minutes. The three subtests

---

[9]A. I. Gates and W. MacGinitie, *Gates-MacGinitie Reading Tests: Readiness Skills* (N. Y.: Teachers College Press, Columbia University, 1939, revised 1968).

[10]M. L. Harrison and J. B. Stroud, *Harrison-Stroud Reading Readiness Profiles* (Boston: Houghton Mifflin, 1949, revised 1956).

[11]J. M. Lee and W. W. Clark, *Lee-Clark Reading Readiness Test* (Monterey, Ca.: California Test Bureau, 1931, revised 1962).

focus on (1) letter symbols, (2) concepts, and (3) word symbols. The test is designed for use with children in kindergarten or first grade.

Metropolitan Readiness Tests[12]

Seven subtests are included in the Metropolitan Readiness Tests. The six required subtests focus on areas similar to those emphasized in major tests of reading readiness. These areas include (1) word meaning, (2) listening, (3) matching, (4) alphabet, (5) numbers, and (6) copying. Two forms of the test are provided. Administration time is approximately sixty-five to seventy-five minutes. The seventh test is optional and also largely unique among reading readiness tests. The seventh test requires the child to "draw a man." Results of the "draw a man" test can provide information on the child's general maturity, perceptual abilities, visual-motor coordination, and the like.

Murphy-Durrell Reading Readiness Analysis[13]

Three subtests are provided for assessing abilities and skills related to (1) sound recognition (phonemes), (2) letter names, and (3) rate of learning words. One form of the test is provided and it can be administered in approximately eighty minutes. The test is designed for use with kindergartners and first graders.

Individual Tests in Specific Areas of Reading Readiness

Formal group tests of reading readiness generally contain subtests that are sufficient for determining the strengths and weaknesses shown by most children in the special abilities required for beginning reading. Sometimes, however, there are children for whom results from group tests are inconclusive, or for whom there are other indications that a more detailed examination of certain specific abilities is required. In these cases, depending on the purpose(s) of the test, individual tests such as the ones described below may be administered by the classroom teacher or by specialists.

The Wepman Auditory Discrimination Test[14]

The Wepman Auditory Discrimination Test consists, largely, of a series of paired words from which the learner selects the words in a pair that sound alike or different as the case may be. Provisions are made for comparisons and contrasts of all the consonant and vowel sounds reproduced in

---

[12]G. H. Hildreth, N. L. Griffiths, and M. E. McGauvran, *Metropolitan Readiness Tests* (N. Y.: Harcourt Brace Jovanovich, Inc., 1933, revised 1965).

[13]H. A. Murphy and D. D. Durrell, *Murphey-Durrell Reading Readiness Analysis* (N. Y.: Harcourt Brace Jovanovich, 1949, revised 1965).

[14]Joseph M. Wepman, *Auditory Discrimination Test* (Chicago, Ill.: Language Research Associates, 1958).

initial, medial, or final positions. Designed for individual administration, the test is available in two forms and requires approximately ten minutes to administer.

The Slingerland Screening Tests[15]

The Slingerland Screening Tests are designed to aid in assessment of maturational readiness for learning tasks required in schools. Offered for use in assessing strengths and weaknesses of sensory-motor modalities specifically related to language learning, these tests provide information additional to that usually gained from results of conventional tests of reading readiness. Information can be gathered regarding abilities and concepts related to (1) phonemic-graphemic correspondencies, (2) number symbols, and (3) geometric forms. The tests can be administered individually or in typical classroom groups.

Frostig Developmental Test of Visual Perception[16]

Designed to provide measures of various kinds of abilities in the area of visual perception, the Frostig Developmental Test of Visual Perception can be administered in a group or individually. Measures are included for five perceptual abilities: (1) eye-motor coordination, (2) figure-ground relationships, (3) constancy of form or shape, (4) position in space, and (5) spatial relationships. Responses require abilities to (1) draw continuous lines of various types (2) identify figures against backgrounds varying in complexity, (3) recognize various geometric figures in various sizes, textures, positions and shadings, (4) discriminate reversals and rotations of figures presented in series of schematic drawings, and (5) analyze and copy simple forms and patterns.

Formal Procedures and Materials for Assessing General Needs in Reading

Several different types of formal procedures and materials can be used to gain an overview of learners' general reading abilities. Ordinarily, it is essential for a teacher to have information related to learners' general proficiencies in reading early during an instructional period. This type of general information is the minimum required to initiate organizational schemes and begin selection of instructional strategies and materials essential for providing an effective instructional program. Several general types of formal tests can be used to gather that information needed early in the instructional period. Included among types of formal tests that can be used to provide this information are standardized group tests of achievement and reading survey tests.

---

[15]Beth H. Slingerland, *Screening Tests for Identifying Children with Specific Language Disabilities* (Cambridge, Mass.: Educators Publishing Service, 1962).

[16]M. Frostig, *Administration and Scoring Manual for the Marianne Frostig Developmental Test of Visual Perception* (Palo Alto, Ca.: Consulting Psychologists Press, 1966).

Any standardized test, as the term implies, requires administration under specific conditions and according to specific directions.* A definition such as presented by Noll and Scannell highlights the special characteristics of standardized tests. According to these authors:

> Standardized Tests. Tests carefully developed by experts according to accepted purposes, administered according to standardized procedures. Used to obtain comparable measures in different classes or different schools. Interpreted in terms of norms or scales that have been predetermined.[17]

Complete standardized tests or batteries are designed to measure performance in a number of subject areas. When detailed information about performance in a specific area is desired, however, a standardized test provides only limited input. Generally, an achievement test samples few skills and abilities required specifically in reading.

There are times and situations, however, necessitating use of a standardized achievement test to indicate some of the needs of learners in a class. Matters such as time, cost, and other factors can dictate such an expediency. Furthermore, for some learners, gross indications of proficiency in reading as indicated by results from a standardized test may be adequate for initial decisions about their instructional program.

One of the greatest limitations of standardized achievement tests as assessment measures in reading is the lack of scope in information related to specific skills and abilities required in reading. According to Roger Farr, "The most serious deficiency in using standardized tests to diagnose reading achievement is the lack of discriminant validity (the validity of tests as measures of distinct skills or abilities)."[18]

Included among many criteria suggested for making good choices when a standardized test of achievement must be used to provide information about reading ability are the following:

1. The test should be suitable in terms of the purposes for which it is to be used.
2. Despite the name of the test, specific items should be examined in order to determine exactly what the test does measure.
3. The manual should be examined carefully in order to determine if the norm groups used during standardization of the test are suitable for the comparisons that should be made for learners in the class.

Standardized tests of achievement usually are provided by the schools and administered according to regularly scheduled times. Because of this, it is often possible to obtain learners' scores on previously administered tests from school records. In such cases, other types of procedures and materials should be used to gain initial information more directly related to learners' specific strengths and

---

*This topic is discussed in Chapter 6 of this text.

[17]Victor H. Noll and Dale P. Scannell, *Introduction to Educational Measurement*, Second edition (Boston: Houghton Mifflin, 1972), p. 567.

[18]Roger Farr, *Reading: What Can be Measured?* (Newark, Del.: International Reading Association Fund, 1969), pp. 80–81.

weaknesses in reading. Among widely used standardized achievement tests are the following:

Iowa Every-Pupil Tests of Basic Skills, Multilevel Edition[19]

The multilevel edition of the Iowa Every-Pupil Tests of Basic Skills encompasses grade levels from three to six. Five separate tests are included with emphases on (1) vocabulary, (2) reading comprehension, (3) language skills, (4) work-study skills, and (5) arithmetic skills. Of fifteen scores that can be obtained from administration of the complete battery, the largest number of these relate either directly or indirectly to reading skills and abilities. Two forms of the test are available. Administration of the complete test requires approximately four and one-half hours of time spread over four sessions.

Three types of norms are provided including (1) grade percentile for individuals, (2) grade percentiles for school averages, and (3) special percentile norms for regional areas, Catholic schools, and large city schools.

The vocabulary test emphasizes basic meaning or definitions of words. The test of reading comprehension measures a limited number of basic comprehension skills and abilities. The language skills test places major emphasis on skills required in written expression.

California Achievement Tests[20]

Five levels are included in the complete tests: Lower Primary, Grades 1–2; Upper Primary, Grades 2.5–4.5; Elementary, Grades 4–6; Junior High School, Grades 7–9; and Advanced, Grades 9–14. Two forms are available for both levels of the primary batteries and four forms are available for the elementary and high school batteries. The advanced level provides three forms. Among skills and abilities related directly to reading for which scores can be obtained are reading vocabulary and reading comprehension. Types of scores available are grade placement scores, percentile ranks, standard scores, and stanines.

Sequential Tests of Educational Progress (STEP)[21]

Four levels, including grades 4–6, 7–9, and upward comprise the Sequential Tests of Educational Progress. At least two forms are available for each level. Each battery contains seven tests with major focus on the communication skills. Test items are of multiple-choice and essay types. Various testing times are required for administration of the subtests, but the time required for the entire test can be approximately eight hours. All parts of the battery are group-administered except the listening test which must be administered on an

---

[19]H. F. Spitzer, E. Horn, M. McBroom, H. A. Greene, and E. F. Lindquist, *Iowa Every-Pupil Tests of Basic Skills* (Boston: Houghton Mifflin, 1956).

[20]Ernest W. Tiegs and Willis W. Clark, *California Achievement Tests* (Monterey, Ca.: California Test Bureau, 1957 edition, 1963 norms).

[21]*Sequential Tests of Educational Progress (STEP)* (Princeton, N. J.: Cooperative Test Division, Educational Testing Service, 1956, revised 1963).

individual basis. Major emphasis in the tests is on application and understanding rather than on recall of factual information. Level four (grades 4–6) for example, emphasizes abilities to recall ideas, translate ideas and make inferences, analyze motivation, analyze presentation, and criticize.

Metropolitan Achievement Tests[22]

Six batteries (grades 1–12) comprise the total Metropolitan Achievement Tests. A vocabulary test and a reading test are included at all levels of the test. The elementary, intermediate, and advanced levels of the test have four forms each, while the high school battery is available in two forms.

Survey Tests for Assessing Specific Reading Abilities and Skills

Standardized survey tests in reading share many of the same characteristics as those of standardized tests of achievement. However, there is a major difference between standardized tests of achievement and reading survey tests in primary emphasis. Reading survey tests focus specifically on skills and abilities required in reading, while standardized tests of achievement generally include many other areas of the curriculum in their concerns. Since sole focus of reading survey tests is on skills and abilities in reading, these make possible a more detailed analysis of a learner's strengths and weaknesses in reading. At the same time, survey tests in reading generally require a longer time for administration than is required by administration of a subtest in reading provided as a part of an achievement battery.

Some of the purposes served by reading survey tests include: (1) identification of levels of overall reading performance; (2) comparison of a learner's performance with that of an appropriate age- or grade-level norm group; and (3) attainment of a profile, or graphic picture, of a learner's overall achievement in reading. Descriptions of some important tests categorized as reading survey tests follow.

Gates-MacGinitie Reading Tests[23]

Six separate tests are included in the Gates-MacGinitie Reading Survey Tests. Levels of the test include Primary A for grade 1, Primary B for grade 2, and Primary C for grade 3. Each of these tests, designed for learners in the early grades, is available in two forms. Vocabulary and comprehension abilities are stressed. Primary CS, designed for grades two and three, consists of three forms and provides information related to speed and accuracy in reading. Survey D for grades 4–6 and Survey E for grades 7–9 consist of three forms each.

[22]Walter N. Durost, Harold H. Bixler, Gertrude H. Hildreth, Kenneth W. Lund, J. Wayne Wrightstone, et al., *Metropolitan Achievement Tests* (N. Y.: Harcourt Brace Jovanovich, 1931, revised 1966).

[23]A. I. Gates and W. MacGinitie, *Gates-MacGinitie Reading Tests* (N. Y.: Teachers College Press, Columbia University, 1926, revised 1965).

Survey D and Survey E provide information related to a learner's speed and accuracy, vocabulary development, and comprehension abilities. Testing time varies from forty to fifty minutes. All the tests are easy to administer and score and can be given to an entire class at once.

Lee-Clark Reading Test[24]

This test is useful for assessing abilities and skills of learners at first and second grade levels. Two forms are provided at each level. Testing time is approximately fifteen minutes for the first level, primer level, and approximately twenty-five minutes for the second level, first-reader level. The tests are easy to administer and score. Initial Teaching Alphabet editions are available for both levels of the test.

California Reading Test[25]

This series of tests can be used to gather information about reading skills and abilities of learners at all levels between grades one and nine. Two forms are provided for the lower primary grades, one and two. These tests focus on vocabulary and comprehension abilities. Approximately thirty-five minutes testing time is required. Two forms for upper primary, grades 2.5–4.5, provide scores related to vocabulary and comprehension. Each test for the upper primary grades requires approximately fifty minutes testing time. For testing at the elementary and junior high school levels, four forms are provided. Emphasis is on vocabulary and comprehension abilities. Tests at the elementary and junior high school levels require, respectively, sixty and eighty minutes for administration.

Some Limitations of Reading Survey Tests

Certain characteristics inherent in reading survey tests limit their value for locating the exact needs of some learners in reading. Reading survey tests, for example, do not reveal the exact nature of causes that may lie at the root of some of the weaknesses a learner may show in reading. Perhaps more importantly, reading survey tests fail to assess strengths and weaknesses that relate to many important skills and abilities in reading. Therefore, adequate assessment of the needs of some learners requires use of more precise measures of assessment.

More Precise
Formal Measures of
Reading Abilities

It is not often that classroom teachers are required to engage in detailed analysis of a learner's needs in reading merely for the practical purposes related to initial instructional activities. Thorough acquaintance with

[24]J. M. Lee and W. W. Clark, *Lee-Clark Reading Test* (Monterey, Ca.: California Test Bureau, 1965).

[25]E. W. Tiegs and W. W. Clark, *California Reading Test* (Monterey, Ca.: California Test Bureau, 1957, revised 1963).

learners' needs can be acquired through the continuous types of assessment that accompany the instructional process as it develops. The type of special attention that must be given to the needs of learners who have special problems also becomes clearer as instruction proceeds. Occasionally, however — even at the point of initial assessment — more precise information is needed about a learner's strengths and weaknesses in particular reading areas than that input obtained through use of general measures. More precise measures of performance can be obtained through use of reading diagnostic tests, special types of inventories, and other tests focused on specific abilities and skills in reading.

Stanford Diagnostic Reading Test[26]

Designed for learners in grades ranging from 2.5–8.5, the Stanford Diagnostic Reading Test produces scores related to several areas in reading. Seven scores can be obtained for level one, grades 2.5–4.5. Eight scores can be obtained for level two, grades 4.5–8.5. Specific subtests in level one focus on reading comprehension, vocabulary, auditory discrimination, syllabication, beginning and ending sounds, blending, and sound discrimination. Subtests in level two focus on reading comprehension from which three scores—literal, inferential, and total comprehension—are obtained. Other scores obtained from level two subtests include vocabulary, syllabication, sound discrimination, blending, and rate of reading.

Durrell Analysis of Reading Difficulty[27]

Individually administered, the test has time requirements which are prohibitive for many teachers in classroom situations. Designed to assess specific strengths and weaknesses in several areas of reading, subtests include silent and oral reading, listening comprehension, word analysis, phonetics, faulty pronunciation, writing, and spelling. Materials of the test consist chiefly of paragraphs graded in difficulty, a simple tachistoscope, and a set of cards. Measures of visual memory of words, letter-recognition, auditory analysis of word elements, rate of learning words, and listening comprehension are provided for nonreaders. An outstanding feature of the test is a detailed checklist of possible difficulties or errors. Such a list can be valuable in alerting the classroom teacher to specific abilities required in reading. Nevertheless, valid interpretation of the Durrell Analysis of Reading Difficulty requires the expertise of an experienced examiner.

Gates-McKillop Reading Diagnostic Tests[29]

These tests can be used with learners in grades one through six. Individually administered and requiring several hours for administration, these tests are seldom practical for use in the classroom. Their contents, however, reveal components of reading in which specific strengths and weaknesses may be identified. This feature makes the test, in and of itself, of some value to the

[26]B. Karlsen, R. Madden, and E. F. Gardner, *Stanford Diagnostic Reading Test* (N. Y.: Harcourt Brace Jovanovich, 1966).

[27]Donald Durrell, *Durrell Analysis of Reading Difficulty* (N. Y.: Harcourt Brace Jovanovich, 1955, new edition).

[28]A. I. Gates and A. McKillop, *Gates-McKillop Reading Diagnostic Tests* (N. Y.: Bureau of Publications, Teachers College, Columbia University, 1962).

classroom teacher. Among subtests in the Gates-McKillop tests are those designed to measure abilities related to word meaning, sentence meaning, speed of reading, spelling, and word recognition.

The Classroom Reading Inventory (CRI)[29]

The Classroom Reading Inventory by Nicholas J. Silvaroli is one of a number of resources that provide detailed knowledge of learners' strengths and weaknesses in reading. Unlike most formal diagnostic tests in reading, the Classroom Reading Inventory can be administered by the classroom

---

Figure 1

Specific Instructions
for administering Form A, Form B, and Form C

Part I ■ GRADED WORD LISTS - Form A, B or C

PURPOSE: To identify specific word recognition errors and to estimate the approximate starting level when the child begins reading the oral paragraphs in Part II.

PROCEDURE: Present the graded words lists, starting at the PP (Pre-Primer) Level, and say:

"Pronounce each word, if you are not sure or do not know the word, at least tell me what you think it is."

Discontinue at the level in which the child mispronounces or indicates he does not know 5 of the 20 words in a particular grade level (75%). Each correct response is worth five points.

As the child pronounces the words, at each level, the teacher should record all word errors on the Inventory Record.° Corrected errors are counted as acceptable responses on Part I.

		Example		
1	was	saw		(error)
2	day	+		
3	three	DK	(don't know)	(error)
4	farming	+		

After the child reaches the cut-off point (75%), his *oral reading* level should be *started* at the highest level in which he successfully pronounced all (100%) 20 words in the list.

Part II ■ GRADED PARAGRAPHS - Form A, B or C

PURPOSE: (1) To estimate the child's INDEPENDENT and INSTRUCTIONAL reading levels.
(2) To identify word recognition errors made during oral reading and to estimate the extent to which the child actually comprehends what he reads.

LEVELS: Four levels may be identified through the use of the Classroom Reading Inventory. However, most classroom teachers are concerned with the child's Independent and Instructional Levels.

Source: Nicholas J. Silvaroli, *Classroom Reading Inventory* (Dubuque, Ia.: William C. Brown Co. 1973), p. xi. Used by permission.

[29]Nicholas J. Silvaroli, *Classroom Reading Inventory* (Dubuque, Ia.: William C. Brown Co., second edition, 1973).

teacher in relatively short periods of time. Results of the test can be interpreted easily by classroom teachers who are inexperienced with standard diagnostic techniques. The Classroom Reading Inventory includes three parts: (1) graded word lists, (2) graded oral paragraphs, and (3) a graded spelling survey. Materials similar to those typically found in elementary school programs are offered in the inventory. Word lists and paragraphs are designed to be used on an individual basis. The spelling survey can be used with the class as a total group. Types of information made available through use of the Classroom Reading Inventory can be seen in Figure 1.

The Botel Reading Inventory[30]

Through a phonics mastery test, a word-recognition test, and a word-opposites test, the Botel Reading Inventory provides information related to several areas in reading achievement. Learners' reading levels, their knowledge of selected phonics, and related skills can be determined through use of the inventory. The test is appropriate for use with children whose reading levels are at fourth or lower grade levels.[31] The phonics mastery test provides information related to knowledge of sounds represented by single consonants, consonant blends, consonant digraphs, rhyming elements, vowels, and skills related to syllabication. Interpretation of test results is simplified through use of the accompanying manual.

Oral
Reading Tests

Tests that reveal strengths and weaknesses as a learner reads orally are useful in several ways. Results from oral reading tests can be used to supplement information obtained from other sources. During progress of the test, the teacher has an opportunity to observe the kinds of difficulty a learner may be experiencing. The areas of reading difficulties itemized in the forms provided for recording the learner's performance are useful for emphasizing components of reading ability. Administration of oral reading tests, however, is time-consuming and often impractical for the classroom teacher.

Gilmore Oral Reading Test[32]

Useful for analyzing the reading abilities of learners in grade levels one through eight, the Gilmore Oral Reading Test measures accuracy of oral reading, comprehension of materials, and oral reading rate. The test can be used conveniently in most classrooms, since it requires about fifteen minutes for administration.

---

[30]Morton Botel, Cora L. Holsclaw, and Gloria C. Cammarata, *The Botel Reading Inventory* (Chicago: Follett Publishing, 1961, revised 1966).

[31]Ira E. Aaron, "Botel Reading Inventory" in *The Sixth Mental Measurements Yearbook*, Oscar K. Buros, ed. (Highland Park, N. J.: Gryphon Press, 1965), p. 834.

[32]John V. Gilmore, et al., *Gilmore Oral Reading Test* (N. Y.: Harcourt Brace Jovanovich, revised 1968).

Included in the manual[33] is a system for recording errors during the reader's performance. Types of errors assessed during the performance include substitutions, mispronunciations, hesitations, repetitions, insertions, omissions, disregard of punctuation, and words for which help must be given.

The Gray Oral Reading Test[34]

The major purposes of the Gray Oral Reading Test include assessment of oral reading skills and abilities and assessment of difficulties a learner may have in reading. Provisions are made for recording errors related to total and partial mispronunciations, omissions, substitutions, insertions, repetitions, and hesitancies.

Assessing Needs of Learners Through Informal Procedures

Adequate assessment of needs of learners requires use of informal procedures. Results from these procedures are important for validation of information obtained from formal procedures and materials. In addition, informal measures are the only practical methods available to the classroom teacher for assessment of many affective behaviors of young children. Factors such as work habits, for example, are best assessed through informal approaches.

Informal procedures and materials often can be devised by the teacher to serve purposes unique to the situation. In contrast to standardized tests, informal procedures and materials generally are criterion-referenced rather than norm-referenced. As such, informal measures can be constructed or selected to conform closely to purposes defined by the situation. Criterion-referenced measures can be constructed so that learners are required to perform actual tasks related to objectives rather than to answer questions as is often required in norm-referenced measures.

Informal procedures and materials can be used to serve many of the same purposes served by formal ones. Both affective and cognitive behaviors can be assessed through informal means.

Informal Assessment of Affective Behaviors

Affective behaviors—such as interests, attitudes, appreciations, and the like—are recognized as factors important not only in themselves, but influential also in their effect upon development of cognitive skills and abilities required in reading. Yet, in many approaches to need assessment, these factors tend to be neglected or slighted. A variety of informal measures can be used to provide information related to affective behaviors.

---

[33]*Manual of Directions, Gilmore Oral Reading Test* (N. Y.: Harcourt Brace Jovanovich, 1952), pp. 8–9.

[34]Helen M. Robinson and William S. Gray, eds., *Gray Oral Reading Test* (Indianapolis, Ind.: Bobbs-Merrill, 1963).

Careful observation of the behaviors shown by learners in various situations often can substitute for use of more time-consuming and complex procedures. As Walter B. Barbe states, "No interest inventory will measure interest better than the teacher's observation."[35] Observation must be distinguished, however, from mere incidental looking. To be effective, observation must be planned and directed toward well-defined purposes. Moreover, its results should be recorded according to an appropriate technique.

Techniques for Observing and Recording Information*

Depending on the purposes set for observation of affective behaviors, procedures and techniques such as those in the following list are typical of those that can be used for making observations and recording the results.

1. *Techniques for recording observations*
   a. Anecdotal records
   b. Rating scales
   c. Checklists
   d. Questionnaires
   e. Autobiographies
2. *Typical situations in which to observe*
   a. Interviews
   b. Conferences
   c. Informal conversation between teacher and learner
   d. Discussions in class groups
   e. Conversations shared by groups of learners
   f. Story time
   g. Library periods
   h. Free-time periods
   i. Instructional periods

As suggested by this list of situations in which observation can be carried out, the typical school day affords numerous opportunities for gaining information about learners. Besides situations typically experienced during the school day, learners' daily products can reveal pertinent information.

Materials for Informal Assessment of Reading Skills and Abilities

Informal procedures and materials may be used by the classroom teacher in assessment not only for affective behaviors, but also for

---

[35] Walter B. Barbe, *Educators' Guide to Personalized Reading Instruction* (Englewood Cliffs, N. J.: Prentice-Hall, 1961), p. 97.

*This topic is discussed more fully in Chapter 6 of this text.

cognitive skills and abilities. Many informal procedures and materials serve equally well whether affective or cognitive behaviors are under consideration. There are a number of informal procedures and materials, however, designed for the direct purpose of assessing skills and abilities in reading. Among the variety of informal approaches that can be used in informal reading assessment, two approaches of particular importance are the informal reading inventory and the cloze procedure.

The Informal Reading Inventory (IRI)

The informal reading inventory—often referred to as the IRI—can provide opportunity for the teacher to make structured observations and records of the nature of an individual's overall performance in reading. The inventory can be designed to produce information related to specific components of reading, such as sight vocabulary, word-analysis skills, and basic and higher comprehension skills and abilities. Depending upon the way the inventory is used, information related to attitudes, interests, thinking, and language abilities also can be attained.

An exact definition of an informal reading inventory is difficult to give. As the word "informal" implies, the nature of an informal reading inventory is not regulated according to hard and fast guidelines or rules. Johnson and Kress have referred to the technique as a "detailed study of a reader's entire performance in the area of reading and in those language and thinking functions related to reading."[36] Harris and Smith have described it simply as a "series of paragraphs graded in terms of reading difficulty."[37] Informal reading inventories can be developed so completely and thoroughly as to fit the broad description given here in the first instance. Or they can be viewed in so limited a way as to make the description given in the second instance an appropriate one. Inventories fitting descriptions ranging between these two extremes are found in practice. The nature of any particular IRI depends upon the purposes it is designed to serve in a particular situation.

It is understandable and desirable that specific characteristics of an informal reading inventory may vary considerably from one instance to another. Very complete and comprehensive inventories are often developed by groups of teachers and utilized throughout some school districts or schools. Sometimes individual teachers construct inventories for their own unique uses. Since the purpose of the inventory is the ultimate guide for its nature, variation is to be expected.

Both the procedures and materials in construction and utilization of an inventory are unstandardized. Norms generally are not established: individuals' performances are not compared with those of others. Generally, comparisons are made between an individual's performance and standards previously and arbitrarily established as ideal by the maker of the measure.

Several general purposes can be served through use of an informal reading inventory. A teacher can gain general information related to an individual's outstanding

---

[36]Margaret Seddon Johnson and Roy A. Kress, *Informal Reading Inventories* (Newark, Del.: International Reading Association, 1965), p. 3.
[37]Larry A. Harris and Carl B. Smith, *Reading Instruction Through Diagnostic Teaching*, p. 120.

strengths and weaknesses in reading. Principally, however, an informal reading inventory serves the specific purpose of determining levels of competency that a learner may show in reading various levels of materials. Determination of levels of reading is important for both organizational and instructional purposes. Grouping for instruction or the selection of suitable materials for a group of learners are both procedures that are performed best if the teacher has information pertaining to levels at which the particular learners are reading.

An individual's ability to read varies with the level of difficulty he or she encounters in reading materials. Some materials may be of such nature that the individual can read them with ease and without assistance. In other words, the individual can read the materials at an *independent reading level.* The same individual may be able to read other materials satisfactorily that are at a higher level of difficulty with a minimum amount of help—thus, reading the materials at an *instructional level.* When reading materials are too difficult for the individual— both in word-recognition and in comprehension—these may be said to be at the *frustration level* of the individual. The *listening* or *hearing capacity level* indicates the level at which the individual can understand the meaning of a selection to a high extent if the material is read aloud, although he or she may lack skills required to decode the symbols.

Criteria accepted for levels of reading performance vary somewhat according to the developer and user of an informal reading inventory. The criteria offered by Johnson and Kress approximate many that are suggested by various authorities. According to Johnson and Kress, criteria for the levels include the following:

1. *Independent level*
Word Recognition	99% accuracy
Comprehension	90% or above
2. *Instructional level*
Word Recognition	95% accuracy
Comprehension	75% or above
3. *Frustration Level*
Word Recognition	90% accuracy, or less
Comprehension	50% or less
4. *Hearing capacity level*
Comprehension	75% or above

Materials used in an informal reading inventory also are likely to vary according to the situation and purposes the inventory is expected to serve. Generally, materials used in the inventory should exemplify the types of materials used in the instructional setting. Any, or all, of the following forms of materials may be used: (1) graded word lists for timed and/or untimed exposures to the individual in order to assess his sight vocabulary and word-analysis skills; (2) one or two sets of graded paragraphs to be read orally and/or silently by the individual in order to reveal his ability related to word skills and comprehension skills; (3) questions based on the reading selections designed and used to assess the individual's comprehension abilities; and (4) prepared forms upon which may be recorded the

---

[38] Margaret Seddon Johnson and Roy A. Kress, *Informal Reading Inventories*, pp. 5–13.

number and nature of errors the individual may make in responding to all phases of the inventory.

Procedures involved in administration of the inventory consist mainly of (1) presenting the word lists for the individual's timed and/or untimed responses, recording any errors that are noted, and (2) having the individual read the graded paragraphs either silently or orally, or both, and respond to questions designed to reveal the nature and extent of his comprehension. Both word lists and paragraphs are presented according to an ascending order of difficulty, beginning at the level at which the individual can respond easily and correctly and ending at the frustration level.

Informal reading inventories can be adapted for individual or group administration. They can be constructed and used in highly technical ways so that they become suitable as clinical procedures. In typical classrooms, however, important information about the reading skills held by the learners can be attained through types of inventories that are simple and nontechnical, both in format and in uses.

It is a relatively simple matter for classroom teachers to construct their own informal reading inventories. Lists of words, or paragraphs, can be selected from many sources. For example, basal readers provide a ready source for graded materials. The chief consideration is that the materials represent several different levels of difficulty and that they relate to the materials appropriate for the learners in the instructional situation. Detailed help for constructing and using informal reading inventories is available in many sources.*

The Cloze Procedure

Designed to provide an uncomplicated approach to determination of the readability† of materials,[39] the cloze procedure can be adapted to provide an informal approach to assessment of levels of reading ability.

In essence, the cloze procedure consists of (1) selecting a series of passages to be read by the learner or learners, (2) deletion of every fifth (or nth) word from each passage, and (3) having learners supply the words they believe were deleted.

Use of the cloze procedure can serve several purposes, including the following:
1. Finding out whether reading abilities of learners are sufficient for reading the materials to be used in their instruction
2. Finding out whether materials for independent reading are suited to the independent reading levels of the learners under consideration

---

*One source from which detailed information may be obtained regarding informal reading inventories is:
Frazier R. Cheyney, "The Informal Reading Inventory; How to Construct It, How to Use It," in *The First R: Readings On Teaching Reading*, S. L. Sebesta and C. J. Wallen, eds. (Chicago: Science Research Associates, 1972), pp. 225–28.

†Widely known readability formulas for determining difficulty of a selection include the Flesch Formula of Readability and the Dale-Chall technique. Among other procedures required in these formulas, each requires a count of either the number of syllables per word, the number of words per sentence, or both. The Dale-Chall approach also requires a count of the number of uncommon words used in each sentence.

[39] John R. Bormuth, "The Cloze Readability Procedure," *Elementary English*, 45 (April, 1968), p. 429.

3. Determining the nature of assistance learners will require in order to handle certain materials
4. Grouping individuals whose strengths and weaknesses in reading seem to be similar
5. Providing a basis for estimation of the nature of a learner's concepts and thinking abilities[40]

Obviously, the cloze procedure is most suitable for use with learners who have already acquired some basic skills in reading. For most effective results, procedures for construction, administration, and scoring should be followed closely. Detailed information regarding use of the cloze procedure can be found in any of the sources cited here.

Need Assessment, Diagnosis, and Evaluation

Comparisons can be made among the processes of need assessment, diagnosis, and evaluation. Despite the frequency with which these terms are used interchangeably, some significant differences in the nature of each process can be identified. Identification of some of the similarities and some of the differences among these processes helps to clarify the unique nature of each process.

Need Assessment and Diagnosis

The processes of need assessment and diagnosis are related but not identical. Both processes focus on determination of learners' strengths and weaknesses, but they do so to differing degrees of intensity. Diagnosis is a broader and deeper process of which need assessment is only a part.

Need assessment, generally, is characterized by use of less technical procedures and materials than those required in the process of diagnosis. Need assessment is an appropriate term for use in the description of the types of appraisal that are feasible in classroom situations. The term diagnosis describes more precisely the nature of appraisals made in clinical situations.

In both the processes of need assessment and diagnosis, recognition is given to the importance of underlying causes of any difficulties that may be found on the parts of the learners under consideration. The process of diagnosis, however, is a more systematic and in-depth probing of the causes of difficulties. In need assessment, only the most apparent causes are within the teacher's range of analysis. Consequently, the process of need assessment achieves its major effectiveness when its results are sufficient to indicate instructional priorities.

---

[40] John R. Bormuth, "The Implication and Use of the Cloze Procedure in the Evaluation of Instructional Programs" (Los Angeles, Ca.: University of California, 1967, Report No. 3). John R. Bormuth, "Comparable Cloze and Multiple-Choice Test Comprehension Scores," *Journal of Reading* (February, 1967), p. 295.

Need Assessment and Evaluation
of Achievement

Need assessment is a specialized aspect of the broader process of evaluation. Evaluation of achievement is an integral part of effective instruction in reading. Evaluation focuses on determination of the extent to which instructional objectives are achieved by learners.[41] Evaluation of achievement, therefore, assumes prior identification of instructional objectives. In the absence of recognized instructional objectives, there exists no basis for determination of that portion of a learner's achievement that is a result of instruction. Results of need assessment are essential in determining instructional objectives. Thus, one major difference between the processes of need assessment and evaluation lies in the relation each has to instructional objectives.

For need assessment and for evaluation of achievement, both quantitative and qualitative data are essential. Both processes require use of a variety of procedures and materials to acquire such data. Both are based on major principles stipulating comprehensive and continuous approaches; and both require attention throughout an instructional period, although each requires emphasis at varying times. Need assessment is emphasized prior to and during instruction, while evaluation receives its greatest emphasis during and after instruction has occurred. Effectiveness of each process generally is increased in proportion to the degree that all persons affected by it are permitted active and informed participation in it.

Problems in
Need Assessment

Several factors related to need assessment limit the degree of accuracy and precision in its results. Consequently, results of need assessment in a classroom should be considered tentative—rather than final—indications of instructional directions.

Some problems in need assessment arise because of lack of available instruments for appraising learner-characteristics. In some cases, needed materials and other resources, such as time, are not available to the classroom teacher. For many personality variables believed to affect reading ability, formal procedures and materials that are useful in classroom situations have not been designed.

Problems arise from various other sources. Error of measurement is a basic characteristic of educational measurement, even when the greatest care is taken in the use of formal measures. Mistakes can be introduced in interpretation of the results of both formal and informal measures. Frequently teachers lack competencies essential for accurate collection and analysis of information. The large number of variables affecting an individual's performance in reading intensifies the complexity of accurate assessment of his needs in reading.

---

[41]Norman E. Gronlund, *Measurement and Evaluation in Teaching*, Second Edition (N. Y.: Macmillan, 1971), pp. 7–8.

Some General Competencies Required of Classroom
Teachers For Assessment of Needs in Reading

1. Ability to apply knowledge related to the influences of growth and development that should be considered in determination of a learner's needs in reading.
2. Ability to apply knowledge related to the influence of environmental factors on a learner's reading needs.
3. Ability to interpret a learner's reading needs in light of biological and environmental factors that impinge upon them.
4. Ability to identify characteristics of a learner that are indicative of strengths or weaknesses in reading.
5. Ability to select, administer, and interpret the results of formal procedures and materials in assessment of needs in reading readiness and in reading.
6. Ability to develop and execute plans for assessing needs of all individuals comprising a classroom instructional group.
7. Ability to develop and execute plans for obtaining detailed evidence of an individual's needs in reading.
8. Ability to distinguish between those needs of a learner that can be met in a classroom situation and those that require attention of specialists.
9. Ability to select and use formal procedures and materials for assessing needs related to specific aspects of reading.
10. Ability to select and use informal procedures and materials to assess the nature of learners' affective behaviors.
11. Ability to determine whether information desired can be attained best through use of standardized achievement tests or through use of reading survey tests.
12. Ability to distinguish between the types of information that can be attained best through the use of reading survey tests or diagnostic tests in reading.
13. Ability to use efficient ways to record information resultant from need assessment approaches.
14. Ability to use the results of need assessment to improve effectiveness of instruction and learning.
15. Ability to identify causes of learners' difficulties in reading.

SUMMARY

The importance of need assessment is emphasized by its primary and recurrent role in instruction, its influence on effectiveness of individualization of instruction, and its effect on the nature of subsequent instructional tasks.

In reading instruction, need assessment can be described as a process of gathering information related to strengths and weaknesses shown by learners in skills, abilities, and affective behaviors in reading development. The basic process involves (1) deciding what information is to be gathered, (2) using procedures and materials for gathering the information, and (3) using the information as a basis for determining organizational and instructional strategies.

Since behaviors related to reading are numerous and pervasive, a variety of procedures and materials must be used in the process of need assessment. Both quantitative and qualitative data, and both formal and informal approaches are essential in gathering information related to all factors affecting reading ability.

Need assessment bears many characteristics similar to diagnosis and evaluation. Yet, there are significant differences characterizing the nature of each process. Need assessment differs from diagnosis chiefly in the degree and intensity of the investigation. It differs from evaluation mainly in terms of the times during the instructional process in which it is emphasized, and its role in relation to instructional objectives. Need assessment is emphasized prior to and during instruction. Evaluation is emphasized during and after instruction. Need assessment is essential for determination of appropriate instructional objectives. Evaluation depends on objectives previously determined as the focus of instruction.

Several competencies are required of teachers for implementing the process of need assessment in the classroom. Among these are knowledge, skills, and abilities for gathering information, and for using it to improve organizational and instructional strategies.

Review Questions

1. In what ways can the strengths of learners be recognized in the instructional program? **(1.1)** *

2. Why should instruction be designed to emphasize strengths of learners? **(1.1)**

3. How can the weaknesses shown by learners in reading be used as guidelines for the nature of instruction essential for meeting learners' needs? **(1.1)**

4. How can the results of need assessment be used to improve classroom organization for reading instruction? **(1.2)**

5. Explain how results of need assessment can be used to help determine the nature of instructional strategies essential for a particular group of learners. **(1.2)**

6. How do results of need assessment affect the types of objectives that should be set forth for a reading program? **(1.2)**

7. Describe some specific and desirable attitudes toward need assessment for which a teacher should be held accountable. Explain why the attitudes you describe are significant and reasonable ones to be expected of teachers. **(1.3)**

8. How do results of need assessment contribute to improving effectiveness of individualizing instruction? **(1.4)**

9. Define "need assessment" as it pertains to reading instruction. **(2.1)**

10. What are some basic understandings that a teacher must have in order to determine what constitutes a "need" in reading? **(2.3)**

11. Why is the teacher's concept of reading important in determination of a learner's needs in reading? **(2.3)**

12. Why is it essential to use a variety of procedures for assessing a learner's needs in reading? **(3.1)**

13. What differences exist between procedures and materials used in need assessment? **(3.2)**

---

*Boldface numbers in parentheses refer to the numbered behavioral objectives at the beginning of the chapter.

14. How might procedures and materials used in need assessment be categorized?   (**3.3**)

15. What is the most important criterion to use in determination of the appropriateness of procedures and materials to be used in need assessment?   (**3.4**)

16. Is it feasible for a teacher to assess the needs of each learner in a class group? Why, or why not?   (**3.5**)

17. What factors must be considered by the teacher who attempts to assess needs of each learner in a total class group?   (**4.1**)

18. Outline a tentative plan for assessing the needs of learners in a class at the beginning of an instructional period.   (**4.2**)

19. Make a list of procedures and materials that can be used to gather information about learners in a class.   (**4.3**)

20. What would you consider to be an adequate variety of materials to be used for surveying needs of a class prior to planning instruction in reading?   (**4.3**)

21. Define the term "reading readiness."   (**5.1**)

22. Prepare a list of questions that you think should be answered in determining an individual's readiness for reading.   (**5.2**)

23. Describe the factors about which information should be gathered in order to assess an individual's readiness for reading.   (**5.2**)

24. Make a list of formal materials that can be used in assessing readiness for reading.   (**5.3**)

25. Describe differences that exist between formal and informal measures of reading readiness.   (**5.3**)

26. List skills that are specifically related to reading that a learner could be expected to show as part of his readiness for formal instruction in reading.   (**5.4**)

27. What procedures should a teacher use in order to determine, specifically, whether a particular test of reading readiness is suitable for learners in his situation?   (**5.5**)

28. List characteristics that tend to be common to many tests of reading readiness.   (**5.6**)

29. Select two tests of reading readiness and describe the kinds of information they can provide. Point out essential differences between the two tests.   (**6.1**)

30. Select a particular factor related to reading readiness and give an example of an individual test that might be used to provide information about this factor.   (**6.2**)

31. What specific skills and abilities should be examined in order to assess a learner's needs in reading?   (**7.2**)

32. Distinguish between characteristics of survey tests in reading and tests essential for determining specific needs of an individual.   (**7.3**)   (**7.4**)   (**7.5**)

33. If you were faced with the prospect of gathering information related to the needs of all learners in a total class group, what procedures would be of major concern to you?   (**7.4**)

34. What procedures and materials would you consider to be important in determining specific strengths and weaknesses an individual may show in reading?   (**7.4**)

35. What materials would you obtain and administer in order to survey general needs of all learners in a total class group? Why would you make these selections?   (**7.5**)

36. List specific behaviors that are included in the general term "affective behaviors."   (**8.1**)

37. Why should the nature of a learner's affective behaviors be of concern in reading instruction?   (**8.1**)

38. In what specific ways do quantitative and qualitative measures of assessment differ? **(8.2)**

39. What is meant by the term "techniques of observation"? **(8.3)**

40. List and describe major characteristics of an informal reading inventory. **(8.4)**

41. Explain how an informal reading inventory can be used to gather information about needs of learners. **(8.5)**

42. Give a description of the cloze procedure. Explain the steps required in its use. **(8.6)**

43. How can the cloze procedure be used to provide information about needs of learners? **(8.7)**

44. How might results obtained from use of an informal reading inventory affect decisions that the teacher must make regarding appropriate instructional strategies? **(8.5)**

45. In what ways are need assessment and diagnosis alike? **(9.1)**

46. What is the relationship between need assessment and evaluation of achievement? **(9.2)**

47. How do the processes of need assessment and evaluation differ? **(9.2)**

48. Why should results of need assessment be considered tentative? **(10.1)**

49. State some of the problems that often accompany efforts by a teacher to determine needs of learners? **(10.2)**

50. Among the problems you have stated, which are within the teacher's power to solve? **(10.2)**

51. What basic competencies must a teacher possess in order to assess learners' needs in reading? **(11.0)**

Selected References

1. Anderson, Paul S., *Language Skills in Elementary Education,* second edition. N.Y.: Macmillan, 1972.

2. Bloom, Benjamin S., J. Thomas Hastings, and George F. Madaus, *Handbook on Formative and Summative Evaluation of Student Learning.* N. Y.: McGraw-Hill, 1971.

3. Bond, Guy L., and Miles A. Tinker, *Reading Difficulties: Their Diagnosis and Correction.* N. Y.: Appleton-Century-Crofts, 1967.

4. Cheyney, Frazier R., "The Informal Reading Inventory: How to Construct It, How to Use It." In *The First R: Readings on Teaching Reading,* eds. S. L. Sebesta and C. J. Wallen. Chicago: Science Research Associates, 1972.

5. Culhane, J. W., "Cloze Procedures and Comprehension," *The Reading Teacher,* 26 (December, 1972), 299–302.

6. DeBoer, John J., and Martha Dallmann, *The Teaching of Reading.* N. Y.: Holt, Rinehart, and Winston, 1970.

7. Farr, Roger, *Reading: What Can be Measured?* Newark, Del.: International Reading Association, 1969.

8. Farr, Roger, and Nicholas Anastasiow, *Tests of Reading Readiness and Achievement.* Newark, Del.: International Reading Association, 1969.

9. Gagne, R., *The Conditions of Learning.* N. Y.: Holt, Rinehart, and Winston, 1965.

10. Glaser, R., "Instructional Technology and the Measurement of Learning Outcomes," *American Psychologist,* 18 (1963), 519–21.

11. Goodman, Yetta M. "Reading Diagnosis — Qualitative or Quantitative?" *Reading Teacher,* 26 (October, 1972), 32–37.

12. Gottman, John Mordechai, and Robert Earl Clasen, *Evaluation in Education.* Itasca, Ill.: F. E. Peacock Publishers, 1972.

13. Gronlund, Norman E., *Measurement and Evaluation in Teaching,* second edition. Englewood Cliffs, N. J.: Prentice-Hall, 1971.

14. Harris, Albert J., *How to Increase Reading Ability.* N. Y.: David McKay Co., 1961.

15. Harris, Larry, and Carl B. Smith, *Reading Instruction Through Diagnostic Teaching.* N. Y.: Holt, Rinehart, and Winston, 1972.

16. Henderson, Judith E., and Perry E. Lanier, "What Teachers Need to Know," *The Journal of Teacher Education,* 24, No. 1 (Spring, 1973), 4–16.

17. Johnson, Margaret Seddon, and Roy A. Kress, *Informal Reading Inventories.* Newark, Del.: International Reading Association, 1965.

18. Kaufman, Roger A., "A System Approach to Education: Derivation and Definition," *A. V. Communication Review,* 16, No. 4 (Winter, 1968), 415–25.

19. Mehrens, W. A., and I. J. Lehmann, *Standardized Tests in Education.* N. Y.: Holt, Rinehart, and Winston, 1969.

20. Sweigert, Ray L. Jr., "Assessing Needs to Achieve Relevancy," *Education,* 91, No. 4 (1971), 315–18.

21. Wilson, Robert M., *Diagnostic and Remedial Reading,* second edition. Columbus, Ohio: Charles E. Merrill, 1972.

3 Objectives for Reading Instruction

Soundness of a program of reading instruction depends on how well the learners for whom it is designed achieve clearly defined objectives. Through objectives set forth for immediate guidance of day-to-day learning experiences, the major goals of reading instruction are approached and gradually achieved.

Authorities in reading instruction and leaders in the accountability movement agree on the necessity for clear direction if a program of instruction is to be effective. Illustrative of the importance assigned to clarity of directions as a need in reading instruction are the words of Albert J. Harris, "Since reading is a highly complex activity involving the learning of many specific skills, instruction should be planned with highly specific outcomes in mind."[1] Felix M. Lopez expresses a similar concern for the importance of direction in any educational undertaking, "The clearer the idea you have of what you want to accomplish, the greater your chance for accomplishing it."[2] Regardless of the perspective, whether from the standpoint of reading instruction particularly, or from that of educational accountability generally, a sense of clear direction is viewed as vital in achieving effectiveness.

Those persons directly involved in providing instruction in reading for learners in classrooms should be accountable for using clear, meaningful objectives to direct instruction and learning.

---

[1]Albert J. Harris, *How to Increase Reading Ability* (N. Y.: David McKay Co., 1962), p. 17.
[2]Felix M. Lopez and Associates, "Accountability in Education," *Phi Delta Kappan*, 52 (December, 1970), p. 231.

Behavioral Objectives

The content of Chapter 3 is presented in such a way that after reading it, an individual

1.0   Understands the nature of objectives
    1.1   Defines the term, "behavioral objective"
    1.2   Explains how objectives in reading instruction are similar to those in other areas of the curriculum
    1.3   Explains how objectives in reading instruction differ from those in other areas of the curriculum
    1.4   Explains why a variety of types of objectives are essential in reading instruction
    1.5   Describes the interrelated nature of all objectives sought through reading instruction

2.0   Recognizes the various roles of objectives in reading instruction
    2.1   Explains how objectives help to keep instruction focused on individuals, rather than being aimed vaguely toward an entire class as a homogeneous entity
    2.2   Explains how objectives can be used to facilitate planning for instruction
    2.3   Explains how objectives can be used to guide the efforts of learners to improve their own reading ability
    2.4   Describes how objectives serve as guides for selection of instructional materials
    2.5   Describes the role of objectives in guiding teaching procedures
    2.6   Explains the role of objectives in evaluation of achievement

3.0   Recognizes characteristics of objectives that are pertinent in reading instruction
    3.1   Differentiates between general and specific objectives
    3.2   Differentiates between the importance of stated and unstated objectives
    3.3   Differentiates between objectives pertaining, primarily, to cognitive behaviors and those focused on development of affective behaviors
    3.4   Selects objectives suitable for long-range plans
    3.5   Selects objectives suitable for short-range plans

4.0   Obtains objectives from various sources
    4.1   Identifies sources from which objectives may be selected
    4.2   Identifies sources from which objectives may be derived
    4.3   Explains how needs of learners constitute a source of objectives
    4.4   Explains how the local school and community contribute to determination of objectives for reading instruction
    4.5   Explains how objectives may be selected or derived from instructional procedures and materials
    4.6   Identifies professional texts that can be used as sources of objectives
    4.7   Suggests a variety of sources of objectives

5.0   Recognizes problems that may arise in relation to determination of objectives
    5.1   Describes the relationship of objectives to scope and sequence of instruction
    5.2   Explains how objectives may be used so that these do not interfere with the scope of instruction

6.0   Recognizes problems that may arise in relation to statement of objectives
    6.1   Identifies problems related to communication
    6.2   Suggests solutions to problems related to communication

6.3 Explains how the tendency to proliferate objectives may be avoided

6.4 Suggests ways in which stated objectives may be used, yet not limit the scope of instruction

7.0 States objectives in reading instruction

7.1 States general objectives for developing skills in word recognition

7.2 States general objectives for developing skills in comprehension

7.3 Selects specific objectives in terms of general objectives

7.4 Selects objectives in terms of all pertinent domains of learning

7.5 Identifies guidelines that may be used for assessing the quality of objectives

The Nature of Objectives

Objectives are statements that describe the behaviors expected of individuals as a result of learning. Many psychologists and educators agree that learning pertains to changes in behavior brought about under prescribed conditions. Paul H. Mussen describes learning as "changes in behavior or performance as a consequence of experience."[3] According to M. W. Travers, "Performance represents the observable behavior of the individual. Performance is his response. Modifications of the response indicate that learning has occurred."[4] Ernest R. Hilgard refers to learning as "the process by which an activity originates or is changed through training procedures."[5] These views of the nature of learning are widely accepted. Taking from these definitions a focus on behaviors and behavior change, teachers can deliberately seek such change by setting objectives for instruction that are directed toward specific behaviors.

Objectives in reading instruction share many characteristics with objectives in any area of the curriculum. As do objectives in any area of the curriculum, objectives in reading instruction indicate ends or products of learning, focus on the learner, and refer to observable behavior. But the majority of objectives in reading instruction also relate, directly, to knowledge, understandings, skills, attitudes, and interests essential for performing the act of reading and for using reading effectively. Because of the nature of reading, objectives for instruction in it include behaviors that may be classified in any domain of learning.

Objectives as Ends or Products of Learning

Objectives represent deliberately planned outcomes of instruction, often referred to as "ends" or "products" of learning. The meaning of these terms, however, must be considered a special one in two major ways. In the first place, an end or product of learning is not necessarily final in the sense that it is permanent or requires no further modification. Ends or products implied

---

[3]Paul H. Mussen, *The Psychological Development of the Child* (Englewood Cliffs, N. J.: Prentice-Hall, 1963), p. 14.

[4]M. W. Travers, *Essentials of Learning* (N. Y.: Macmillan, 1962), p. 29.

[5]Ernest R. Hilgard, *Theories of Learning* (N. Y.: Appleton-Century-Crofts, 1948), p. 4.

in objectives often are tentative, merely marking the conclusion of a phase of learning, as well as signalling the beginning of a subsequent phase. In the second place, ends or products of learning are usually considered relative to the individual. The achievement of an objective at the desired level of competency represents success for a particular individual. For one person, successful achievement may not be identical with successful achievement for another.

Focus on the Learner

The learner is, invariably, the subject of any meaningful objective.[6] An objective, correctly stated, is an explicit description of the way in which the learner is expected to perform, act, or behave, as a result of instruction. A behavioral objective must be differentiated clearly from statements that merely describe procedures anticipated by teachers for the conduct of a learning experience. It must be distinguished, also, from statements that describe content or activities that comprise a learning experience.

Objectives Include Observable Behavior

Objectives that should be sought in reading instruction, and for which accountability is to be assumed, must describe types of behavior that can be observed or otherwise indisputably substantiated. The behavior may be a condition in the learner, a state shown by the learner, a skill applied by the learner, or any action by the learner that becomes apparent after he has achieved an intended learning. Some changes sought as a result of reading instruction are highly tangible and can be observed directly. Other changes, because of their intangibility, must be perceived through indirect means.

Objectives Relate to Cognitive and Affective Behaviors

Objectives in reading instruction are comprehensive in their relationship to all categories of learning indicated in the cognitive and affective domains. For instance, objectives sought through reading instruction comprise behaviors that are related to the categories of knowledge, comprehension, skills, application, analysis, and synthesis, all areas categorized in the cognitive domain in the *Taxonomy of Educational Objectives*.[7] Affective behaviors classified in the taxonomy, as those of receiving, responding, valuing, organizing, and characterizing by values,[8] are sought, as well, through instruction in reading. Some behaviors of a psychomotor nature are also of concern in reading instruction because these behaviors, directly or indirectly, facilitate acquisition of behaviors directly involved in reading.

---

[6]Robert F. Mager, *Preparing Instructional Objectives* (Palo Alto, Ca.: Fearon Publishers, 1962).

[7]Benjamin S. Bloom, ed., *Taxonomy of Educational Objectives: Handbook I, Cognitive Domain* (N. Y.: David McKay Co., 1956).

[8]David R. Krathwohl, B. S. Bloom, and B. B. Masia, *Taxonomy of Educational Objectives: Handbook II, Affective Outcomes* (N. Y.: David McKay Co., 1964).

Objectives Relate to Major Goals
of Reading Instruction

Major goals of reading instruction stipulate that each learner learn how to read, and that he enjoy and use reading in enrichment of his life. All objectives in reading instruction should lead, ultimately, to achievement of these major goals. Knowledge, understandings, and skills related to the major goal of knowing how to read require development of numerous behaviors. These behaviors run the gamut from those required to master basic prereading skills and attitudes through basic decoding and comprehension abilities to those required in higher competencies in all aspects of reading. Having the desire to read and using reading for both functional and pleasurable purposes require development of numerous behaviors of an affective nature. Objectives focused on behaviors required for achievement of either of the major goals of reading instruction are sought simultaneously and continuously throughout all phases of the program.

Objectives for an Entire Class and for Individuals

Some objectives sought through reading instruction represent basic behaviors intended for achievement by all members of a class group. These objectives represent minimum essential behaviors required of all learners at a particular stage of development. Tests and other procedures used in determination of achievement related to these objectives are structured so that complete mastery of the objectives may be seen. Behaviors included in objectives designed for mastery by an entire class group generally are those categorized at the lower levels of the classification of educational objectives. These objectives accommodate what is known of similarities among learners in terms of their personal needs as well as in terms of the demands of society.

Objectives set for achievement by individuals, because of the uniqueness of individuals, allow for the differences found among learners. Some learners can be expected to achieve more, and at a higher level, than their classmates. Objectives set for maximum achievement according to individual differences are required in an effective program of instruction.

General and Specific Objectives

Both general and specific objectives are required in effective reading instruction. General and specific objectives serve different functions, yet they are interdependent and interrelated. General objectives represent major categories of behaviors identified as desirable for achievement of learners over a long-range period. The term "long-range" refers to periods of time that may vary in length. Expectations for achievement of some general objectives may continue throughout school-life and beyond school for learners. Others should be achieved, perhaps, during the elementary-school years. Others may be sought for a particular school term. Still others are set for achievement during an extensive unit of study, during a series of lessons, or during a single learning experience. For instance, the general objective "understands the meaning of democracy" would normally require a longer period for achievement than would the objective "knows the characters in the story." General objectives can be stated to represent various levels of generality.

Specific objectives are used to define the behaviors included in the general objectives but not specified there. These may be established as expectations for achievement by learners during short-range periods. These periods of time may comprise single learning experiences, or brief series of learning experiences. Behaviors included in specific objectives, as the term implies, are specific and observable. It is upon the specific objectives that accountability must ultimately depend.

Stated and Unstated Objectives

Objectives for which accountability can be claimed are those that are not only anticipated, but also stated, prior to the process of instruction. Stated objectives are sought consciously and are evaluated as an integral part of the teaching-learning process. Correctly stated objectives clearly communicate the intent of instruction. In order that objectives communicate the intent of instruction to all persons concerned, they must almost invariably be written as well. Objectives, defined and written, leave little room for equivocation regarding the intent of instruction.

Some results of instruction, however, are independent of objectives foreseen prior to instruction. Some critics of the objectives method cite the unseen ends of instruction as reasons for not stating objectives. There should be no conflict between whether objectives are stated or unstated prior to instruction. Stated objectives are those that are basic to accountability. A teacher cannot be held accountable for outcomes that are unforeseen; although at times, these outcomes may be desirable.

Unstated outcomes of instruction, on the other hand, may be detrimental to its effectiveness. The term "functional objectives" has been used to describe unstated outcomes sometimes accompanying the teaching-learning process. According to Gronlund, unstated or functional outcomes can reduce effectiveness of a program by creating a discrepancy between what is thought to be sought and that which is actually sought. Such a discrepancy must be removed if improved instruction and optimal learning conditions are to prevail.[9]

Unstated ends of instruction, whether positive or negative in their influence on teaching and learning, cannot be held as evidence of accountability. Accountability requires that objectives, of observable and measurable dimensions, give guidance to instruction and learning. Accounting must be made in terms of the degree to which anticipated objectives are represented in behaviors of learners at the conclusion of an instructional period.

Roles of Objectives in Reading Instruction

Objectives serve several important roles in the teaching-learning process. Included among these roles are those of (1) helping the teacher maintain perspective during instruction, (2) facilitating essential planning,

---

[9]Norman E. Gronlund, *Measurement and Evaluation in Teaching* (N. Y.: Macmillan, 1971), p. 34.

(3) encouraging opportunities for involvement by learners in their own learning, (4) providing direction for selection of instructional procedures and materials, and (5) providing a basis for effective evaluation.

Developing and Maintaining a Perspective During Instruction

Objectives help the teacher develop and maintain a perspective toward the essential focus of instruction, and the place and significance of all other important aspects of the program. The focal concern of instruction is to cause and facilitate learning. Objectives keep this concern before the teacher, thereby decreasing the possibility that instruction will be directed in meaningless ways.

Objectives also improve possibilities for keeping the instructional program balanced in terms of the variety of behavioral changes desired of learners. Attention and effort can be directed, proportionately, toward development of all pertinent types of behavior, both affective and cognitive. At the same time, objectives lessen the incidence of unnecessary repetition of instructional efforts.

Facilitation of the Process of Planning

Objectives simplify development of meaningful plans for all phases of instruction. Essential elements of a typical plan for instruction include (1) statement of objectives, (2) description of procedures and materials to be used during instruction, and (3) description of procedures for evaluation of achievement. Once objectives for a learning experience have been determined, the nature of plans for remaining aspects of instruction are clarified to a great extent. After objectives have been defined, the major question to be answered is whether or not subsequent tasks planned in instruction offer the most effective way to help learners achieve the objectives.

Direction for Learners' Efforts

Objectives serve both teachers and learners alike. Teachers need clear objectives to provide direction for all phases of the instructional process. Learners need objectives to clarify the importance, nature, and direction of a particular learning. As much as is possible, learners should become actively and directly involved in their own learning. One way to make sure this is done is to engage learners in recognition and acceptance of objectives.

The need for active participation by learners to help achieve the greatest value from their efforts has been widely recognized. One writer has asserted that individuals "learn in response to their needs and perceptions, not those of their teachers."[10] Another has stated that "if the youngster accepts educational objectives as his own, he is willing to undertake the activities that will result in the modification of his behavior."[11]

---

[10] Robert E. Bills, "Believing and Behaving: Perception and Learning" in *Learning More about Learning*, Alexander Frazier, ed. (Washington, D.C.: Association for Supervision and Curriculum Development, 1959), p. 63.

[11] John F. Travers, *Learning: Analysis and Application* (N.Y.: David McKay Co., 1965), p. 17.

Part of the teacher's role in achieving accountability in reading instruction is recognition of the importance of permitting learners to participate in setting and accepting objectives for their own learning. In engaging learners in this phase of their learning, the teacher must take into consideration several characteristics of the learners. The ages of the learners, their present levels of competency in reading, and their past experiences related both to reading and to the task of planning for themselves are characteristics that help determine the amount and kind of participation of which the learners are capable. All learners cannot, and need not, participate in planning objectives to the same extent.

It is also the teacher's responsibility to devise means by which learners' participation in setting and accepting objectives may be realized. Depending on the characteristics of the learners, opportunities for doing this may occur through conferences, interviews, encouragement of independent work, provision of tasks that assure success for the learners, and teacher-attitudes that permit learners the privilege of making their own mistakes.

Guide for Selection of Instructional
Procedures and Materials

Objectives play an important role as guides for selection of procedures and materials that may be needed in a program. Yet, objectives do not prescribe any particular approach as being generally more productive than another. The value of procedures and materials must be decided in terms of the specific objectives under consideration. Many approaches are available for use in a program of reading instruction. Whether or not any approach or any combination of approaches will be beneficial for learners must be decided on the basis of objectives defined for their achievement.

Basis for Evaluation of Achievement

Meaningful evaluation of achievement is based on objectives. In the absence of objectives, no criteria exist for determining whether progress in learning has been made. Objectives constitute a standard against which decisions regarding the relative or absolute progress of learners may be assessed. Mere use of testing or other measurement or evaluative techniques is pointless in the absence of objectives.

Sources of Objectives
in Reading Instruction

Objectives must be either derived from appropriate sources or selected from sources of prepared objectives for use in the program of reading instruction. The term "derived" is used here to refer to objectives perceived and constructed by the teacher. "Selected" objectives are those chosen from lists of objectives prepared and suggested by others. There are numerous sources from which teachers can derive or select objectives that are suitable for use in particular situations.

The Needs of Learners as Sources of Objectives

Instruction in reading should be directed toward development of behaviors required in reading and also behaviors relevant to the needs of the learners. Clues for objectives that are needed in a situation can be detected from several factors pertinent to the learners. These factors include the mental and physical potentialities of the learners, their experiential backgrounds, their language development and habits, their present competencies in reading, and their interests and attitudes. All of these factors and others interact in various ways to affect the nature of objectives needed in a particular situation. Results of initial and continuous need assessments made of the learners in a class comprise an important resource from which objectives may be derived.

The Local School and Community

Many objectives for reading instruction can be derived from information related to the local school and community. Social and economic conditions, expectations, and values in the school and in the surrounding community should be influential in determining the nature of objectives that are desirable in a particular learning situation.

The way in which learners are organized for instruction in a particular school emphasizes the importance of certain objectives. For example, reading instruction in an open classroom, planned and conducted by a team of teachers, necessitates some objectives that differ from those required in a self-contained classroom in which one teacher is responsible for all phases of instruction.

Some objectives are implicit in the manner in which learners are allowed to progress through the various levels of a school. For example, in many schools, learners are promoted to successively higher grade levels on the basis of their achievement at previous grade levels. In such a case, teachers at various grade levels expect that learners promoted to those grades will have achieved certain levels of competency in reading. Often, contents of the curriculum guide in use at a particular school or in a particular school district will have contributed to the nature of these expectations. Contents of curriculum guides constitute another source for selection or derivation of objectives that are to be sought in a particular situation.

Expectations held by parents and others in the community influence and even dictate some of the objectives to be sought in reading instruction. Expectations held about methods of instruction, use of the community as a learning resource, nature of homework assignments, and even the moral, ethical, and political tendencies in the community often influence the types of objectives that should be given priority in a reading program.

Instructional Procedures and Materials

Some objectives appropriately sought through reading instruction can be derived or selected from procedures and materials used in the program. Although it is desirable, it is not always possible to determine essential objectives prior to determination of procedures and materials that will be used in the program. In many classrooms, procedures and materials of instruction are, for the most part, predetermined for the teacher. From a practical viewpoint, therefore, such procedures and materials must serve a dual purpose in relation to objectives. They must become sources of objectives as well as a means through which objectives are achieved.

Basal-reader materials, widely used as core materials throughout the schools, can be used as sources of objectives. These materials, relatively comprehensive in terms of knowledge and skills required in reading instruction at various levels of the school, often contain explicitly stated objectives. In other cases, objectives are implicit in the materials. Frequently, objectives selected from basal-reader materials must be modified to meet the unique needs of learners in a particular situation. Sometimes, too, objectives selected from these sources will require restatement in order to conform to requirements for accountability. Care must be taken to make sure that statements offered as objectives are not merely statements of proposed teaching procedures or subject matter to be explored.

Materials sometimes termed "supplementary" for use in reading instruction can yield objectives that are important in a particular situation. For instance, in the book *An Activities Handbook for Teachers of Young Children*, by Croft and Hess,[12] several skills required in readiness for reading are identified. Purposes are stated for activities in phrases such as "recognizing sounds," "identifying and grouping objects beginning with the same sound," or "matching identical symbols."[13] These general purposes, with little modification, easily become specific objectives.

Some instructional materials contain lists of specific objectives identified for achievement as a result of studying the content and/or engaging in the suggested activities. An example of a list of this type is the list in the teacher's guide accompanying materials in the Phoenix Reading Series.[14] Objectives stated in behavioral terms and related to major skills in reading are ready for use in situations in which they are appropriate.

Statements of "teaching objectives" initiate plans for each lesson included in *Teacher's Manuals and Keys*, a guide book supplied for use with learning materials in the "Early-to-Read" I/T/A Program.[15] Objectives appropriate for learners can be derived from ideas included in the stated "teaching objectives." For example, both of the teaching objectives stated for a workbook lesson on "Reading from Left to Right"[16] utilize the infinitive forms, "to teach" and "to encourage," respectively, signalling that orientation of the objectives is from the standpoint of the teacher. These statements, however, can be rearranged into objectives that describe learner behavior. Stated from the standpoint of the learner, an objective such as "to teach the numerals 1, 2, 3, in sequence"[17] might become "identifies the numerals, etc."

As in the case of materials, procedures used in instruction can be used as sources for objectives. Procedures such as discussion, explanation, conversation, for exam-

[12] Doreen J. Croft and Robert D. Hess, *An Activities Handbook for Teachers of Young Children* (Boston: Houghton Mifflin, 1972), pp. 15–33.

[13] Croft and Hess, *An Activities Handbook for Teachers of Young Children*, pp. 15–33.

[14] Marion Gartler and Marcella Benditt, *et al., The Phoenix Reading Series, Level A, Teacher's Guide* (Englewood Cliffs, N. J.: Prentice-Hall, 1974), pp. 289–94.

[15] Albert J. Mazurkiewicz and Harold J. Tanyzer, *Easy-to-Read I/T/A Program Revised, Phase 1, Teacher's Manuals and Keys* (N. Y.: I/T/A Publications, 1966).

[16] Mazurkiewicz and Tanyzer, *Easy-to-Read I/T/A Manual*, p. 3.

[17] Mazurkiewicz and Tanyzer, *Easy-to-Read I/T/A Manual*, p. 25.

ple, may suggest changes that should occur in the behaviors of the learners. Procedures which require learners to seek information in classroom libraries or other libraries may reveal the utility of seeking objectives related directly to procedures.

Professional Textbooks in Reading Instruction

Many modern professional texts in the teaching of reading reflect the demands of educational accountability in the new emphasis being placed on behavioral objectives. Many modern texts include illustrative lists or other models of objectives to be achieved through instruction. These texts in reading are also useful as sources of objectives. From such sources, objectives can be selected, modified, and supplemented with others for effective use in instructional programs.

In the text *Competency in Teaching Reading*, by Carl J. Wallen, the author asserts that objectives constitute one of two major elements involved in "interactive teaching."[18] Categories of various types of reading-skill objectives are treated as integral parts of testing and teaching procedures described here.

In *Patterns of Teaching Reading in the Elementary School*, Lawrence E. Hafner and Hayden B. Jolly present an "Outline of Reading Skills and Statements of Behavioral Objectives" that have been developed by the Wisconsin Research and Development Center for Cognitive Learning at the University of Wisconsin at Madison.[19] Teachers can use a list of objectives such as this for acquiring an overall view of skill components in the reading process and for selecting objectives to use in specific situations.

Other Sources of Objectives

Numerous other resources can be used for help in obtaining objectives that can be adapted or selected outright for use in reading instruction. In *Selecting Appropriate Instructional Objectives*, Gronlund[20] offers detailed assistance for formulation of objectives in various subject areas. Application of these ideas is helpful in deriving or selecting objectives for use in reading instruction.

The major sourcebook, *Handbook on Formative and Summative Evaluation of Student Achievement* by Benjamin S. Bloom and others,[21] offers ideas for the content of objectives and for ways in which objectives may be organized to conform with all categories in the various domains of learning. A reading teacher can use the sections pertaining to the language arts for assistance in deriving or selecting objectives relevant to reading instruction.

---

[18] Carl J. Wallen, *Competency in Teaching Reading* (Chicago: Science Research Associates, 1972), p. 12.

[19] Lawrence E. Hafner and Hayden B. Jolly, *Patterns of Teaching Reading in the Elementary School* (N. Y.: Macmillan, 1972), pp. 319–42.

[20] Norman E. Gronlund, *Selecting Appropriate Instructional Objectives* (N. Y.: Macmillan, 1970).

[21] Benjamin S. Bloom, J. Thomas Hastings, and George F. Madaus, *Handbook on Formative and Summative Evaluation of Student Learning* (N. Y.: McGraw-Hill, 1971).

The Instructional Objectives Exchange (IOX)[22] collects, prepares, and distributes objectives for use in various subject areas. Related especially to concerns in reading are "Objectives on the Decoding Skills of Reading," "Reading Comprehension," and "Structural Analysis." Eva L. Baker explains the function of the IOX:

> IOX collects objectives in subject matter areas from school districts dispersed nationally. Its research assistants revise objectives which have not been clearly stated, and provide sets of test items to measure them.[23]

Criteria for Selecting or Deriving Objectives in Reading Instruction

Regardless of whether objectives are selected or derived by the teacher and regardless of the sources from which the objectives are obtained, their value in a particular situation depends on the extent to which they meet several criteria. Some of these criteria are that objectives should:

1. Represent those behaviors related to development of understandings, skills, attitudes, and interests in reading.
2. Represent concerns that are appropriate in terms of needs of the learners for whom they are selected.
3. Accommodate present competencies acquired by the learners for whom they are selected.
4. Be compatible with the value systems of the school and its community.
5. Be amenable to achievement through use of available resources.
6. Provide direction, consistently, toward the major goals of reading instruction.

Considerations in Determination of Objectives

Several considerations require attention in the process of obtaining objectives which are, at the same time, both appropriate and practical in a learning situation. Efforts should be made to ascertain that objectives derived or selected are within the scope and sequence determined for a particular program of instruction. Furthermore, objectives should serve their function and yet not restrict concerns deemed important in a program.

Objectives and the Scope and Sequence of Instruction

A teacher should know the scope and sequence expected in a program prior to setting objectives for instruction. Scope refers to the range of subject content to be explored and the skills to be developed during the

---

[22] *Catalog 1974* (Los Angeles, Ca.: Instructional Objectives Exchange, 1974).

[23] Eva L. Baker, "The Instructional Objectives Exchange: Assistance in Goal-referenced Evaluation," *Journal of Secondary Education* 45, No. 4 (April, 1970), pp. 158–62.

course of instruction. Sequence refers to the order in which elements in the program will be introduced and developed.

Clues for the scope and sequence of instruction arise from many sources. One of these is the curriculum guide in use in the particular school district. Another is the nature of materials and other resources provided for use in the instructional program. Still another is the nature of the teacher's knowledge of what is expected of learners at a particular level of development and what he or she knows of those for whom instruction is planned. All of these determinants must be considered in the process of obtaining appropriate objectives.

Consideration must be given as well to the amount of time allocated for various periods of instruction. Extended periods of instruction involve the major segments of time into which the school year is divided in particular schools. These may be six-week periods, semesters, or the like. Generally, at conclusion of these periods of time, reports of learners' progress are made. Long-range plans guided by general objectives should be used as a basic guide for instructional concerns during these extended periods. Short-range plans guided by specific objectives are needed for the briefer periods of time usually including daily or weekly concerns in a classroom.

Determination of which objectives, and how many objectives, are appropriate in terms of the scope and sequence of concerns to be encountered in a program may constitute a challenge for many teachers.

Objectives as Limiting Influences on the Scope of Instruction

Critics, questioning the value of objectives in education, have pointed to the possibility that objectives may be used in such a way as to become limiting influences on the scope of instruction. Conceding that objectives may be of value when applied to simple and easily defined skills, Arthur Combs has warned that objectives "applied without clear understanding of their limitations . . . can be wasteful and inefficient—even on occasion, destructive of the very ends we seek."[24] Others have asserted that the teacher's potential may be lost if his attention is focused so much on objectives that complete coverage of all important concerns is neglected. Many persons have expressed the fear that learning "specifics" may preclude learning the "generals" so important in any area of the curriculum.[25]

The problem of how to use objectives in such ways that they do not become limiting influences, either on the scope of instruction or on the type of concerns included in that scope, must be faced by teachers of reading. Several considerations can help prevent the problem from being an unsolvable one.

It should be considered that although objectives provide direction for other important phases of instruction, they are not intended as inflexible standards. Objectives that are recognized and deliberately sought do not preclude achievement

---

[24] Arthur W. Combs, *Educational Accountability: Beyond Behavioral Objectives* (Washington, D. C.: Association for Supervision and Curriculum Development, 1972), p. 6.

[25] Arthur M. Cohen, "Junior-College Objectives: Reactions and Criticisms," *School and Society*, 97 (Summer, 1969), pp. 330–33.

of others unforeseen prior to instruction. Knowledge of specified objectives can free the teacher and the learner to accomplish more. Stated objectives need not limit the number of behavioral changes that are actually realized as a result of instruction.

Not only is it unnecessary that specified objectives limit the number of changes actually brought about in learners, but they need not limit the nature of behaviors developed. Objectives at the lower levels of behaviors, categorized in the cognitive domain, are easier to state and to evaluate than those classified at higher levels, in the cognitive or affective domains. Difficulty in defining and evaluating objectives at higher levels of learning, however, should not discouarge efforts to be as exact as possible both in recognizing and deliberately seeking these in the program. Properly conceived and properly sought objectives in the cognitive domain aid in development of many desirable behaviors in the affective domain. Daniel Tanner has reminded us that "although the term 'domain' implies a separation of spheres of activity, in effective learning, these spheres are marked not by separation, but by continuity and interdependence."[26]

Problems Related to Stating Objectives

Tasks involved in statement of objectives for reading instruction sometimes are accompanied by problems pertaining to communication and the tendency to proliferate the number of objectives.

The Problem of Communication

One of the problems that must be faced in the statement of objectives is how to make sure that the objectives communicate clearly the intent of instruction to any person involved or interested in the results sought in a particular situation. Many terms used in reading education tend to convey different meanings to different persons. Even the term reading, itself, is defined variously according to the user's beliefs about the nature of reading or according to the perspective from which reading is viewed. The same behaviors in reading may be identified by different terms by different persons. Conversely, behaviors which are essentially different may be identified by the same term. Yet, if objectives are to fulfill their potential in accountability, they must communicate clearly the changes proposed for learners.

Educational jargon and other types of speech that limit communication with the general public and with learners must be omitted from objectives if they are to communicate the intent of instruction and learning. Behaviors must be described in simple terms and in terms whose meanings are widely understood and accepted.

Limiting the Number of Stated Objectives

Contemplation of all the abilities, skills, and affective behaviors essential in effective reading yields large numbers of objectives impor-

---

[26] Daniel Tanner, *Using Behavioral Objectives in the Classroom* (N.Y.: Macmillan, 1973), p. 5.

tant in a program of instruction. How to limit the number of objectives so that they are realistic in terms of actual use and actual achievement can be a problem. Too many stated objectives can result in confusion rather than in clarification of intent.

General objectives determined for an extended period of time or an extended unit of work should be stated first. Each general objective stated should be subjected to rigid evaluation in terms of its potential for meeting the needs of particular learners, requirements of the curriculum, and possibilities for achievement within the resources available in the situation. If the number of general objectives is limited sufficiently, the number of specific objectives needed becomes lessened.

The number of specific objectives identified to define each general objective should be limited to just enough to conclude that the learner's achievement of the general objective is satisfactory. Only the most important and meaningful behaviors needed to amplify meaning of the general objective are essential.

Another factor that can help to limit the number of objectives needed is the level of generality expressed in each general objective. An attempt should be made to avoid including broad statements of behaviors that are difficult to define in the general objectives. Emphasis should be placed on behaviors that have possibilities for realistic achievement. Both general and specific objectives should focus on behaviors that can be described by terms that tend to have similar meanings for most persons. Compare, for example, meanings generally held of terms such as knows, understands, or identifies with meanings generally held of terms such as feels, believes, or envisions. It is easier to identify behaviors essential in indicating that a learner knows, understands, or identifies something than it is to substantiate what he feels, believes, or envisions.

How to State
Objectives in
Reading Instruction

Objectives in reading instruction should not only be recognized by the teacher, but should be stated as well, if they are to perform their roles in effective instruction and also in accountability. More than a verbal claim must be made if objectives are to be considered operant in a program of instruction. Statements of clear, precise objectives for reading instruction necessitate attention to certain technological aspects of the task.

Importance of General Objectives
as First Concerns

In stating a list of objectives, attention should first be given to the general objectives contemplated for an aspect of instruction. From the general objectives, the nature of specific ones needed will become apparent. General objectives provide a framework essential for giving meaning, importance, and continuity to specific objectives.

Focus on Learner Behavior

The subject of an objective stated for instructional purposes is, invariably, the learner. Because this is the case, the subject of the objective need not always be stated. For the classroom teacher, it is often economical, in terms of time and effort, simply to state the behavior sought and omit direct reference to the subject. Omission of the subject, however, requires that the objective be so clearly stated from the orientation of the learner that there will be no confusion regarding its focus.

Terms used to initiate a statement of intent such as, "to introduce," "to develop," and the like, are seldom useful in an objective designed to describe anticipated learner behavior. These infinitive forms almost always refer to performances to be made by the teacher in the process of an instructional activity. Statements similar to the following, for example, sometimes are mistaken for behavioral objectives for learners:

1. To introduce ten words from a list of basic sight words.
2. To present the main characters in the story.
3. To develop interest in the poem.

The subject is omitted from each of the examples stated above, yet there can be no doubt about who will do the "introducing," the "presenting," the "developing." Any statement of a similar focus does not meet the specification of a behavioral objective for learners. Note the emphasis in the following examples:

1. Recognizes ten words from a list of basic sight words.
2. Identifies the main characters in a story.
3. Appreciates poems about animals.

Although specific ways in which the learner will show the behavior required in each of the general objectives in the examples are not clear, it is immediately clear that the subject of concern is the learner.

Identification of Products of Learning

Because objectives describe the nature of a learner's behavior at conclusion of a phase of instruction, this behavior can be considered a product. The way in which an objective is stated should emphasize the nature of the product expected, rather than the process of learning that is occurring. Nor should an objective merely indicate that a learner has the ability to show a behavior. The choice of words used to describe the behavior expected determines whether a process, an ability, or a product will be communicated by the objective.

Certain words are descriptive of some type of the process of learning, rather than descriptive of the product resultant from learning. For example, words such as "achieves," "learns," "develops," etc. indicate behaviors in the process of developing a product, not the product itself. Products of learning are more clearly indicated by terms such as "knows," "understands," "demonstrates," or "uses," etc. This is illustrated in the pairs of examples which follow. Note how the choice of verbs used to initiate each statement shifts emphasis from process as in examples numbered 1 to a product as in examples numbered 2.

1. Learns how to use the components of compound words as clues to word recognition.
2. Uses the components of compound words as aids to word recognition.

1. Achieves understanding of contextual clues as aids to word recognition.
2. Understands uses of contextual clues as aids to word recognition.

A distinction should, likewise, be made between statements that describe actual behavior and those that refer to ability. Behavior or performance can be observed. Ability, as such, can only be assumed to exist. Behavior is a manner of acting or performing; ability is the power or capacity to act or perform. If an objective is to communicate clearly what the learner does at completion of instruction, it must describe actual behavior, not ability believed to underlie the behavior. Merely to state that the learner has ability to act or perform leaves the objective open to varied interpretations. For this reason, statements such as the following are inadequate as objectives that identify products of learning.
1. Ability to discriminate between the sounds "b" and "d."
2. Ability to follow directions.
3. Ability to summarize the sequence of events in a story.

In each of these examples, the question of what the learner does to indicate that the ability exists remains unclear. The types of behaviors expected of the learner are left to the imagination of the reader.

Inclusion of One Behavior Per Objective

Only one behavior or one category of behaviors should be included in each objective. In the case of a general objective, a category of behaviors may be indicated. A specific objective should convey a specific intent.

There are several reasons for concentrating on one behavior per objective. In this way, the potential of an objective for clear communication is increased. The possibility that attention will be diverted from the central intent of the objective is lessened. Persons concerned with the objective are not forced to interpret the relative importance of the behaviors included. The process of evaluating achievement of the objective is simplified.

In the following example of objectives, taken from plans prepared by a teacher, lack of focus and difficulty of evaluating achievement of the objectives are apparent.
1. Asks questions and discovers answers by deduction.
2. Knows the spelling list and recognizes the misspelled words.
3. Uses listening skills. Is alert to the story.

Avoid Unnecessary Words

Loading an objective with numerous modifiers complicates interpretation of its meaning. No amount or type of modifiers can improve potential for communication of a badly stated objective. A good approach to formulation of an objective that communicates clearly the intent of instruction is to use only as many words as are necessary to make its point, and no more. For example, the objective, "Becomes aware of what fairy tales really say," is not improved in quality by addition of the extraneous term, "really."

Stating Objectives in the Cognitive Domain

Although its uses are not limited to the provision of categories of objectives for use in reading instruction, the *Taxonomy of Educational Objectives* (Bloom, 1956[27]; Krathwohl, 1964[28]) is an important aid in determining appropriate objectives for reading instruction. The taxonomy can be used for assistance in acquiring sufficient comprehensiveness in a list of objectives, whether the list is prepared for an extended period of work or for a single learning experience. Using the taxonomy as a reference can prevent concentration of objectives on a narrow range of concerns.

The taxonomy consists of a classification of areas of learning arranged in hierarchical order into which objectives appropriate for any area of the curriculum can be placed. Handbook I of the taxonomy includes categories in the cognitive domain pertaining to knowledge and development of intellectual abilities and skills. Handbook II pertains to the affective domain emphasizing outcomes of education that relate to feelings or humanistic attributes. Both parts of the taxonomy are of particular interest in reading instruction.

Objectives determined to be essential in a particular program of reading instruction can be viewed as adequately comprehensive when these are balanced in their relationship to all applicable categories in both the cognitive and affective domains. Categories in the taxonomy overlap and are integrally interdependent and interrelated. Not only *should* objectives in many applicable categories be sought simultaneously, but any appreciable success in their achievement *demands* that their interdependence and interrelatedness be recognized.

Categories in the cognitive domain include (1) knowledge, (2) comprehension, (3) application, (4) analysis, (5) synthesis, and (6) evaluation.[29] A brief description of each category in the cognitive domain and illustrative objectives related to reading instruction are presented in Table 1, pages 72–73.

Stating Objectives in the Affective Domain

Affective objectives have been defined as those that are primarily related to attitudes, interests, appreciations, and other emotions.[30] An individual's feelings are immensely influential on the development of cognitive abilities and skills. To an extent, quite the reverse is also the case. Some feelings are greatly affected by an individual's achievement in cognitive areas.

---

[27] Bloom, editor, *Taxonomy of Educational Objectives: Handbook I, Cognitive Domain.*

[28] Krathwohl, Bloom, and Masia, *Taxonomy of Educational Objectives: Handbook II, Affective Outcomes.*

[29] Bloom, *Taxonomy of Educational Objectives: Handbook I Cognitive Domain*, pp. 201–7.

[30] Blaine Nelson Lee and M. David Merrill, *Writing Complete Affective Objectives: A Short Course* (Belmont, Ca.: Wadsworth Publishing, 1972), p. 2.

Table 1   Major Categories in the Cognitive Domain of the Taxonomy of Educational Objectives with Reading Objective Examples

Description of Major Category	*Illustrative Objectives in Reading*
1 Knowledge: Remembering or recalling information previously learned	1.1 Identifies the main character(s) in a story
	1.2 Relates sequence of events in a story
	1.3 Identifies speech sounds represented by initial consonants
	1.4 Names the vowels
	1.5 Recites a phonic generalization
	1.6 Defines a term
2 Comprehension: Understanding the meaning of material (at lowest level of understanding), translating, interpreting, predicting consequences or effects	2.1 Retells a story
	2.2 Summarizes a selection
	2.3 Gives an example of a phonic generalization
	2.4 Draws a picture related to the theme of a story
3 Application: Uses what is learned or read in new and concrete situations	3.1 Applies rules of syllabication by dividing given words into syllables
	3.2 Bakes a cake according to directions given in a recipe
	3.3 Shifts the accent in given words according to the context in which they are used
	3.4 Uses the index to locate a specific topic in a book
	3.5 Follows written directions in completing independent work
	3.6 Determines pronunciation of a word by applying phonic skills
4 Analysis: Distinguishes the component parts of material in order to clarify its structural organization; identifies relationships between/among the parts, ideas or organizational principles; determines author's purposes	4.1 Points out implied meanings in a selection
	4.2 Distinguishes between facts and opinions stated in a selection
	4.3 Identifies the unstated assumptions in a selection
5 Synthesis: Combines ideas or parts to form a new idea or thing: a unique communication, a plan of operation, or a set of abstract operations	5.1 Writes an original story based on the theme of a story
	5.2 Presents a plan for sharing a story
	5.3 Categorizes, according to types,

Note: Descriptions of each category presented here are based on and paraphrased from explanations given in Bloom, *Taxonomy of Educational Objectives: Handbook I, Cognitive Domain.*

Description of Major Category		Illustrative Objectives in Reading
Table 1 (Continued)		
		propaganda techniques encountered in a selection
	5.4	Plans a dramatization of a story
6 Evaluation: Judges the value of ideas, materials, procedures on the basis of specified criteria.	6.1	Appraises ideas in a selection in terms of the author's purposes
	6.2	Compares themes in two selections in terms of their application to the solution of a defined problem
	6.3	Validates information by checking several sources
	6.4	Reevaluates past conclusions in light of new information

Participation by an individual in any experience designed for achievement of cognitive objectives requires use of his affective attributes. For instance, ability to receive—or "attend"—usually is a prerequisite for achieving success in any school-related activity. Affective behaviors, although frequently neglected in formal plans for learning experiences in reading, are not only important but, in reality, cannot be separated from cognitive concerns.

Affective behaviors are less tangible than those of a cognitive nature. As such, they are more difficult to define or specify than cognitive ones. Compared with cognitive objectives, affective objectives are not generally measurable in a quantitative sense. Extent of their presence or absence, or of their rate of development, must be reported on the basis of subjective evidence.

Difficulties involved in defining or evaluating affective objectives, however, are not sufficient to justify their neglect in plans, or implementation of the plans, in reading instruction. Their development should not be left entirely to chance, although accountability for these as products of instruction cannot be claimed in the same sense as that claimed for development of cognitive behaviors.

The taxonomy of affective outcomes of education prepared by Krathwohl, Bloom, and Masia[31] can be helpful in determination of affective objectives in reading instruction. Categories of affective outcomes identified in the taxonomy include (1) receiving, (2) responding, (3) valuing, (4) organization, and (5) characterization by a value or value complex. These categories are arranged — as are the ones in the taxonomy of cognitive objectives — according to a hierarchical continuum. They can be used by the teacher as a guide or set of criteria by which objectives in reading instruction can be appraised for suitability of content and comprehensiveness. Descriptions of each of the categories and objectives illustrative of categories are presented in Table 2.

---

[31] Krathwohl, Bloom, and Masia, *Taxonomy of Educational Objectives: Handbook II, Affective Outcomes*, pp. 176–85.

Table 2 Major Categories in the Affective Domain of the Taxonomy of Educational Objectives with Reading Objective Examples

Description of Major Category	Illustrative Objectives in Reading
1 Receiving: Awareness, willingness to pay attention, listens	1.1 Notices differences in alphabetic symbols 1.2 Notices likenesses in alphabetic symbols 1.3 Detects rhyming elements in words 1.4 Identifies words that begin alike
2 Responding: Reacts overtly to an experience; participates; volunteers action; achieves satisfaction from participation	2.1 Completes work voluntarily 2.2 Asks questions related to an oral selection 2.3 Selects books to read for personal enjoyment 2.4 Asks questions related to story
3 Valuing: Attaches worth to various phenomena; accepts values; shows preference for certain values; becomes committed	3.1 Completes assigned work 3.2 Supports point of view with evidence 3.3 Handles books properly 3.4 Applies work-study skills, independently 3.5 Joins classroom book club
4 Organization: Organizes personal values into a system; determines relationships among values; establishes priorities	4.1 Compares characteristics of a story form liked with those of a form disliked 4.2 Suggests probable sources of bias in both sides of an argument 4.3 Fits oral presentation into allotted time limits
5 Characterization by a value or value complex: develops a characteristic life style; acts consistently in accordance with the values, beliefs, or ideals that comprise his philosophy	5.1 Explains why he uses self-discipline 5.2 States reasons why he prefers certain types of books

Note: Descriptions of each category presented in Table 2 are based on, and paraphrased from, the taxonomy of affective outcomes by Krathwohl, Bloom, and Masai.

Competencies Required of Teachers

In order to facilitate utilization of objectives in the instructional program in reading, competencies such as the following are helpful:

1. Ability to utilize information resultant from need assessment as a source of objectives in reading.

2. Ability to identify objectives for learners whose needs, abilities, and interests differ.
3. Ability to utilize content and skills in reading as sources of objectives.
4. Ability to state general objectives for long- and short-range plans.
5. Ability to relate specific objectives to general objectives.
6. Ability to use information related to the nature of the school as a resource for objectives relevant in reading instruction.
7. Ability to locate sources from which objectives needed in reading instruction may be selected.
8. Ability to use the community in which the school exists as a resource for determining objectives relevant in the reading program.
9. Ability to assess the relative importance of stated and unstated objectives in reading instruction.
10. Ability to differentiate between types of evaluation data required for accountability related to achievement of cognitive and affective objectives.
11. Ability to select instructional procedures and materials to lead to achievement of identified objectives.
12. Ability to relate objectives to both instructional and evaluation procedures.
13. Ability to involve learners, according to their levels of development, in recognition and acceptance of objectives pertinent in their reading instruction.
14. Ability to differentiate between objectives essential for long-range plans and those essential for immediate achievement.
15. Ability to determine feasible solutions to problems related to the use of objectives in the reading program.
16. Ability to state objectives that meet criteria for clear communication of intent.

SUMMARY

Like objectives in any area of the curriculum, objectives in reading instruction are descriptions of behaviors which learners are expected to show as a result of learning. Behavioral objectives are practical applications of the concept that learning means changes in behavior brought about under certain conditions. Objectives in reading instruction are identifiable and specific behaviors resultant from instruction. They indicate the conscious intent of teachers to produce identifiable evidence that learning has occurred. Objectives provide a basis for evaluation upon which claim to accountability can be made.

Objectives in reading instruction or in any area of the curriculum focus on the learner. Any other focus removes the statement from the category of those designed to indicate intent for student learning. Care should be taken to differentiate objectives from statements that merely describe teaching procedures or content.

Objectives in reading instruction relate to cognitive and affective behaviors. All behaviors are interrelated and interdependent, regardless of categorization. An attempt should be made to achieve balance in the types of objectives defined for reading instruction. It must be recognized, however, that different types of data are required for accountability related to different types of objectives.

Objectives serve many different roles in an instructional program. Among these roles are their functions as means for (1) helping teachers to maintain a perspective toward many other aspects of the instructional program, (2) facilitating the process of planning, (3) serving as guides for the selection of strategies and materials to be used in the program, and (4) providing a basis for evaluation of achievement.

Varied sources exist from which objectives for reading instruction may be derived or selected. Sources should include the needs of learners and requirements made by the process of reading.

The quality of objectives can be determined, in part, by their potential for clear communication of instructional intent. Teachers should master technological aspects related to stating objectives in reading instruction. Several competencies facilitate the effective utilization of objectives in an instructional program in reading.

Review Questions

1. Of the following statements, select the one that most closely exemplifies your concept of an objective for reading instruction. Explain why you presume your choice to be correct. **(1.1)** **(1.2)** **(1.3)***
   a. To introduce a phonic generalization related to pronunciation of a diphthong.
   b. To present several examples of digraphs.
   c. Selects several examples of words that contain digraphs from a list of selected words.
   d. Identification of irregular, function words.
2. What are major characteristics of the reading process? What are implications of these characteristics for the types of objectives required in a comprehensive approach to reading instruction? **(1.4)**
3. State several reasons why affective objectives are important in achievement of objectives in the cognitive domain. **(1.5)**
4. Why should objectives in the cognitive domain and those related to the affective domain be sought simultaneously in a program of reading instruction? **(1.5)**
5. What is the major function of objectives in reading instruction? **(2.1)**
6. Explain how objectives help to focus attention on achievement by an individual, rather than on that of a class as a group. **(2.1)**
7. Why should objectives be selected prior to selection of instructional procedures? **(2.2)** **(2.5)**
8. Suggest ways by which learners can be made aware of objectives for improvement of their own efforts to learn. **(2.3)**
9. Suggest techniques that may be used by a teacher to make first graders aware of, and receptive of, objectives to be sought during a learning experience. **(2.3)**
10. Suggest ways by which learners in the intermediate grades may participate in selecting objectives. **(2.3)**
11. What arguments substantiate the claim that evaluation of achievement is impossible if objectives are not identified prior to instruction? **(2.6)**
12. Prepare a list of general and specific objectives that are appropriate for a short-range

---

*Boldface numbers in parentheses refer to the numbered behavioral objectives at the beginning of the chapter.

plan for a reading activity for learners of a grade and age level of your choice. **(3.1)** **(3.5)**

13. What are some limitations that might be expected in instructional effectiveness when instruction is given in the absence of stated objectives? **(3.2)**

14. How would you defend the statement, "I know the objectives for this learning experience although I cannot put them into specific statements"? **(3.2)**

15. Prepare two lists of objectives. Include cognitive objectives in one list and affective behaviors in the other. What objectives in each of the lists might be sought through similar types of learning experiences? **(3.3)**

16. Prepare a list of general and specific objectives that would be suitable for an extended period of instruction related to a major topic or set of skills in reading? **(3.4)**

17. Make a list of sources that may be used in obtaining objectives for reading instruction for learners in a grade level of your choice. From the list you have compiled, indicate those sources from which objectives must be derived and those from which objectives may be selected. **(4.1)** **(4.2)**

18. How do needs of a learner influence the nature of objectives that should be used in his instruction? **(4.3)**

19. State several specific ways in which each of the following may be used as sources for objectives:
    a. The local school
    b. The community
    c. Instructional materials and procedures **(4.4)** **(4.5)**

20. List several sources from which objectives for reading instruction may be obtained. **(4.6)** **(4.7)**

21. State several characteristics that help to determine whether an objective clearly communicates the intent of instruction. **(6.1)**

22. What procedures should be followed to make sure that statement of an objective clearly identifies the behavior intended? **(6.2)**

23. Make a list of guidelines that can be used to prevent extension of a list of specific objectives beyond the limits of practical use. **(6.3)**

24. How might objectives be used to broaden, rather than limit, the scope of instruction? **(6.4)**

25. Prepare a plan for a lesson on some phase of word-recognition that you might teach to learners in a grade level of your choice. Identify the general and specific objectives that are to be sought. **(7.1)**

26. Select a story suitable as the basis for a lesson in reading at a grade level of your choice and do each of the following:
    a. State a general objective related to word recognition for which this story might be used as a means for achievement. **(7.1)**
    b. State a general objective related to comprehension for which this story might be used as a means for achievement. **(7.2)**
    c. For each general objective, state the specific objectives you would need for determining achievement of the general objective. **(7.3)**
    d. Make a list of affective behaviors that the story might be helpful in achieving. **(7.4)**

Make a list of guidelines or criteria by which the quality and appropriateness of general and specific objectives might be assessed.

Selected References

1. Aylesworth, Thomas G. and Gerald M. Reagan, *Teaching for Thinking*. Garden City, N. Y.: Doubleday, 1969.
2. Beatty, Walcott H., editor, *Improving Educational Assessment and an Inventory of Affective Behavior*. Washington, D. C.: Association for Supervision and Curriculum Development, 1969.
3. Bloom, Benjamin S., editor, *Taxonomy of Educational Objectives: Handbook I, Cognitive Domain*. N. Y.: David McKay Co., 1956.
4. Bloom, Benjamin S., J. Thomas Hastings, and George F. Madaus, *Handbook on Formative and Summative Evaluation of Student Learning*. N. Y.: McGraw-Hill, 1971.
5. Gagne, R. M., "Educational Objectives and Human Performance" in *Learning and the Educative Process*, J. D. Krumboltz, editor. Chicago: Rand McNally, 1965, pp. 1–24.
6. _____, *The Conditions of Learning*. N. Y.: Holt, Rinehart, and Winston, 1965.
7. _____, "The Implications of Instructional Objectives for Learning" in *Instructional Process and Media Innovations*, R. A. Weisgerber, editor. Chicago: Rand McNally, 1968, pp. 505–16.
8. Girod, Gerald R., *Writing and Assessing Attitudinal Objectives*. Columbus, Ohio: Charles E. Merrill, 1973.
9. Gronlund, Norman E., *Stating Behavioral Objectives for Classroom Instruction*. N. Y.: Macmillan, 1970.
10. Kearney, Nolan C., *Elementary School Objectives*. N. Y.: Russell Sage Foundation, 1953.
11. Krathwohl, D. R., B. S. Bloom, and B. B. Masia, *Taxonomy of Educational Objectives: Handbook II, Affective Outcomes*. N. Y.: David McKay Co., 1964.
12. Lee, Blaine Nelson, and M. David Merrill, *Writing Complete Affective Objectives: A Short Course*. Belmont, Ca.: Wadsworth Publishing, 1972.
13. Lindvall, C. M., editor, *Defining Educational Objectives*. Pittsburgh: University of Pittsburgh Press, 1964.
14. Mager, Robert F., *Developing Attitude Toward Learning*. Palo Alto, Ca.: Fearon Publishers, 1968.
15. _____, *Preparing Instructional Objectives*. Palo Alto, Ca.: Fearon Publishers, 1962.
16. Plowman, Paul, *Behavioral Objectives in Reading*. Unit 8. Chicago: Science Research Associates, 1969.
17. Popham, W. James, E. W. Eisner, H. J. Sullivan, and Louise L. Tyler, *Instructional Objectives*. A.E.R.A. Monograph Series on Curriculum Evaluation, No. 3. Chicago: Rand McNally, 1969.
18. Popham, W. James, and Eva L. Baker, *Set of 7 Illustrative Filmstrips with Accompanying Audio-Taped Narrations and Instructor's Manual*. Los Angeles: VIMCET Associates, 1967.
    (1) "Appropriate Practice"
    (2) "Educational Objectives"
    (3) "Establishing Performance Standards"
    (4) "Evaluation"
    (5) "Perceived Purpose"
    (6) "Selecting Appropriate Educational Objectives"
    (7) "Systematic Decision-Making"

19. _____, *Systematic Instruction.* Englewood Cliffs, N. J.: Prentice-Hall, 1970.

20. Skinner, B. F., *The Technology of Teaching.* N. Y.: Appleton-Century-Crofts, 1968.

21. Sullivan, H. J., *Improving Learner Achievement through Evaluation by Objectives.* Inglewood Ca.: Southwest Regional Laboratory for Educational Research and Development, 1968.

22. Tanner, David, *Using Behavioral Objectives in the Classroom.* N. Y.: Macmillan, 1972.

23. Tyler, R. W., *Basic Principles of Curriculum and Instruction.* Chicago: University of Chicago Press, 1950.

24. _____, "Some Persistent Questions on the Defining of Objectives" in C. M. Lindvall, editor, *Defining Educational Objectives.* Pittsburgh: University of Pittsburgh Press, 1964, pp. 77–83.

25. Walbesser, Henry H., *Constructing Behavioral Objectives.* College Park, Md.: College of Education, University of Maryland, 1968.

4 Individualizing Reading Instruction

The importance of the individual is a major concern in educational accountability. Effective instruction cannot be achieved by attempting to force all learners into a common mold. Accountability's thrust is toward making instruction count for each person.

Reading itself is an individual matter. Not only is development of competence in reading relative to variables affecting each person differently, but the uses of the reading skill are also largely unique to an individual. Usually, reading is not a social activity in which numerous persons share simultaneously. Instead, reading is a silent and unique communication shared privately between an author and an individual.

Accountability demands that instruction be directed to each learner. Yet, in many classrooms where reading is taught, everything is limited except the number of individuals who must be taught to read. Personnel, facilities, materials of instruction, time, and other factors frequently are less than are desirable for adequately meeting individual needs and requirements.

While the importance of individualizing instruction is recognized among advocates of accountability and among persons primarily concerned with effective reading instruction, many plans for achieving it tend to be highly impractical in typical classroom situations. Often, financial resources for implementing such plans are inadequate. Yet, the need for individualizing instruction in reading must be met if students are to learn to read in the most effective way possible. Thus, the task of individualizing instruction must be achieved within the constraints found in most situations.

Ultimately, individualization of instruction is more a reflection of the teacher's attitudes and competencies than it is a matter of certain routines, physical accommodations, or availability of other resources. Individualizing instruction is a process of humanizing the approaches used in instruction. It is a method of receiving and dealing with human beings. As such, it can be achieved in any classroom, to an appreciable degree, regardless of the physical constraints within the situation.

Behavioral Objectives

The content of Chapter 4 is presented in such a way that after reading it, an individual

1.0   Understands the necessity for individualizing reading instruction

     1.1   Predicts the range of ability often characteristic of a classroom group of learners

     1.2   Describes linguistic differences that may be found among learners in a classroom group

     1.3   Describes differences in experiential and cultural backgrounds that may be found among learners in a classroom group

     1.4   Identifies different types of learning modalities that may be preferred by individuals

     1.5   Describes how similarities among individuals in a classroom group may be used to facilitate individualization of instruction

2.0   Understands the meaning of individualized instruction

     2.1   Identifies the meaning of terms used to indicate individualized reading instruction

     2.2   Describes characteristics of individualized reading as a formalized approach to reading instruction

     2.3   Distinguishes individualization of instruction from a discrete approach to reading instruction

     2.4   Explains the basic philosophical ideas underlying the formalized approach to individualized reading instruction

     2.5   Describes types of problems often encountered in using the formalized approach to individualized reading instruction

     2.6   Identifies principles that can be used as a practical guide to individualized instruction

3.0   Knows conventional approaches used for individualizing reading instruction

     3.1   Describes school-wide grouping plans

     3.2   Describes methods of grouping within classrooms

     3.3   Explains how effective teaching can be viewed as a means for individualizing instruction

4.0   Understands how to plan for individualization of instruction

     4.1   Identifies facets of instruction that should involve cooperative planning by teacher and learners

     4.2   Suggests ways in which the daily schedule for reading instruction can be arranged

     4.3   Explains the importance of planning for the arrangement of instructional materials in the classroom

     4.4   Suggests plans for arranging learning space in the classroom

4.5 Explains reasons for planning with (a) individuals, (b) small groups, and (c) the total class

5.0 Knows various strategies and materials that can be used for individualizing reading instruction

5.1 Describes types of programmed materials

5.2 Identifies types of multi-media approaches

5.3 Describes steps in the construction of "modules"

5.4 Explains how modules can be used for individualizing reading instruction

5.5 Explains how learning stations or centers can be used for individualizing reading instruction

6.0 Understands that individualization of instruction is not dependent on a specific approach or method of instruction

6.1 Describes the nature of an approach to reading instruction

6.2 Identifies special features of some widely used approaches to reading instruction

6.3 Compares advantages of selected approaches for individualizing instruction

7.0 Understands how learners can be helped to develop independence in reading

7.1 Explains how independence in reading requires effective development of skills in reading

7.2 Explains the importance of the teacher's attitudes in helping learners develop independence in reading

7.3 Suggests ways by which learners can be encouraged to develop independence in reading

8.0 Knows types of competencies required of teachers for individualizing reading instruction

8.1 Identifies competencies needed for helping learners develop independence in reading

8.2 Identifies competencies needed for utilizing limited resources to maximum advantage

8.3 Identifies competencies needed for utilizing classroom space to maximum advantage

The Necessity for Individualizing Reading Instruction

The necessity for individualizing reading instruction is based, of course, on the existence of differences among individuals in a classroom group. Much verbal recognition is given to the significance and pervasiveness of these differences, yet, success in meeting the challenge of individualization often becomes overwhelming in the realities of the classroom environment. The tendency for teachers to view learners in a classroom as a homogeneous group is common. This tendency, no doubt, is given impetus by a number of factors related to school organization and to the manner in which learners are admitted to, and allowed to progress through, the various levels of the school.

Many persons have tended to equate chronological ages of learners with grade levels of the schools. They also equate certain content and skills with a particular grade level or relegate certain content and skills to a grade level. It is not unusual to hear a teacher speak of his or her role in instruction as being clearly defined in terms of inflexible requirements inherent in a grade level. Such teachers expect learners in a classroom to have identical needs, abilities, and attributes, and identical obligations to meet requirements of the grade level.

The range of differences among and within individuals comprising any class group is great. Differences pertain not to just one characteristic, but to numerous characteristics related to all variables of human development and behavior. They are related, also, to environmental and experiential backgrounds of learners.

Differences Related to Abilities and Achievement

Often learners are assigned to classroom units on the basis of ability or achievement. Regardless of the base used for grouping learners in a classroom, there still must be concern for the differences that are shown among individuals. For instance, if learners are tested and grouped in classrooms according to similar test scores, many other differences still exist. If a class is identified on the basis of the number of years learners have attended school, differences are present. Despite generalized conceptions held by many persons that learners at certain grade levels are similar in chronological ages, the disparities can be surprising. Labels such as grade-level indications or descriptive terms such as gifted, slow, average, or disadvantaged are practically useless in terms of differences that inhere and remain among and within the individuals in the groups.

Results of several studies have underscored limitations in attempts to determine and maintain homogeneous groups on the basis of ability or achievement. Balow found that formation of so-called homogeneous groups on the basis of achievement test scores did not reduce individual variations to an appreciable degree.[1] Results from other studies have been comparable to those reported by Balow.[2] Cook, on the basis of his research, reported that the spread found for the middle 96 percent of first-grade children studied was between three and four years.[3] McNemar found mental ages of first graders tested, when distributed according to the curve of normal probability, showed a range of four to eight years for 95 percent of the children. In grade six, variability in mental ages among learners was double that found among first graders.[4]

---

[1] Irving H. Balow, "Does Homogeneous Grouping Give Homo-Geneous Groups?" *Elementary School Journal,* 63 (October, 1962), pp. 28–32.

[2] Bruce Balow and James Curtin, "Reading Comprehension Scores as a Means of Establishing Homogeneous Classes," *Reading Teacher,* 19 (December, 1965), pp. 169–73.

Joseph Justman, "Reading and Class Homogeneity," *Reading Teacher,* 21 (January, 1968), pp. 314–16, 334.

[3] Walter W. Cook, *Grouping and Promotion in the Elementary School* (Minneapolis, Minn.: University of Minnesota, 1941).

[4] Quinn McNemar, *The Revision of the Stanford-Binet Scale: An Analysis of Standardization Data* (Boston: Houghton Mifflin, 1942), pp. 23–25.

Excellent teaching likewise fails to lessen individual differences in ability and achievement among individuals in class groups. Effective teaching serves, instead, to increase the spread of differences in achievement. According to Harris, "Uniformity of achievement in a class is more apt to indicate neglect of abler pupils than generally effective teaching."[5]

Linguistic Differences

There is a close relationship between a learner's linguistic abilities and his rate and extent of achievement in reading. Differences in linguistic abilities among learners in a class may be pronounced. Depending on the part of the country in which a school is located, a class group may be reflective of pronounced differences in the types of dialects and other types of regional speech spoken by individuals. Many dialects are found throughout the United States, some regional in nature. Some may be related to whether the learner has an urban, rural, or suburban background. As Smith and Harris have indicated, "Environmental language, therefore, becomes one more variable for the reading teacher to weigh in making his diagnosis and in planning instruction for individuals and groups."[6]

Linguistic differences among individuals in a class may be so pronounced that they are not easily overlooked as factors to be considered in making instruction compatible with special differences shown by particular learners. Differences related to dialect or bilingualism, for example, tend to be quite obvious. Other differences related to linguistic abilities, however, may be very subtle, such as those related to an individual's ability to listen, to understand meanings expressed by others, and to express his own ideas clearly and freely.

An individual's linguistic abilities are closely related to other important factors about himself, including his self-concept, his intelligence, and the opportunities for verbalization afforded and encouraged in his background. Differences in linguistic abilities may require differentiation in the types of instructional materials that can be used effectively with various individuals. Some instructional materials in reading are inappropriate for certain individuals because the meanings conveyed may be difficult or even unintelligible to the learners.[7]

Differences in Experiential and Cultural Backgrounds

Each learner's motivations, values, beliefs, attitudes, habits, and other behavior patterns resultant from his experiences in the environment and his cultural milieu are peculiar to himself. Differences related to these

[5] Albert J. Harris, *How to Increase Reading Ability* (N. Y.: David McKay Co., 1961), p. 96.

[6] Larry A. Harris and Carl B. Smith, *Reading Instruction Through Diagnostic Teaching* (N. Y.: Holt, Rinehart and Winston, 1972), p. 16.

[7] Edmund W. Gordon and Doxey A. Wilkerson, *Compensatory Education for the Disadvantaged* (N. Y.: College Examination Board, 1966).

Kenneth S. Goodman, "Dialect Barriers to Reading Comprehension," *Reading and Inquiry*, International Reading Association Conference Proceedings, 10 (1965), pp. 240–42.

factors must be considered in plans, procedures, and materials to help an individual profit from reading instruction. Instructional approaches that may be effective for an individual whose experiences have equipped him with rich, varied, and well-developed concepts, interests, and motivations required for progress in reading are not equally effective for the learner whose background may have been just the opposite.

Differences in Favored Learning Modality

That there is no one best method for teaching reading to all learners is widely recognized. A significant factor underscoring this point of view is that of the differences shown in learning style preferences. According to deHirsch, modality strengths and weaknesses should largely determine the method of teaching.[8]

According to the modality concept, each learner has a particular sensory channel for learning to read that is superior for him. There are assumed to be three basic learning modes: (1) the visual modality which emphasizes the sense of sight, (2) the auditory modality which calls, primarily, upon the sense of hearing, and (3) the kinesthetic modality which pertains to the sense of touch. No one of these modes is mutually exclusive, in the case of most learners.[9] Most learners benefit through learning experiences that provide for mutual reinforcement of all senses.[10] Yet, for example, a learner with strong auditory and visual modalities would benefit more from a sound-symbol approach to instruction, while one with weak auditory and strong visual modalities might profit more from use of programmed materials. Differences in preferred learning styles are important in determining ways in which instruction should be individualized in a class.

Similarities Among Learners

Although a great amount of attention and concern must be focused on differences that necessitate individualization of instruction, some attention must be given to the similarities that also exist among individuals in a class. While similarities among learners do not necessitate differentiation in instruction, these facilitate the task of individualizing instruction where needed. Similarities among individuals make possible many different grouping arrangements that serve, also, to meet the needs of individuals. Many objectives in reading instruction are basically the same for all individuals. Many other objectives actually require participation by the peer group, or must be sought in audience situations in order to be achieved. Individuals tend to be highly similar, for example, in their needs for interaction with others and for realization of success in personal achievements and acceptance by others.

---

[8] Katrina deHirsch, *et al.*, *Predicting Reading Failure* (N. Y.: Harper and Row, 1966).

[9] J. David Cooper, "Learning Modalities and Reading" in *Individualizing Reading Instruction: A Reader*, Larry A. Harris and Carl B. Smith, editors (N. Y.: Holt, Rinehart and Winston, 1972), pp. 115–21.

[10] Harris and Smith, *Reading Instruction Through Diagnostic Teaching*, p. 3.

The Meaning of
Individualized Reading

Many terms are used to refer to individualized reading instruction. Two well-known terms are "individualized reading" and "personalized reading." Jeannette Veatch, a proponent of the concept of individualized reading, described it, in part, as a "new reading program . . . based upon the idea that children can and do read better, more widely, and with vastly increased interest when allowed to choose their own reading materials."[11] Walter B. Barbe used the term "personalized reading" and referred to it as "essentially a program which teaches the child to read on an individualized basis."[12] Mary C. Austin and Coleman Morrison described individualized reading as an attempt to "focus attention on each child, first by allowing him to select his own reading materials and then by giving him an opportunity to confer with his teacher for instructional and diagnostic purposes alone and/or in small groups."[13]

Implied in each of these viewpoints is the idea that certain unique operations are required in individualizing reading instruction. In the first instance, it can be seen that learners are expected to *choose* their own reading materials, rather than have these assigned. In the second, each learner is required to "read on an individual basis." In the third, each learner is expected to confer with his teacher either alone or in the company of others in small groups for purposes of skill development and diagnosis. Taken together, these brief statements summarize the major elements that have been promoted widely as individualized reading.

Individualized reading, from this perspective, has been referred to as an "approach," a "system," an "organizational device," and even a "method of teaching reading." It is widely believed that, in order to have individualized reading instruction, certain conditions and certain prescribed procedures must be implemented. These include (1) making available to learners a wide variety of books generally classified as children's literature, (2) permitting each learner to *search* among these materials and *select* those that he wishes to read, (3) permitting each learner to read at his own rate, and (4) providing individual conferences between teacher and learner.

Underlying these conceptions of individualized reading instruction is the philosophy regarding growth, behavior, and development of children as advanced, principally, by Willard C. Olson.[14] According to Olson,

> Individualized reading is primarily concerned with reading as it meshes into and promotes child develop-

---

[11] Jeannette Veatch, "Children's Interests and Individualized Reading," *The Reading Teacher,* 10 (February, 1957), p. 160.

[12] Walter B. Barbe, *Educator's Guide to Personalized Reading Instruction* (Englewood Cliffs, N. J.: Prentice-Hall, 1961), p. 15.

[13] Mary C. Austin and Coleman Morrison, *The First R: The Harvard Report on Reading in Elementary Schools* (N. Y.: Macmillan, 1963), p. 87.

[14] Willard C. Olson, *Child Development* (Boston: D. C. Heath, 1949).

ment in its many aspects — physical, mental, social, emotional, linguistic, and experiential.[15]

Jeannette Veatch has explained the application of Olson's philosophy to reading instruction:

> The traits of seeking, self-selection, and pacing are inborn characteristics of man and animals. When creatures explore their surroundings they exhibit seeking behavior. When they take something from that environment to promote their own growth, they show the process of self-selection. When they use whatever they have selected, they pace the consumption at the proper rate for their own development . . . .
>
> In an individualized reading program seeking, self-selection, and pacing also come into play. For example, children use seeking behavior to explore the classroom or library book supply. They will seek, if the supply is sufficient, a book that is right for their reading development at that time. Further, children will read those selected books at the pace that is most suitable to their needs.[16]

Problems in Implementing Certain Concepts of Individualized Reading Instruction

Conceptions of individualized reading instruction as outlined in the steps above often cause teachers to view individualized reading as a formidable task accompanied by many problems. The typical self-contained classroom sometimes accommodates as many as thirty or thirty-five children. Problems such as how to make sure that each learner can conduct his reading activities in an independent manner without disruption of others in the classroom, or how to provide enough suitable materials so that learners of varying tastes, abilities, motivation, and interests can, in a real sense, search out and select their own materials remain unsolved for many teachers. Other unsolved problems relate to how the teacher can become familiar with, and maintain familiarity with, the wealth and variety of materials required. Robert C. Auckerman has called attention to the way individualized reading is often perceived and subsequently neglected by teachers.

> The fact that more than 80 percent of elementary teachers are basal-reader oriented is an indication of the problem of initiating an individualized reading program into any school system. Teachers would have to be convinced that the individualized reading approach is, indeed, better and would have to make a commitment to learn how to make

[15] Willard C. Olson, "Seeking, Self-Selection, and Pacing in the Use of Books by Children," *The Packet* (Lexington, Mass.: D. C. Heath, 1952), pp. 3–10.

[16] Jeannette Veatch, *Individualizing Your Reading Program* (N. Y.: G. P. Putnam's Sons, 1959), pp. 7–8.

it succeed. Reaction to change of such a radical nature often precludes even a modest try at individualized reading.[17]

Principles of Individualized Reading: A Practical Consideration

It is essential that the concept of individualized reading instruction be implemented in any program in which accountability is sought. Individualized reading instruction need not be regarded as a rigid set of procedures that must be implemented in a uniform way in all classrooms where reading is taught. Individualization might be thought of as a quality of instruction, rather than as a set of procedures. As a quality, individualization may accompany any approach or method of instruction.

Stated simply, individualized reading instruction is a matter of providing for each individual the kinds of experiences for learning that most nearly meet his or her unique needs. Individualized reading instruction begins with determining the learner's needs and it proceeds in the light of objectives most appropriate for meeting those needs. In essence, the definition for diagnostic teaching offered by Dorris M. Lee is equally adequate as a definition for individualized reading. According to Lee, diagnostic teaching requires that "teachers organize a classroom and the learning situation so that, within reasonable limits, each child can work at what are his next steps in the areas of his greatest concerns and in the ways that are most effective for him."[18]

Accountability demands that desired changes sought through instruction become manifest in each learner, not in a group, or in some proportion of that group. Consequently, instruction must be individualized in the sense that it is conducive to the growth and development of each person. Effective instruction does not permit a choice as to whether or not instruction will be individualized. In the words of James E. Allen, then Assistant Secretary for Education and United States Commissioner of Education, "So long as there is one boy or girl who leaves school unable to read to the fullest extent of his capability, we cannot escape the charge of failure in carrying out the responsibility entrusted to us."[19] Principles involved in individualized instruction, viewed simply and practically, are ones that can be, and should be, implemented in any reading program, regardless of the label by which the program is called.

Individualized instruction is a way of looking at learning and at the conditions that make learning possible in classrooms. In this view, learning is perceived as an individual matter. Each learner must be helped to recognize his own objectives for learning and pursue these at his own rate and according to his own abilities.

---

[17] Robert C. Aukerman, *Approaches to Beginning Reading* (N. Y.: John Wiley and Sons, 1971), pp. 387–88.

[18] Dorris M. Lee, *Diagnostic Teaching* (Washington, D. C.: Department of Elementary, Kindergarten, Nursery Education, E/K/N/E, NEA, 1966), pp. 6–7.

[19] James E. Allen, Jr., "The Right to Read — Target for the 70's," Address delivered at the 1969 Annual Convention of the National Association of State Boards of Education, Century Plaza Hotel, Los Angeles, Ca. (September 23, 1969).

In fostering learning, the role of the teacher takes many forms. The teacher must provide an appropriate setting and intellectual and social climates for learning by each individual. In so doing, the teacher — at various times — serves as a diagnostician, a planner, a designer, a helper, a counselor, and sometimes a manager. At times, also, a teacher must serve the role required of a dispenser of knowledge. Virtually never, however, is the teacher required to direct every move a learner makes in the process of learning.

Individualized reading instruction does not mandate a particular set of procedures or materials, but it is facilitated if instructional procedures and materials are developed and selected on the basis of certain principles. Arthur Heilman has helped to put individualized reading into perspective:

> An effective individualized reading program, of necessity, must rest on a rather broad base. It may include, but cannot be limited to, children selecting books; reading these at their own rate; and, occasionally reporting to the teacher on their reading. Individualized reading does not exclude practices which may be thought of as integral parts of other instructional approaches.[20]

Opportunity should be provided for each learner to develop his full potential, regardless of the form of classroom organization for learning that may be in effect. Whether the learner does individual work, works as a member of a small group, or has an experience involving the entire class is not significant in and of itself. What is important is whether or not the experience provided is what the learner needs, at that point in time, to further his development toward the objectives deemed important for him.

Each learner should be given opportunity to learn about and freedom to develop skills, concepts, interests, and attitudes that he needs, regardless of those deemed important for, and in process of development by, other members of the class. What is desirable for one individual does not, necessarily depend on, or even relate to, that which may be desirable for another. There are times, however, when the needs of one individual are the same as those of others in the class. At such times, it is both efficient and profitable for all concerned that development of desired behaviors of the learners involved be sought simultaneously. According to Alexander Frazier, "Individualization may be conceived of chiefly as freeing the learner to run a specified course as fast as he can."[21] That course can take any form of group or individual endeavors.

Each learner should be permitted to develop skills and concepts that he needs in reading regardless of the content specified in materials adopted in the curriculum and also regardless of grade-level requirements. Course content or grade-level requirements are valuable as guides, but these should not be given precedence over

---

[20] Arthur W. Heilman, *Principles and Practices of Teaching Reading*, Second edition (Columbus, Oh.: Charles E. Merrill, 1967), p. 364.

[21] Alexander Frazier, Esther E. Schatz, Mary E. Willsberg, and Roberta Utterback, *Making Sure of Skill Development in Individualized Reading* (Columbus, Oh.: College of Education, The Ohio State University, 1965), p. 2.

the needs and abilities of the learner. It is equally ineffective either to try to stretch a learner or to try to reduce him to fit a particular set of requirements.

The teacher's qualifications are also important in individualizing reading. The teacher should understand the process of reading, and the nature of skills involved in development of ability in reading well enough to prescribe and select those that should be of concern to an individual learner.

Each learner should be helped to develop independence in reading and in learning. The tasks involved in this process do require an expenditure of time and patience, but it is time and patience well spent. What is done to help an individual develop independence in learning should be considered an integral part of reading instruction. Less time will be required for this as the learner matures and as he gains experience in the tasks of independent learning.

Each teacher should consider and help each learner realize that reading is a very special tool required by each person for coping with present and future problems. At the same time, learners should be helped to see reading not only as an aid in solving problems in the basic requirements of living, but also as a means to many pleasant and rewarding experiences. Each learner should be helped to understand and appreciate the utility of learning to read, reading to learn, and the pleasures of reading to read.

Individualized reading should be conceived of as a factor in facilitating independent reading, but not as synonymous with independent reading. Individualized reading does not mean leaving the learner on his own to develop concepts and skills in reading without significant help from the teacher. Each learner must be permitted to grow into reading, but his growth requires guidance. Reading is a complex process involving acquisition of many concepts and skills. A learner should not be expected to develop these on his own.

Conventional Approaches to Individualizing Reading Instruction

Many proposals and plans have been set forth and implemented, with varying degrees of success, for the purpose of accommodating individual differences in reading. Some of these have involved organizational schemes for the entire school or within each classroom unit. Some have involved use of additional personnel or special materials. Others have relied on effective teaching alone as an adequate means for achieving individualization.

School-Wide Grouping Plans

The conventional way in which learners are assigned to classrooms, in some schools, is a first step in an effort to reduce the breadth and variety of differences found among a group of learners. In some schools, learners are assigned to classrooms on the basis of chronological age at entrance into school.

For instance, all six-year-old children are assigned to first grade. This plan amounts to a type of heterogeneous grouping. In schools in which this plan forms the major basis for classroom units, special provisions generally are made by the school as a whole, or by individual teachers, to further accommodate differences among the learners. Among these provisions may be special classes for gifted or for slow learners, acceleration or enrichment plans, inter*class* or inter*grade* groupings, or subgroups within classrooms.

Interclass grouping involves grouping learners of a single grade level according to their abilities or achievement in reading. For instance, learners in third grade may be grouped according to above average, average, or below average in reading ability or achievement. At a scheduled time for instruction in reading, all learners assumed to be at the same particular level go to the teacher designated to provide instruction appropriate for that level.

Intergrade grouping is similar to interclass grouping, except that several grade levels—rather than a single grade—may be involved. Under the plan, learners are grouped for reading instruction on the basis of their reading grade, regardless of their assigned grade in school. All learners from each of the grade levels included are instructed in reading at the particular grade level at which they are reading. For instance, if fourth, fifth, and sixth grades are included, learners in any of those three grades who may be reading at fourth-grade level are instructed in reading at the fourth-grade level. Similarly, those learners reading at either the fifth- or sixth-grade levels are taught reading at the grade level deemed appropriate for them.

Homogeneous grouping is used throughout all grades in some schools in an effort to limit the range of differences among learners in various classrooms. Scores from intelligence or achievement tests usually must be used to determine ability or achievement levels of learners. Those who are believed to be similar in ability or achievement are then grouped together in classrooms.

Homogeneous groups usually are established on the assumption that if individuals are matched on one factor, such as ability or achievement, there will be a high degree of similarity in their instructional needs. It has been found, however, that because of their intra-individual differences, learners who are similar with respect to one factor are not necessarily similar in other factors.[22] Therefore, classroom units believed to consist of individuals of similar characteristics continue to reflect significant differences. Hence, further efforts by the teacher at the classroom level are essential in order to achieve an appreciable degree of individualization in instruction.

Nongraded instruction in all basic-skill subjects or in reading only is an organizational plan sometimes used in recognition of individual differences. Nongrading is a special way of grouping learners according to their "development, achievement, or ability," rather than according to chronological ages or grades.[23] Un-

---

[22] Marvin Y. Burr, *A Study of Homogeneous Grouping in Terms of Individual Variations and the Teaching Problem* (N. Y.: Teachers College, 1931).

[23] Lloyd K. Bishop, *Individualizing Educational Systems* (N. Y.: Harper and Row, 1971), p. 18.

graded primary units indicate the removal of grade designations from first through third grades. In nongraded elementary schools, grade indications are removed throughout all grades in the elementary school. According to Goodlad and Anderson, nongraded organization is "designed to implement a theory of continuous progress; since the differences among children are great and since these differences cannot be substantially modified, school structure must facilitate the continuous educational progress of each pupil."[24]

Grouping Within Classrooms

One of the most widely used methods for coping with the range of differences among individuals involves formation of subgroups within classrooms. Ability and achievement are the most commonly used bases for the grouping. Frequently, three or more groups are formed by the teacher early in a school year, and often learners placed in the groups remain in them for the duration of the year. That this method is widespread was evident in the report of the study by Austin and Morrison:

> Regardless of the way in which schools organized children into classes, grouping within a classroom was considered essential by administrators and supervisors, and teachers were expected to group pupils for reading instruction even when the range of ability in their classroom was not a wide one.
>
> . . . With few exceptions . . . children were placed in groups according to reading ability as determined by test scores, teacher observation and evaluation, and previous classroom performance. In the primary grades, three reading groups were found to be the most common.[25]

Grouping on the basis of ability or achievement has many limitations. These bases are usually insufficient for accommodating the variety of differences found among learners in a class. Achievement and ability do not comprise all of the purposes for which grouping in reading instruction is needed. Some undesirable practices have resulted from use of these limited bases to meet the needs of individuals, and also from the manner in which the groups are conducted. One undesirable result is the psychological ramifications of naming groups in unfortunate ways. Also, some grouping arrangements have tended to generate fixed attitudes among members of a group. Once assigned to the "slow" group, for instance, learners are sometimes automatically expected to be slow readers permanently.

Effective Teaching as a Means of Individualizing Instruction

As indicated earlier in this chapter, effective teaching does not, necessarily, decrease the range of differences found among individuals

---

[24] John I. Goodlad and Robert H. Anderson, *The Nongraded Elementary School* (N. Y.: Harcourt Brace Jovanovich, 1959), p. 52.

[25] Austin and Morrison, *The First R: The Harvard Report on Reading in the Elementary Schools*, p. 76.

in a class. As learners progress through the grade levels of the elementary school, differences found among members of a class generally become greater as the grade level becomes higher. Some proposals for meeting the challenge of individual differences, however, have claimed that an effective teacher, sensitive to children's individuality is more influential than grouping schemes.[26] A conclusion reached by Daisy M. Jones from results of a study in which she compared the outcomes of individually planned teaching with a prescribed curriculum program was that perhaps an able teacher, given freedom to work creatively, is more important than any mechanical scheme, however ingenious.[27]

It seems that there is no simple, clear-cut solution to the problem of individualizing reading instruction. A combination of the most promising features of several plans and proposals and a teacher concerned with the significance of the individual comprise what is probably the most practical and effective approach to the problem, generally. Specifically, each teacher working within constraints in his particular situation and aware of principles that should be implemented in individualization of instruction can utilize several procedures and materials to increase opportunity for each individual in the classroom to progress in terms of his potential.

Planning for Individualizing Instruction

Making reading instruction meaningful to each person in the classroom requires careful and detailed planning related to several aspects of the program. Plans must be made for (1) scheduling time for individual and group work in which the teacher will be directly involved with the learners; (2) scheduling time in which learners will be engaged in independent work either individually or in groups; (3) arranging materials for maximum ease and convenience in use and storage; (4) organizing classroom space to accommodate individual and group activities; and (5) planning with individuals, small groups, and the total class.

Arranging the Daily Schedule

There is no set formula for arranging the time in a school day for maximum benefit to all classes under all circumstances and in all types of schools. Details of time arrangements must be worked out by each teacher in a particular situation. Details are always affected by constraints that vary from situation to situation. There are some general considerations, however, that can be meaningful.

As a general rule, it is a good idea to plan the schedule for reading instruction within large blocks of time. The time that is available might be divided into large

---

[26] Darrell Holmes and Lois F. Harvey, "An Evaluation of Two Methods of Grouping," *Educational Research Bulletin*, 35 (1956), pp. 213–22.

[27] Daisy M. Jones, "Experiment in Adaptation to Individual Differences," *Journal of Educational Psychology*, 39 (1948), pp. 257–72.

blocks for (1) teacher-directed individual and small-group work, (2) teacher-directed total class work, and (3) independent work by individuals and groups. The way in which the blocks of time should be arranged, and also the amount of time allocated for each will vary according to the levels of the learners. For example, a teacher who must work with first graders will arrange and organize time differently from one who works with sixth graders.

A typical arrangement of time at the first-grade level might resemble the following:

9:00– 9:20	Planning with the total class
9:20– 9:40	Guided reading activity with individuals or small groups
9:40–10:00	Guided reading activity with individuals or small groups
10:00–10:30	Reading activities involving total class
10:30–10:50	Guided reading activity with individuals or small groups
10:50–11:30	Independent activities, total class

At the sixth-grade level, the division of time might be similar to the following:

9:00– 9:15	Planning with total class
9:15–10:15	Independent reading, total class
10:15–10:45	Teacher-directed activities with individuals or small groups

Arranging Instructional Materials

Plans must be made for arranging and storing materials so that learners can obtain these when needed with minimal interruptions to other learners and to the teacher. Most learners will need help in learning how to accept and meet the responsibilities of obtaining and caring for materials. Several routines, such as the following, will have to be worked out so that materials can be used with ease. Generally, learners should be made aware of the importance of each of the following and of specific ways in which they can:

1. Share materials
2. Care for materials in use
3. Replace materials after use
4. Select materials according to objectives sought
5. Select only those materials needed at the moment
6. Handle mistakes
7. Cooperate with others in use of materials
8. Use good manners
9. Avoid interrupting others
10. Respect the rights of others
11. Observe necessary rules and regulations
12. Replace materials obtained from files (perhaps modules)
13. Use special centers for independent work (perhaps learning stations)

Learners, at any level, can participate in formulation of pertinent rules and regulations. Generally, essential rules and regulations will be more effective if learners suggest and accept these than if rules are thrust upon them by the teacher. A group of learners working under the direction of a student teacher worked out the following procedures for use of the learning stations established in the classroom. The "rules" were displayed on a chart where, in the words of a child, "Everyone (could) see them easily." Although wordy—and at times ungrammatical—the rules represented the consensus of the group and made a contribution to effective use of the materials.

> "If we can't work together at the stations we have to go back to our desks and do some other lessons by ourselves."
>
> "We'll help each other."
>
> "We'll stay at the station where we start for the full time until we complete it."
>
> "It's good to have conversations, but they should be quiet conversations."
>
> "We'll take turns with the materials. There are enough for everyone to have a turn."
>
> "We have to read over the directions and follow them carefully because we are working on our own."
>
> "It's important to be a good listener. We learn from other people at the station."

Arranging Learning Spaces in the Classroom

Individualized instruction and independent learning are encouraged in an environment that permits freedom of movement and affords well-defined spaces for specific kinds of activities. Various types of learning areas, made as attractive and functional as possible, should be established in the classroom. Regulations for utilization and care of these areas should be clearly understood and accepted by each learner in the classroom.

The physical characteristics of each classroom will influence the extent to which learning spaces can be established effectively. More numerous and more varied types of areas can be established in a well-equipped, spacious, open classroom than are possible in smaller and more closed quarters. Many things can be done, however, by an enterprising teacher to improve use of space in almost any kind of situation. Modern classrooms are equipped, for the most part, with movable furniture that facilitates flexible arrangements. In many cases, teachers are free to effect arrangements of classroom space to serve requirements of the instructional program.

Little more than imagination is required in order to devise and arrange areas where individuals can read quietly and with some degree of privacy. Sometimes the addition or arrangement of bookcases or small rugs can increase the privacy and comfort levels of a reading area.

As much as is feasible, an area of the classroom, removed somewhat from the reading area, should be identified for those activities that tend to be somewhat disruptive or distracting. Activities such as painting, constructing or playing games often are extensions of ideas gained from reading experiences. Sometimes the opposite is true. These and other similar experiences frequently stimulate children to want to read and to feel a need for reading.

Plans should be made not only for organizing the classroom into attractive and inviting areas for learning, but also for enlisting cooperation of the class in all aspects of the planning. Learners should become acquainted with the teacher's plans, but they should also have opportunities to offer their own suggestions for organizing spaces and utilizing and caring for these.

Planning With Individuals

In a sense, all effective planning with learners in a classroom involves planning with individuals. Even if planning is done with the members of a small group or with the total class, communication should be made with all individuals. To the extent that communication with a group involves the attention and participation of each member of the group, planning can be considered to be effective. Techniques of planning, however, may differ depending on whether one individual or several are involved.

Much of the planning with the class can be done efficiently and effectively in small groups or with the total class. Some planning has to be done, however, on a one-to-one basis between the teacher and the individual concerned.

Learners must be taught how to become engaged in and conduct learning experiences for themselves. More time must be spent and planning must be more detailed for younger and less experienced learners. Learners of any age or at any grade level will require some instruction and help in learning how to make decisions that are valuable to their learning related to reading or to their behavior in the classroom as they engage in various instructional activities.

Planning in a conference situation on a one-to-one basis between teacher and learner is required when matters pertaining uniquely to the individual are under consideration. Individually prescribed instruction is an example of a concern that requires planning directly with the individual. A learner generally requires help in understanding (1) objectives set for his achievement, (2) various alternative objectives, (3) how to keep essential records, (4) how to assess his progress and achievement of the objectives, and (5) how to secure help from the teacher or another source.

Planning With Small Groups

Those concerns that are unique to small groups organized for particular purposes should be planned in group sessions with all members of the group. Problems that involve cooperation of all members in arriving at solutions require participation in planning by all members. In the small-group setting, learners can be helped to understand methods and procedures related to group decisions and group process.

Participation in planning in a small-group setting affords personal advantages for some learners. Members of the group can interact with each other in a relatively protective environment. A small audience of peers can be less formidable to learners who tend to be shy and reluctant to express ideas publicly. Planning, unlike many other learning activities, does not require extensive preparation on the parts of learners. Those who may enjoy few successes in academic matters may experience roles of active participation and even leadership in small planning groups.

Techniques of planning used in the small groups should take varied forms. The precise nature of desirable techniques will depend on the backgrounds of the learners, their ages, abilities, and the like. If the learners are very young, construction and use of experience charts or role-playing techniques may be advantageous. If learners are in the intermediate grades of the elementary school, brainstorming or techniques of simulation may be appropriate. Simply telling and retelling learners what to do should be avoided as much as possible. Regardless of their ages, learners can devise many of their own procedures under the skillful guidance of a perceptive teacher.

Planning With the Class

Much of the planning needed in general by all members of the class can be taken care of with the total class. Some of the concerns in reading that require attention of all members of the class include (1) how to select a book at the proper level of difficulty, (2) how to use the classroom library without disturbing others, (3) how to obtain and replace materials, and (4) what standards to observe in the process of sharing information. These and similar matters require attention and participation in planning by all members of the class.

Generally, it is better to focus attention of the class on one concern at the time, rather than attempting to plan several procedures at once. Aids such as charts, the chalkboard, bulletin boards, and the like, on which are listed or illustrated results of planning or suggestions can reinforce the ideas which result from planning sessions.

Assignment of responsibilities for routine duties in the classroom is an example of one aspect of planning that should involve all members of the class. Cues for techniques to be used in planning will stem from characteristics of the group. Levels of maturity of class members should be a primary consideration in determining techniques of planning. Generally, techniques for planning with the total class are discussion, explanation, role-playing, committee work, and the like.

Strategies and Materials for Individualizing Instruction

Individualized reading instruction does not depend simply on whether or not each learner works alone. The important thing is that each person is permitted to seek achievement of objectives appropriate to his needs. There are many occasions and many reasons, however, for a learner to work alone in seeking achievement of objectives uniquely important to him or her. In any classroom where individualization of instruction is attempted, strategies and materials should be provided to facilitate individual learning activities when needed.

Many materials and other resources are available for individualizing learning activities. Numerous technological aids, tradebooks, and other commercial materials can be used to assist in the task. Some materials can also be developed by the teacher and the learners. However, none of these can be considered to be inherently effective.

The principle that there is no one best method for teaching reading to all learners at all times holds equally true for strategies and materials for individualizing instruction. There is no one best strategy or set of materials to guarantee success of individualized learning or independent work for all learners in every situation. The teacher in a particular classroom has a tremendous influence on the effectiveness of individualized instruction. The teacher must make decisions related to selection, organization, and use of strategies and materials that will meet the needs of particular learners. These decisions must be based on information about learners that is often available only to the teacher.

Most strategies and materials for individualizing reading instruction cannot be classified strictly on the basis of whether they are restricted to development of any single aspect of reading. Skills involved in word recognition and comprehension are closely related. Often it is difficult and also undesirable to attempt to focus on developing skills in one aspect without reference to other closely related ones. However, objectives stated for instruction generally specify discrete behaviors that can be categorized as emphasizing the need for certain types of learning experiences. On this basis, some materials and procedures are more valuable for development of skills related to one aspect of reading than to another. Characteristics of several strategies and materials that can be adapted to fit requirements of individualization of instruction in various situations are described below.

Programmed Instructional Materials

The term "programmed materials" implies the nature of the types of learning materials to which it refers. Programmed materials provide tasks arranged systematically and sequentially to permit an individual to proceed at his own pace toward achievement of predetermined objectives. All programmed materials have certain well-defined characteristics including the following: (1) a predetermined objective or set of objectives, (2) presentation of content in small, discrete steps ranging from the simplest to the most complex in the series, (3) presentation of the content in a type of format that permits the learner to proceed through the steps independently and at his own rate, and—in many cases—(4) immediate feedback to the learner as to the correctness or incorrectness of his response.

Programmed instructional materials for reading are available in several different forms. Some forms are similar to conventional textbook-type materials and, within themselves, contain all that is necessary to enable the learner to perform the tasks and make his responses. Other forms require use of additional equipment such as teaching machines, cassettes, or tape recordings for the complete learning experience. The most easily accessible, and most widely used, programmed instructional materials are those in textbook format.

Among examples of programmed reading materials in textbook formats are the Sullivan Associates' Programs.[28] This is a series of programs designed, primarily,

---

[28]Cynthia Dee Buchanan and M. W. Sullivan, *Programmed Reading* (Manchester, Mo.: Webster/McGraw-Hill, 1971).

for children in initial and early stages of reading instruction in the elementary schools. The materials are offered as a basal reading program for the primary grades and as a corrective reading program for learners in the middle- and upper-grade levels.

Included among the materials are reading readiness kits designed to prepare children for beginning formal instruction in reading. Contents of the kits emphasize the names of letters of the alphabet and the sounds these represent, colors, left-to-right directions, and other skills and concepts important in beginning reading. Based on a linguistic approach that emphasizes sound-symbol relationships, the programmed books are available for each of twenty-one levels of competencies ranging from beginning reading instruction through the primary grades. Placement tests are available for determining the level at which an individual should begin work in the materials.

Another set of programmed materials presented in textbook format are "Lessons for Self-Instruction in Basic Skills: Reading."[29] These materials are designed for learners who have developed basic skills in word-recognition and in comprehension and are ready for further experiences in auxiliary and higher skills in comprehension. Focus of the materials is on development of skills related to (1) following directions, (2) use of reference materials, and (3) reading interpretation. The teacher can work with small groups of learners whose needs may be similar, or individuals can use the materials independently. Generally, learners' responses are selected from a group of multiple-choice possibilities. Some lessons, however, provide opportunities for the learner to write in his original responses. In either instance, provisions are made for helping the learner understand why a response may be correct or incorrect. These provisions encourage a higher level of learning than is usually possible when the demand is only for recognition of a correct response.

Charles E. Merrill's "Building Reading Power Program"[30] places major emphasis on development of comprehension abilities. Presented in textbook format, these materials are designed for learners whose reading-grade levels are 4.5 and above. Materials in the series are arranged to develop skills and concepts related to (1) context clues, (2) structural analysis, and (3) comprehension skills. For learners who have developed basic competencies in reading, these materials offer opportunity for development of higher competencies independently and individually.

The Peabody Rebus Reading Program (REBUS)[31] provides another example of programmed materials in textbook format. Through use of special water-sensitive inks used in the printing process, a learner is permitted to recognize through color changes if he has marked a correct or incorrect response. Designed for learners just beginning formal instruction in reading, the materials utilize a

---

[29] Miles Midloch, *Lessons for Self-Instruction in Basic Skills: Reading* (Monterey, Ca.: CTB/ McGraw-Hill, 1965).

[30] *Building Reading Power Programs: Comprehension Skills* (Columbus, Ohio: Charles E. Merrill, 1970).

[31] Richard W. Woodcock, Charlotte R. Clark, and Cornelia Oakes Davies, *Peabody Rebus Reading Program* (Circle Pines, Minn.: American Guidance Service, 1969).

vocabulary of picture words (pictorial rebuses) to help the learner develop a concept of the meaning of reading and some of the skills involved in word-recognition and vocabulary development.

Several advantages are common to programmed instructional materials. Each learner can work at his own pace toward achievement of specific objectives particularly suited to his needs. He can proceed toward the objectives through carefully arranged steps. Usually he can achieve a high degree of satisfaction and encouragement from immediate feedback regarding the status of his answers. On the other hand, certain limitations pertain to the materials. Prior competence in reading is required for effective use of several programs. To a large degree, many of the materials are limited to development of the mechanical rather than the thinking aspects of reading.

Multi-Media Approaches

Several programs and materials useful in individualizing reading instruction utilize a variety of media. Because of this, these are capable of accommodating or reinforcing several sensory modalities. Several programs of the Educational Developmental Laboratories are examples of approaches that emphasize use of multi-media. The "EDL Listen and Read"[32] program consists of a series of thirty audiotapes with workbook exercises for each tape. Emphasis is on development of listening abilities and reading skills.

The EDL Aud-X is a machine which makes use of filmstrips and disc recordings. The visual mode of learning is accentuated through the filmstrips that portray a variety of photographs, illustrations, and other graphic materials. The audio dimension is stressed through tapes by which directions are given for the lessons. Operation of the device requires use of the kinesthetic mode.

The controlled reader is a machine that can be used to provide appeal to several sense modalities. This machine exposes material through a slot that travels across the screen from left to right. Most of these machines can be manipulated to start, stop, change speeds, and the like. Depending on the content utilized, attention can be given to development of various skills related to vocabulary, word-recognition, and comprehension.

The EDL Study Skills Library[33] is a set of materials for self-directed learning related, primarily, to development of comprehension and study skills. Each learner can proceed at his own level and rate of development. Upon assessing the individual's instructional level, the teacher can have him begin use of the material at an appropriate level. Each lesson in the series is designed to lead to development of a particular skill, such as interpretation or evaluation. Several steps are provided for progress through each lesson. Steps include (1) an explanation of the skill, (2) an example of the skill, and (3) application of the skill to content in the reading selection. An individual can assess his progress through answer keys provided in the materials.

---

[32] Stanford E. Taylor, and others, *EDL Listen and Read Programs* (Huntington, N. Y.: Educational Developmental Laboratories, Inc.).

[33] H. Alan Robinson, *et al.*, *EDL Study Skills Library* (Huntington, N. Y.: Educational Developmental Laboratories, 1963).

The Visual Symbol Environment[34] is an individualized program based on a perceptual approach to early reading experiences. Prereading and actual reading experiences are provided for learners at the levels of preschool and kindergarten. The program is designed to help children develop basic concepts and improve perceptual skills required in effective reading.

Visual perception skills are developed through use of games and dialogue. Auditory skills are presented and developed through use of the language master machine. Programs can be adjusted to accommodate various dialects by re-recording the cards to fit the language of a particular individual. Accountability measures built into the program include (1) 115 levels of competencies covering a progressive hierarchy of skills, (2) individual records for keeping track of each learner's progress, and (3) cross checks of accuracy to double check each learner's progress.

Several other types of audiovisual equipment and technological devices help to simplify and improve the effectiveness of individualized reading instruction. Among these are transparencies, overhead projectors, films, filmstrips, records, or headphones used in conjunction with a tape recorder. All of these and many other devices can be used to enable an individual to explore his knowledge and skills in reading, and to achieve practice in any area in which it is needed.

Using Modules for Individualizing Reading Instruction

Particularly for learners at the intermediate and upper levels of the elementary school, modules can provide increased opportunities for self-pacing, individualization, or independent learning.

A module can be described, generally, as an organized set of tasks for developing and evaluating an individual's achievement of a specified objective. Ordinarily, a module provides for several important steps. In step one, the individual is presented with a clearly defined objective. Step two provides a rationale that helps him understand the meaning of the objective and its relevance to his needs and interests. In step three, he is given a pretest to determine his needs, if any, in relation to achieving the objective. On the basis of results of the pretest, step four provides either an activity or a number of alternative activities designed to help him achieve the objective. Step five requires him to assess his progress toward the objective, or have it assessed, through use of a posttest.

The terms "pretest" and "posttest" refer to any type of activity or measure that permits the individual's achievement in terms of the specified objective to be observed. These terms do not refer to paper and pencil tests exclusively. Any activity suitable for evaluating behavior called for in the objective can be used. An evaluative activity may be some form of observational technique, actual performance of a task, or development of a product.

If results of the posttest reveal adequate mastery of the objective, all steps required in the module are completed. If adequate mastery is not achieved after an individual has gone through all steps of the module, he may then be required

---

[34]*Visual Symbol Environment Program* (Edina, Minn.: Educators Service).

to repeat any or all parts of the module, or perhaps engage in additional experiences in order to achieve the desired outcome.

Many skills in reading are suitable for development through use of modules. For instance, steps for achieving objectives such as the following can be arranged into modular presentations:
1. Alphabetizes words
2. Uses phonics clues to word recognition
3. Divides words into syllables
4. Uses picture clues to word recognition
5. Interprets information given in a graph
6. Interprets legends of selected maps
7. Uses an appropriate map to gain information related to climate
8. Arranges ideas found in a selection into sequential order
9. Outlines major ideas found in a selection

The format used for presentation of the module can vary according to the preference of the teacher, the resources that are available, or the competencies of the learners. For instance, modules can be presented in the form of a packet of materials, a kit, or simply a page of instructions on which all directions are clarified.

If modules are to be used effectively in a classroom, consideration must be given to several factors. The modules, first of all, must be developed, and their development can cause some problems for the teacher. Learners must be given instructions regarding the use of the modules: this requires time. Most of the problems accompanying construction and use of modules, however, can be solved with little effort.

Prior to actual construction of a module, the teacher should select the specific objective upon which modules will be focused. One objective, or several closely related ones, should be determined as the basis for each module. Materials and activities for each consecutive step included in each module can then be devised. Resources for providing required learning experiences for completion of the modules are usually those normally found in a classroom situation. The richer the environment for learning afforded in a particular classroom, the more resources will be available for helping learners perform tasks required in the modules.

Once modules are constructed, plans must be made with learners for their use. Attention must be given to helping each learner who will use the modules understand what they are, and how and when they are to be used. Planning may involve all learners in the class, or only those individuals whose particular needs and abilities justify use of the modules.

A system for storing, displaying, retrieving, and replacing modules must be worked out in the particular classroom where they are to be used. Any number of ways exist for facilitating these operations, but only the teacher in a classroom can determine the best procedures for use in that particular classroom. Regular file cabinets and filing systems can be used. Containers for the modules and appropriate filing systems can be devised. Modules can be prepared and placed on open shelves from which they may be selected and replaced by individuals who use them.

Establishing and Using Learning Stations

Learning stations in the classroom provide several advantages for the teacher and for learners. For the teacher, opportunities are increased for (1) becoming better acquainted with characteristics of each individual, (2) meeting needs of a large number of individuals at once, and (3) releasing more time for direct work with individuals who require personal guidance and attention. For learners, all styles of learning can be accommodated through use of multi-media in a variety of learning activities. Each learner can work independently at his own rate toward achievement of specified objectives. Through built-in provisions, each learner can evaluate his achievement independently.

Learning stations are an approach to organizing activities that encourages an individual to learn how to learn and how to think independently. These are also helpful in providing opportunities for an individual to accept some responsibility for his own learning. Learning stations should consist of challenging activities that require use of multi-media. As such, their potential for increasing interest in reading can be considerable. Used in a classroom along with a variety of other procedures and materials, learning stations can contribute to individualizing reading instruction. Kaplan and others, explain that

> Learning centers become the vehicles for moving students away from teacher-dominated learning experiences and toward student-selected learning activities. Learning centers organize and direct learning experiences for students by allowing freedom while providing structure.[35]

Specifically, a learning station (or center) in the classroom consists of a set of tasks or activities designed to teach, reinforce, or extend a skill or concept. Each series of tasks or activities included as part of the learning station leads to achievement of a specified objective or set of objectives. The collection of tasks or activities is organized and arranged for independent use by learners.

Several preliminary activities by the teacher are essential to the successful use of learning stations in individualized instruction. There must be clear answers to several questions. These questions include: (1) What is to be learned through use of the stations? (2) How will learners become familiarized with procedures for using the stations? (3) How will interest of the learners become stimulated? (4) What teaching and learning steps are required for each activity included in the stations? (5) What provisions will be built into each activity for learners' self-evaluation of achievement?

Besides considerations related to actual planning and construction of tasks to be included in the learning stations, several activities with the class are essential for their effective use. Learners must be helped to know (1) when to use the stations, (2) how to select appropriate tasks, (3) what to do with completed work, (4) how to seek and get help when needed, and (5) what role the teacher will play in the process.

---

[35] Sandra Nina Kaplan, and others, *Change for Children* (Pacific Palisades, Ca.: Goodyear Publishing, 1973), p. xv.

Once the decision to use learning stations as a means of individualizing instruction has been made, careful planning with the class is essential. At the outset, plans are required to acquaint the total class with procedural concerns. Planning must continue as learning stations undergo changes required for meeting the changing needs of individuals in the class.

Approaches to Reading as Means for Individualizing Instruction

Individualized reading instruction, as pointed out earlier in this chapter, is not synonymous with, exclusive to, or guaranteed by the use of any discrete approach to the teaching of reading. Rather, any approach to reading instruction used by a teacher responding to the needs of individuals in a class can become a means for individualizing reading instruction.

The term "approach" is used here to refer to any organized set of materials—often in conjunction with prescribed procedures—for introducing children to reading and for developing increasingly higher levels of competence in reading. Among other terms used with the same intended meaning are "methods" and "instructional systems." In this sense, "individualized reading" and "programmed reading," referred to earlier in this chapter, are considered by some persons as approaches to reading instruction. Among many other approaches to reading instruction are basal-reader approaches and the language-experience approach. Seldom are these, or other approaches, used discretely. Generally, the approach to reading instruction in a classroom involves use of elements from various approaches.

Basal-Reader Approaches

Basal-reader approaches are so named because of the nature of core instructional materials these provide for use by learners. At the heart of any basal-reader approach is a series of coordinated textbooks to be used by learners at each grade level of the elementary school. These are known as basal readers. Basal readers are graded according to difficulty levels and sequential skill development. Learners are expected to progress systematically through all levels provided by a series of texts.

One of the main features of a series of basal readers is the degree of control used in vocabulary, content, settings of the stories, and sentence structure. Conventionally, words used in stories and other selections in basal readers have been those believed to be a part of the vocabulary of most children. In many series, books designed for use by beginners include words taken from word lists based on frequency of usage by children.[36]

---

[36] Two famous compilations of word lists are the following:

Edward W. Dolch, *Methods in Reading* (Champaign, Ill.: Garrard Publishing, 1955), pp. 373–74.

Henry Rinsland, *A Basic Vocabulary of Elementary School Children* (N.Y.: Macmillan, 1945).

Traditionally, content and settings of stories included in basal texts tended to be reflective of, and even limited to, that believed to be characteristic of neighborhood life as experienced mainly by children of middle-class socioeconomic backgrounds. Modern basal texts tend to be updated and broadened to become representative of a wider range of interests and relevant to experiences of children of varying backgrounds.

Basal-reader approaches to reading instruction tend to be highly structured and complete in terms of materials and procedures required in the teaching of reading. Manuals or guides containing suggestions for teaching and for organizing the class for instruction are included for use by teachers. Among numerous and varied materials comprising a complete basal-reader approach are tests, charts, workbooks, and various types of supplementary and enrichment materials.

A major form of classroom organization for teaching reading in the basal-reader approach has involved grouping learners on the basis of achievement or ability. So much has this been the case that basal readers and "three-group" arrangements for reading instruction in classrooms have become somewhat synonymous. Some differentiation in content and procedures in directed reading and in learners' independent work have been chief devices used for meeting the unique needs of individuals. With a basal-reader approach, it is highly possible to refine the degree to which needs of individuals are met. Modern materials and technological aids provided by many basal-reader approaches facilitate achievement of a close relationship between the needs of a learner and the instruction he or she requires.

The Language-Experience Approach

The language-experience approach focuses directly on involving the learner's experiences in his reading. An effort is made to provide balanced attention to relationships among all aspects of the language arts, including listening, speaking, writing, and reading. Among specific characteristics of the language-experience approach to reading instruction are the following:

1. The activity of reading is closely interrelated and interwoven with all the other language arts.
2. Reading becomes concerned directly with words that arouse meaningful responses in the learners.
3. Learners bring meaning to words used in materials which they develop on the basis of their experiences.
4. The basic philosophy underlying the language-experience approach is usually summarized as: What a child thinks he can say; what he says he can write; what he writes he can read and it can be read by others; and he can read what is written by others.

When a number of learners are involved, as in classroom situations, effective reading instruction requires use of many approaches. Content and procedures associated with an approach, within themselves, do not guarantee that a high degree of individualization will be achieved. Nor do these preclude possibilities for meeting individual needs. Some approaches to reading instruction are more highly structured than others and, thus, the challenge of individualizing instruction may be greater than in those cases in which the approach is largely unstructured. Actual individualization of reading instruction depends on the attitudes and competencies of the teacher rather than on the type of approach used in instruction.

Helping Learners Develop Independence in Reading

Individualizing instruction and independent learning are not synonymous, although many factors influential in fostering one or the other also encourage development of the other. The crux of individualized instruction lies in how closely each learner's needs are met and how well he or she is helped to develop as fully as potential permits. Independent learning relates to the degree of responsibility a learner can accept and meet in terms of personal needs and objectives, and the initiative the learner is capable of in enlarging experiences in positive ways.

A major test of the effectiveness of reading instruction is in how independently learners meet their problems in reading, and how inclined they are to read voluntarily. Ability to solve problems encountered in reading and the inclination to read on a voluntary basis are closely related. An individual who cannot rely upon himself to recognize words or achieve meaning from a reading selection cannot be expected to enjoy reading to the extent that he will choose to engage in it on his own. The same is true of the individual who lacks skills and understandings essential for selecting suitable materials.

Effective Development of Skills

Helping learners acquire independence in reading requires development of several types of skills. These include skills related to the process of reading and also skills related to the location, selection, and use of materials.

Helping learners develop competence in use of decoding skills is of primary importance in development of independence in reading. While word recognition does not represent the complete process of reading, it is crucial in making reading possible. Not only must effective methods be used for teaching skills of decoding, but learners must also be taught to become flexible in their use of the skills. Any method of instruction that encourages learners to develop overreliance on any one technique of word analysis would be limited in its potential for developing independence in reading.

Development of competence in using decoding skills generally requires time and practice. Yet, independence in reading is desirable even during the beginning stages of instruction. The degree to which learners can be expected to show independence in reading, of course, varies according to the developmental levels of the learners. At every level of development, some degree of independence in meeting and solving problems can be shown by learners. Individuals should be taught how to use various resources to enable them to cope with problems of decoding when they lack ability in personal skills. For first graders, this might mean learning how to use picture dictionaries, experience charts, vocabulary cards, or the like. For advanced learners, this might refer to the use of references such as dictionaries and other resources.

Individuals should be taught to select materials for reading that are within range of their abilities and interests. Time should be spent in acquainting them with techniques that can be applied, for instance, in determining whether material might be too difficult. Techniques so simple as counting up to a minimum number of unrecognized words on a page can be used by a first grader to determine whether material is too difficult at his current level. Learners who have developed more competence in reading can be taught to use more sophisticated skills for finding out about the difficulty level of materials.

Abilities related to selection of materials within an individual's range of interests must be developed in indirect ways for the most part. Many learners do not recognize interests that they may have which might be furthered through reading. A large variety of interesting materials read to the class, regardless of the ages and levels of development of the individuals, can help to stimulate interests in reading. Through conferences and interviews with individuals and small groups, interests in reading may be discovered. Attractive displays calling attention to particular materials is another means by which some learners may be helped to recognize interests in reading.

Development and use of learning stations, modules, and various other materials and procedures described earlier for increasing attention and opportunities for individualizing reading instruction all can foster development of skills required in independent learning.

Attitudes of the Teacher

Fostering independent learning in the classroom requires certain attitudes on the part of the teacher. It is important for the teacher to manifest favorable attitudes toward individuals and their worth and toward satisfactions to be gained through reading.

Caring about individuals means respecting human personality and valuing individual achievement. Respect implies a willingness to trust an individual to do some things that are important to him. Part of the teacher's responsibility is to determine areas of concern in which a particular learner can function for himself and on his own. Opportunities should be given learners for gaining experiences conducive to development of independence. Obviously, a learner in the initial stages of learning to read cannot and should not be expected to be held responsible for the types of decisions an older and more experienced learner might make. But, as the learner's independent experience increases, more responsibility will be justified.

Appreciation for an individual's development of skills and attributes essential in independent reading should be apparent in the attitudes of the teacher. Having achievement recognized and praised generally helps to develop an individual's self-concept in positive directions.

Providing Books in the
Classroom Environment

Many types of materials are needed in the classroom environment if learners are to be helped to work independently or under the teacher's guidance in improving their reading achievement level. Most of the materials and resources presented so far in this chapter are of the type which can be used, primarily, in helping learners learn how to read and how to work independently. Learning to read, however, is of little personal value if reading is not used for a variety of purposes and for enjoyment by the individual. Moreover, much improvement in the ability to read is gained through the actual process of reading, rather than through formal instructional procedures. Thus, books are among the most important materials that can be used to provide experiences needed by learners for developing independence in reading and in learning.

Books in the classroom environment should be selected to help all learners in the classroom have access to materials that have personal meaning for them. Characteristics of individuals in particular classrooms can be used to suggest criteria for the selection of books that are right for the learners in that classroom. Teachers should take into account the nature of the learners' backgrounds and select materials that encourage reader-identification with characters and events in stories. Knowledge of topics found to be of interest to learners of certain age groups can be a beginning point in the search for the right books for individuals in the class. Individuals and their unique interests and abilities are the most important factors to be considered if books placed in the classroom environment are to serve their purposes. Aids such as those listed below are also helpful in locating books that may be needed by individuals in a class.

Periodicals and Booklists

1. Baker, Augusta, *Books About Negro Life for Children* (N. Y.: New York Public Library, 1963).
2. *Booklist* (American Library Association), semi-monthly.
3. *Book Review Digest* (H. W. Wilson Co.), annually.
4. *Bulletin of the Center for Children's Books* (University of Chicago Press), monthly.
5. *Childhood Education* (Association for Childhood Education International), monthly, September–May.
6. *Elementary English* (National Council of Teachers of English), monthly, October–May.
7. *The New York Times Book Review* (New York Times), weekly.
8. *The Reading Teacher* (International Reading Association), monthly, September–May.
9. *The School Library Journal* (R. R. Bowker Co.), monthly.

Books and Other Aids

1. Eakin, Mary K., *Subject Index to Books for Intermediate Grades* (Chicago: American Library Association, 1963).
2. _____, *Subject Index to Books for Primary Grades* (Chicago: American Library Association, 1963).
3. Eastman, M. H., *Index to Fairy Tales, Myths and Legends* (Chicago: American Library Association, 1963).
4. Gaver, Mary, editor, *Elementary School Library Association* (Newark, N. J.: Bro-Dart Foundations, 1968; Supplement, 1969).
5. Gillespie, John T., and Diana L. Lembo, *Introducing Books: A Guide for the Middle Grades* (N. Y.: R. R. Bowker, 1970).
6. Huus, Helen, *Children's Books to Enrich the Social Studies: For the Elementary Grades* (Washington, D. C.: National Council for the Social Studies, 1966).
7. _____, *Evaluating Books for Children and Young People*, Perspectives in Reading No. 10 (Newark, Del.: International Reading Association, 1968).

8. Larrick, Nancy, *A Teacher's Guide to Children's Books* (Columbus, Ohio: Charles E. Merrill, 1963).

9. *Paperbound Book Guide for Elementary Schools* (N. Y.: R. R. Bowker, 1966).

10. Phelps, Jennifer L., editor, *New Educational Materials* (Englewood Cliffs, N. J.: Scholastic Magazine, 1970).

11. Rollins, Charlemae, *We Build Together: A Reader's Guide to Negro Life and Literature For Elementary and High School Use* (Champaign, Ill.: National Council of Teachers of English, 1967).

12. Spache, George D., *Good Reading for Poor Readers* (Champaign, Ill.: Garrard Publishing, 1970).

Often children of minority backgrounds find a dearth of materials in the classroom with which they can personally identify. The Challenger Series[37] of books provides for accommodation of some of the special needs and interests of children of varied ethnic backgrounds. Books in the Challenger Series are about black children and Spanish-speaking children. These books are pocket-sized and are available in paperback editions. Titles include: (1) *Challenger: A Multi-Ethnic Reading Unit,* (2) *Challenger: A Spanish-Reading Unit,* and (3) *Challenger: A Black Reading Unit.* Each unit contains from four to eight copies on five to ten topics.

The Bank Street Readers[38] emphasize a multi-ethnic theme expressed through a variety of types of literature, including prose, poetry, drama, fact, and fiction. Content in these books is characterized by language and situations reflective of urban life. While these books can be used as basal readers in the primary grades, they can also be used to supplement materials in the classroom library.

Competencies for Individualizing Reading Instruction

Individualization of instruction does not occur simply because the teacher understands what it means, appreciates its importance, and has attitudes that are favorable toward it. The teacher must be competent in working with individuals, in managing the learning environment and, in short, in implementing procedures that foster individualization of instruction. Several competencies related to assessment of the needs of learners and to determination of objectives were suggested in Chapters 2 and 3 of this book. Such competencies are important also in individualization of instruction. Other competencies essential in individualizing instruction include the following:

1. Adapts activities in reading to the abilities of individuals.
2. Uses small-group instructional activities to meet common needs of several individuals.
3. Involves the total class in reading activities appropriate for large groups.
4. Uses flexible grouping arrangements to meet various needs and interests of individuals.

---

[37] *Challenger Books* (N. Y.: Random House, School Division).

[38] *The Bank Street Readers,* Primary Grades, Revised edition (Riverside, N. J.: Macmillan, School Division, 1972).

5. Uses conferences as needed to improve skills, concepts and attitudes of individuals.
6. Engages in effective planning with individuals.
7. Plans with individuals in groups of varying sizes.
8. Utilizes instructional materials and other resources to meet the needs of individuals.
9. Arranges resources and materials in the classroom so that these are accessible to learners.
10. Sequences learning experiences for individuals, for small groups, and for the total class.
11. Gives clear, explicit directions to learners.
12. Permits all learners to participate in the routine matters related to life in the classroom.
13. Provides opportunities for learners to participate in establishing guidelines for conduct in various classroom and learning situations.
14. Uses positive reinforcement patterns in working with individuals.
15. Gives direct instruction as required by an individual.
16. Instructs an individual at the point where he or she is in development of a concept or skill.
17. Organizes classroom space to accommodate a variety of learning experiences.
18. Utilizes group work to achieve values of group process.
19. Helps learners develop skills in planning.
20. Helps learners develop skills in record-keeping.

SUMMARY

Individualizing instruction is an important factor in determining the extent to which the classroom teacher can be accountable for reading achievement by each learner. Differences among individuals necessitate differentiation in their instruction. Their similarities, however, permit many of their commonly-held needs to be met through grouping arrangements.

Despite constraints found in many classrooms, the teacher is in a unique position to individualize instruction to an appreciable degree. Individualization should be conceived of as a quality in instruction, rather than as a formalized set of procedures. Individualization of instruction is implementation of the concept that each person learns according to his or her own motivations, perceptions, abilities, and experiences. Individualization of instruction requires that each learner's needs and objectives be taken into consideration in the design of learning experiences intended to help the student develop to the fullest potential. Attitudes and competencies of the teacher are often more influential in accomplishing the values of individualized instruction than are organizational patterns and other physical characteristics and resources in a classroom.

Review Questions

1. Explain how differences among individuals in a classroom group often are shown. **(1.1)***

---

*Boldface numbers in parentheses refer to the numbered behavioral objectives at the beginning of the chapter.

2. Suggest several factors to which differences among individuals are related. **(1.1)**

3. Why are homogeneous groups, which are established on the basis of a single factor in which the individuals show similarity, generally inadequate for meeting the needs of individuals? **(1.1)**

4. State specific ways in which each of the following factors might affect an individual's achievement in reading:
   a. Linguistic development **(1.2)**
   b. Experiential background **(1.3)**
   c. Favored learning modality **(1.4)**

5. Identify conventional terms used to refer to individualization of reading instruction. **(2.1)**

6. Describe each special feature of "individualized reading" as a formal approach to meeting the needs of individuals in a classroom. **(2.2)**

7. Explain why individualization of instruction is unlikely to occur as a result of reliance on a specified method or single approach to instruction. **(2.3)**

8. How are the principles of "seeking," "self-selection," and "self-pacing" provided for in the formalized individualized reading approach? **(2.4)**

9. Why is the formalized "individualized reading" approach often difficult to implement in many classrooms? **(2.5)**

10. List several principles that should be observed in any plan for individualizing reading instruction regardless of the specific approach or method that is used. **(2.6)**

11. Describe each of the following types of school organization for meeting the needs of individuals:
    a. Intra-class grouping
    b. Inter-class grouping
    c. Nongraded elementary school. **(3.1)**

12. Describe several procedures teachers have used in accommodating the needs of learners in the classrooom. **(3.2)**

13. Why is effective teaching, alone, sometimes believed to be sufficient for accommodation of individual differences in a classroom? **(3.3)**

14. Indicate several crucial aspects of instruction that should be planned if individualized instruction in reading is to be attempted. **(4.1)**

15. Selecting a grade level of your choice, suggest plans for scheduling formal reading instruction for the individuals in the class. **(4.2)**

16. Categorize the types of materials that should be found in the classroom for reading instruction. How might these be arranged to facilitate use by individuals? **(4.3)**

17. Suggest ways in which space in a classroom might be utilized in order to provide for various activities related to reading. **(4.4)**

18. Identify some of the special considerations and problems that must guide plans made for working with learners in each of the following situations:
    a. Individual conferences
    b. Small-group work
    c. Total class involvement **(4.5)**

19. Describe special features of programmed reading materials; give examples of specific types available for reading instruction. **(5.1)**

20. Describe some specific ways in which programmed reading materials can contribute to individualized reading in a classroom situation. **(5.1)**

21. Describe types of materials included in the general term, "multi-media approaches to reading." **(5.2)**

22. Discuss advantages and limitations that might be expected from the use of multi-media approaches to reading instruction. **(5.2)**

23. Give examples of types of multimedia approaches available for use in reading programs. **(5.2)**

24. Describe the nature of a "learning module." **(5.3)**

25. Explain each basic step in the learning cycle provided by a module. **(5.3)**

26. Describe several ways in which modules can be used to facilitate individualized instruction in reading. **(5.4)**

27. Explain the concept of "learning stations" or "learning centers" for use in individualizing instruction and in encouraging independent learning. **(5.5)**

28. What is meant by a formal approach, method, or instructional system in reading instruction? **(6.1)**

29. Describe special characteristics of each of the following approaches to reading instruction:
    a. Basal-reader approach
    b. Language-experience approach **(6.2)**

30. Is it possible that individualized reading might be achieved through use of any approach to reading instruction? Why or why not? **(6.3)**

31. Describe some procedures that might be used to encourage learners to engage in reading independently. **(7.1)**

32. What effect can attitudes of the teacher have upon development of independence in reading by learners? **(7.2)**

33. Suggest guidelines for encouraging learners to engage in independent reading. **(7.3)**

34. List several competencies needed by teachers for encouraging learners to read independently. **(8.1)**

35. What particular competencies are needed by a teacher for individualizing instruction when resources are limited? **(8.2)**

36. What competencies are needed by a teacher to utilize classroom space advantageously for individualized instruction? **(8.3)**

Selected References

1. Anderson, Robert H., "Ungraded Primary Classes: An Administrator's Contribution to Mental Health," *Understanding Children*, 24 (June, 1955), pp. 66–72.
2. Atkinson, J. W., and N. Feather, editors, *A Theory of Achievement Motivation*. N. Y.: John C. Wiley, 1966.
3. Austin, Mary and Coleman Morrison, *The First R: The Harvard Report on Reading in the Elementary Schools*. N. Y.: Macmillan, 1963.
4. Bales, R. F., *Interaction Process Analysis*. Cambridge, Mass.: Addison-Wesley, 1951.
5. Balow, Irving H., "Does Homogeneous Grouping Give Homogeneous Groups?" *Elementary School Journal*, 63 (October, 1962), pp. 28–32.

6. Baratz, Joan C., and Roger W. Shuy, *Teaching Black Children to Read*. Washington, D.C.: Center for Applied Linguistics, 1969.

7. Barbe, Walter B., *Educator's Guide to Personalized Reading*. Englewood Cliffs, N. J.: Prentice-Hall, 1961.

8. Blakely, W. Paul, and Beverly McKay, "Individualizing Reading as Part of an Eclectic Reading Program," *Elementary English*, 43 (March, 1966), pp. 214–20.

9. Bond, Guy, *Adapting Instruction to Individual Differences*. Minneapolis, Minn.: University of Minnesota Press, 1948.

10. Brogan, Peggy, and Lorene K. Fox, *Helping Children Read*. N. Y.: Holt, Rinehart and Winston, 1961.

11. Burr, Marvin G., "Study of Homogeneous Grouping in Terms of Individual Variation and the Teaching Problem," *Teachers College Record* (October, 1931), pp. 63–64.

12. Carter, Homer, and Dorothy McGinnis, *Teaching Individuals to Read*. Boston: D. C. Heath, 1962.

13. Chall, Jeanne, *Learning to Read: The Great Debate*. N. Y.: McGraw-Hill, 1967.

14. Clymer, Theodore, "Criteria for Grouping for Reading Instruction," Paper presented at 22nd Annual Conference on Reading, University of Chicago (June, 1959).

15. Cook, Walter W. and Theodore Clymer, "Acceleration and Retardation," *Individualizing Instruction*, 61st Yearbook of the National Society for the Study of Education, Part I. Chicago: University of Chicago Press, 1962.

16. Darrow, Helen F., and Virgil M. Howes, *Approaches to Individualized Reading*. N. Y.: Appleton-Century-Crofts, 1960.

17. Esbensen, Thorwald, *Working With Individualized Instruction*. Belmont, Ca.: Fearon Publishers, 1971.

18. Flanagan, John C., "How Instructional Systems Will Manage Learning." *Nation's Schools*, 86 (October, 1970).

19. Goldberg, Miriam L., Harry A. Passow, and Joseph Justman, *The Effects of Ability Grouping*. N. Y.: Teachers College Press, Columbia University Press, 1966.

20. Goodlad, John I., "Ungrading the Elementary Grades," *N. E. A. Journal*, 44 (1951), pp. 170–71.

21. Goodman, Kenneth, *et al.*, *Choosing Materials to Teach Reading*. Detroit, Mich.: Wayne State University Press, 1966.

22. Gray, William, *On Their Own in Reading*, Revised edition. N. Y.: Scott-Foresman, 1960.

23. Groff, Patrick J., "Comparisons of Individualized and Ability Grouping Approaches to Reading Achievement," *Elementary English*, 40 (March, 1963), pp. 258–64; 276.

24. _____, "Helping Teachers to Begin Individualized Reading," *The National Elementary Principal* 43 (February, 1964), pp. 47–50.

25. _____, "Materials For Individualized Reading," *Elementary English*, 38 (January, 1961), pp. 1–7.

26. Hanson, Richard A., "Creating a Responsive Classroom Environment With Learning Centers," in *Individualizing Reading Instruction*, Larry A. Harris and Carl B. Smith, editors. N. Y.: Holt, Rinehart and Winston, 1972.

27. Hillson, Maurie, and Joseph Bongo, *Continuous Progress Education*. Chicago: Science Research Associates, 1971.

28. Jacobs, Leland, "Reading on Their Own Means Reading at Their Growth Edges," *The Reading Teacher*, 6 (March, 1953), pp. 27–32.

29. Johnson, Stuart R., and Rita B. Johnson, *Developing Individualized Instructional Material*. Palo Alto, Ca.: Westinghouse Learning Press, 1970.

30. Keener, Beverly M., "Individualized Reading and the Disadvantaged," *The Reading Teacher*, 20 (February, 1967), pp. 410–12.
31. Kephart, N. C., *The Slow Learner in the Classroom*. Columbus, Oh.: Charles E. Merrill, 1960.
32. Miller, Wilma H., "Organizing a First Grade Classroom For Individualized Reading Instruction," *The Reading Teacher*, 24 (May, 1971), pp. 748–52.
33. Olson, Willard, *Child Development*. Boston: D. C. Heath, 1949.
34. Strang, Ruth, *Diagnostic Teaching of Reading*. N. Y.: McGraw-Hill, 1969.
35. Veatch, Jeannette, *Individualizing Your Reading Program*. N. Y.: G. P. Putnam, 1969.
36. _____, *Reading in the Elementary School*. N. Y.: Ronald Press, 1966.
37. Vite, Irene W., "Individualized Reading: The Scoreboard on Control Studies," *Education*, 81 (January, 1961), pp. 285–90.
38. Wilson, Richard C., and Helen J. James, *Individualized Reading: A Practical Approach*. Dubuque, Iowa: Kendall-Hunt Publishing, 1972.

5 Developing Interests and Attitudes in Reading

Accountability in reading instruction is not achieved by focusing all efforts toward development of measurable skills and concepts to the exclusion of attention to the development of affective behaviors. Affective behaviors, within themselves, are important as part of the ideals of humanistic education. These behaviors are important, also, in facilitating development of cognitive behaviors. The relationship of affective behaviors to accountability has been stated well by Combs.

> A truly comprehensive approach to accountability must take into consideration all aspects affecting the outcomes of schooling, using each for what it can contribute to the total picture with full recognition that all are related and all are required.[1]

Behavioral Objectives

The content of Chapter 5 is presented in such a way that after reading it, an individual
- **1.0** Recognizes relationships between humanistic education and reading instruction
  - **1.1** Specifies types of affective behaviors of primary concern in reading instruction
  - **1.2** Identifies ideals in humanistic education on which reading instruction should focus
  - **1.3** Identifies instructional procedures that contribute, simultaneously, to development of cognitive and affective behaviors

---

[1] Arthur W. Combs, *Educational Accountability: Beyond Behavioral Objectives* (Washington, D. C.: Association for Supervision and Curriculum Development, 1972), p. 2.

115

2.0 Understands the nature of interests and their effect upon development of reading competencies and habits

    2.1 Explains the probable influences of environment and experiences on development of interests

    2.2 Explains importance of structuring procedures and conditions for development of cognitive behaviors so that these contribute to the development of affective behaviors as well

    2.3 Identifies interests that are generally characteristic of learners of various age groups

    2.4 Suggests guidelines for using children's interests to improve the effectiveness of reading instruction

3.0 Understands how factors in the classroom environment affect the development of affective behaviors

    3.1 Explains effects of the teacher's attitudes on the social climate in the classroom

    3.2 Describes teacher competencies that are potentially useful in developing favorable attitudes toward reading

4.0 Understands the importance of readiness in development of interests and attitudes

    4.1 Identifies factors that contribute to types of interests and attitudes that are held by an individual

5.0 Understands how to improve the experiential backgrounds of learners

    5.1 Suggests types of real experiences that can be provided in the classroom for improving concepts held by learners

    5.2 Suggests types of real experiences that can be provided in the school

    5.3 Identifies techniques for helping learners use experiences as a basis for various types of oral expression

    5.4 Suggests ways in which the community can be used as a resource to increase effectiveness of the reading program

6.0 Knows how to improve the social climate in the classroom

    6.1 Identifies factors that influence the social climate in the classroom

    6.2 Suggests procedures that can be used to improve the social climate in the classroom

7.0 Knows how to improve the intellectual climate in the classroom

    7.1 Identifies factors that influence the nature of the intellectual climate in the classroom

    7.2 Suggests procedures that may be used to improve the intellectual climate in the classroom

8.0 Knows how to help learners relate reading to activities in and out of school

    8.1 Identifies techniques for helping learners develop accurate concepts of the nature of reading

    8.2 Explains how reading can be used to increase effectiveness of sharing periods

    8.3 Relates reading and television

    8.4 Identifies ways that reading can be used in content areas

    8.5 Explains the nature of independent reading

9.0 Understands the influential nature of the teacher's interests and attitudes on the development of learners' affective behaviors

    9.1 Distinguishes between the nature of attitudes and the nature of competencies

9.2   Identifies specific attitudes that should be held by teachers

9.3   Explains effects of teachers' affective behaviors on those of learners

10.0   Knows specific techniques that can be used to contribute to the development of learners' interests

    10.1   Identifies techniques that can be used to contribute to each of the following:

        10.1.1   Development of listening habits and abilities

        10.1.2   Appeal of the environment in the classroom

        10.1.3   Creative book reports

        10.1.4   Oral and written expression

        10.1.5   Dramatics

11.0   Recognizes types of competencies required of teachers for development of learners' affective behaviors

Humanistic Concerns in Reading Instruction

Humanistic education consists of all learning experiences that help individuals develop human and humane qualities. Considered from this perspective, all learning activities implemented in the classroom for achievement of objectives in reading can be potentially helpful in pursuit of the ideals of humanistic education.

Ideals of humanistic education are essentially the same as many of the effective behaviors which are developed ultimately through effective reading instruction. Humanistic ideals identified by various writers[2] include the following:

1. An attitude of acceptance and appropriate reaction to change
2. A willingness to examine new ideas and innovations
3. A sense of community and belonging
4. Willingness to participate in affairs that affect oneself and others
5. Attainment of personal meaning and self-actualization
6. Development of a positive self-concept
7. Acceptance and appreciation of the differences among individuals
8. Open-mindedness
9. Critical-thinking abilities
10. Self-direction

A close relationship exists between the ideals stated here and values that are attainable, at least in part, through reading. Progress toward these and related ideas and values should be sought as reading is taught. Attention must be given to development of learners' interests and attitudes. These interests and attitudes are those that influence whether or not learners will actually read once they are

---

[2]Kenneth O. Benne and Bozidar Muntyan, *Human Relations and Curriculum Change* (N. Y.: Dryden Press, 1951).

Combs, *Educational Accountability: Beyond Behavioral Objectives*, p. 23.

John Dewey, *Democracy and Education* (N. Y.: Macmillan, 1923).

Adolph Unruh and Harold E. Turner, *Supervision for Change and Innovation* (Boston: Houghton Mifflin, 1970), pp. 75–77.

taught how to read. Over and above the task of getting learners interested in read-ing for enjoyment or for its utilitarian purposes is the task of helping them sense the broadening influences of reading in their personal development and in their relationships with others.

Several values whose achievement is believed to be facilitated through acquaint-ance with books have been stated by Muriel Crosby. These include the potentiality of books for:

1. Providing insight into differences and similarities of people
2. Giving the reader the vivid and immediate impact of experience
3. Providing opportunity to share the feelings of other human beings — their relation-ships, their predicaments, their joys and sorrows
4. Showing differences among individuals that stem from cultural barriers and helping the reader realize types of problems that may stem from these.[3]

These and other values which reading can encourage comprise an approach to humanistic education. Within the context of humanistic education, development of learners' interests and attitudes affecting their reading can be seen in perspec-tive. Meaningful development of interests and attitudes related to reading cannot be effectively developed through occasional use of techniques and gimmicks de-signed specifically for the purpose. Development of interests and other affective attributes depends upon the total conglomerate of experiences and conditions com-prising the environment, whether in or out of school. In the classroom, humanistic concerns must be considered, even when the attainment of cognitive behaviors is the immediate and direct concern.

Reading affects an individual's ideas and actions, two areas of concern in humanistic education. Several authorities have observed the importance of this influence. E. L. Thorndike stressed the immense importance of interests as an in-fluence on the nature of an individual's thoughts and actions.[4] In a reciprocal way, Russell explained the importance of interests, not only as important factors in humanistic education, but also as important in achievement of competence in reading. According to Russell,

> The development of a permanent interest in reading seems to have a number of social and personal values . . . the health of a democracy is dependent upon a citizenry equipped with some knowledge of the problems faced by the total group.
>
> One of the best ways of becoming a competent reader, as measured by a standardized test or any other instrument, is to do much reading of different kinds of materials. Probably more important, the habit of reading can con-tribute to the child's knowledge of himself, his acquaint-ances, and his world in a way few other activities can.[5]

---

[3]Muriel Crosby, editor, *Reading Ladders for Human Relations*, Fourth edition (Washington, D. C.: American Council on Education, 1963), pp. 3–4.

[4]Edward L. Thorndike, *The Psychology of Wants, Interests and Abilities* (N. Y.: Appleton-Century-Crofts, 1935).

[5]David H. Russell, *Children Learn to Read* (Waltham, Mass.: Blaisdell Publishing, 1961), pp. 362–63.

Guiding instruction in reading in such a way that interests and other affective behaviors are continuous concerns is a practical approach to achievement of humanistic education and achievement of objectives in the cognitive domain.

The Nature of Interests

The nature of interests has been the subject of research by many investigators.[6] It is known that interests can give rise to behavior or result from behavior.[7] This knowledge can be used advantageously in reading instruction. Learners' current interests can be used as a basis for direction of activities and selection of appropriate materials. These established interests can also be used as bases for developing new interests.

Because environmental and experiential factors have significant bearing on the development of interests, attention must be given to structuring the social and intellectual climates of the classroom environment so that these are positive factors in development of learners' reading interests.

Other findings from research on interests also have implications for reading instruction:

1. Interests arise only in situations involving freedom of choice, plus some spontaneity in choosing.
2. There is a reciprocal relationship between interest and ability.
3. Interests can be modified, but true changes are infrequent and slow in occurring.
4. Changes in interest are affected by emotional appeal and personal relationships.[8]

In view of these findings, procedures and conditions established for the primary purpose of developing cognitive ability in reading become important as means for the development of interests. For example, individualization of instruction, important for meeting needs of individuals in achievement of competence in reading is also important for development of interests in reading. Selection of material for instruction in reading requires consideration of the individual's present competence in reading. Competence of the learner in reading is also a consideration in selection of materials or activities for appeal to personal interests. The relationship between the teacher and the learner are influential factors in achievement of objectives in any domain.

Children's Reading Interests

Knowledge of general interests, characteristic of children of various age groups, can be helpful to a teacher in determining procedures to accommodate interests held by individuals. Knowledge of general interests held by groups of children, however, serve only as a guide or starting point for determining unique interests of an individual. Individual differences are reflected in interests just as they are reflected in other factors pertaining to an individual.

---

[6]Arthur T. Jersild and Ruth J. Tasch, *Children's Interests and What They Suggest For Education* (N. Y.: Teacher's College, Columbia University, Bureau of Publications, 1949).

[7]John Dewey, *Democracy and Education* (N. Y.: Macmillan, 1933), p. 147.

[8]Dale B. Harris, "How Children Learn Interests, Motives, and Attitudes," *49th Yearbook, Part I*, National Society for the Study of Education (Chicago: University of Chicago Press, 1950), pp. 129–55.

Several researchers have examined reading interests of boys and girls of various age groups in order to determine if notable differences exist and can be attributed to the sex of an individual. Findings of early studies showed few, if any, sex differences in the reading choices of children before the age of nine years when, according to Terman and Lima, "the divergence is very marked and the breach continues to widen up to adult life . . . ."[9] Later research efforts have corroborated these earlier findings. In general, significant differences do not exist between the types of interests held by boys and girls during the primary grades in regard to topics of reading materials.

Bernice J. Wolfson found the top categories of interests among boys in intermediate grades to include: (1) adventure, (2) sports, (3) physical science, (4) machines, (5) applied science, (6) social studies, and (7) fantasy. For girls of similar ages, top categories of interests were (1) fantasy, (2) personal problems, (3) social studies, (4) sports, (5) adventure, (6) family life, and (7) children.[10]

Marked differences between the reading interests of boys and girls in intermediate grades were also noted by Benjamin F. Jefferson. Jefferson's findings showed that boys preferred stories about war, sports, invention, and exploration. In contrast, girls preferred stories about love, romance, feminine activities, school adventure, child life in other lands, magic and fantasy. Both boys and girls showed preferences for stories about humor and whimsy, self-improvement, realistic animals, and earning money.[11]

On the basis of opinions expressed by more than 24,000 children, G. W. Norvell[12] found that boys' interests favored stories that stressed adventuresome action, physical struggle, human characters, animals, humor, courage, heroism, and patriotism. Boys expressed disfavor for stories that placed emphasis on description, didacticism, fairies, romantic love, sentiment, girls or women as leading characters, and physical weakness in male characters. Interests expressed by girls favored stories that dealt with lively adventure, home and school life, human characters, domestic animals and pets, romantic love, sentiment, mystery, the supernatural, and patriotism. Girls tended not to favor stories depicting violent action, description, didacticism, young children, and fierce animals.

Research results by Ethal M. King indicate that children's interests in reading change as new personal interests develop. Audio-visual aids, television, and films can play important roles in changing reading interests. King also found that preferences of children in the primary grades included fairy tales, realistic stories of everyday life, and animal stories. Children in the intermediate grades preferred stories about mysteries, adventure, animals, and family life.[13]

Some researchers have attempted to determine what relationships, if any, exist between children's socioeconomic backgrounds and their reading interests. There

[9] Helen Huus, "Developing Interest and Taste in Literature in the Elementary Grades" in *Reading as an Intellectual Activity* 8, (1963), pp. 46–50.

[10] Bernice J. Wolfson, "What do Children Say their Reading Interests Are?" *The Reading Teacher*, 14 (January, 1958), pp. 212–18.

[11] Benjamin F. Jefferson, "Some Relationships Between Parents' and Children's Preferences in Juvenile Literature," *Elementary School Journal*, 58 (January, 1958), pp. 212–18.

[12] G. W. Norvell, *What Boys and Girls Like to Read* (Morristown, N. J.: Silver-Burdett, 1968).

[13] Ethal M. King, "Critical Appraisal of Research on Children's Interests, Preferences, and Habits," *Canadian Education and Research Digest*, 7 (1967), pp. 312–26.

is some indication that young children in the inner city prefer reading materials that permit them a high level of reader identification. Implications from such research are that illustrations, settings, and characters in stories selected for children with inner-city backgrounds should depict life with which they are familiar.[14] Results of other studies have indicated just the opposite. Jerry L. Johns investigated reading preferences of children from the inner city in grades four through six to determine if they preferred to read stories or books which contain content and illustrations reflective of life in the inner city. The majority of the children indicated preferences for reading stories which depicted (1) pleasant settings in middle-class suburban areas, (2) characters having positive self-concepts, and (3) characters in positive group interactions.[15] Results of this study indicate that there are still questions to be answered regarding influences of socioeconomic backgrounds on reading preferences. Teachers of children from the inner city — or those dealing with any group of learners — must keep in mind the principle of individual differences when considering the nature of individual interests.

Within the general framework provided by the results of various attempts to determine patterns of children's preferences for reading materials, teachers are provided a starting point for determining the nature of each person's interests. Guidelines such as the following can be used as starters of materials and for determination of meaningful activities.

1. There are variations in interests of children according to ages and grade levels.
2. Girls generally read more than boys, but boys generally have a wider range of interests and read a greater variety of books.
3. Compared with boys, girls usually show an earlier interest in adult fiction of a romantic type.
4. Before approximately age nine, there are no significant differences between the reading interests held by boys and girls.
5. Boys tend to be reluctant to read stories or books written especially for girls; girls show a greater tendency to read books designated as being particularly for boys. Such cross-interests should be encouraged to help both sexes develop wide-ranging interests.
6. Socioeconomic background-levels of learners cannot be assumed to be indicative of the types of materials preferred by the learners any more than sex or any other factor can be assumed as a firm indication of an individual's interests in reading.
7. No single selection or group of materials is likely to satisfy interests of all individuals in any classroom group.

Readiness in Development of Interests and Attitudes

An individual's readiness to begin receiving formal instruction in reading is widely recognized as important in determining the degree of success he is likely to have in beginning reading. Also widely recognized is the

---

[14] Robert Emans, "What Do Children of the Inner City Like to Read?" *Elementary School Journal*, 69 (December, 1968), pp. 119–22.

[15] Jerry L. Johns, "What do Inner-City Children Prefer to Read?" *The Reading Teacher*, 26, No. 5 (February, 1973), pp. 462–67.

continuing importance of readiness as the individual faces increasingly higher and more complex skills and attributes required for achieving cognitive objectives in reading. Less attention is given, however, to the importance of readiness in the acquisition of favorable attitudes on interests in relation to reading. Yet, readiness plays a role in determining how successfully an individual will acquire certain affective behaviors in reading. As in the case of readiness for formal reading instruction, readiness in the development of interests and attitudes is not general in nature. Attention must be given not to *whether* or not an individual is ready to develop favorable attitudes and interests in reading, but to *what* the learner is ready for.

Several factors contribute to the types and levels of interests and attitudes an individual may be capable of developing in reading. The individual's age, competence in reading, and present interests are among factors that should be considered in determining readiness for development of certain affective behaviors.

Age of the Learner

As the results of various studies have shown, the age of the individual can be a significant influence in determining the nature of interests and attitudes he or she is likely to show for certain topics in reading. It is also clear that certain types of activities appeal to children of various ages in various degrees. A fairly clear distinction can be made between topics and activities in which learners at primary grades and those at intermediate grades may take an interest. Consideration of the ages of learners is a prime requisite for success in achieving objectives in the affective domain.

Age of learners is not only significant in terms of topics and activities that might be selected for helping in development of affective behaviors, but it is also an important indicator of the degree of stability that might be expected of their attitudes and interests. The younger the learners, the less stable their interests and attitudes are likely to be. Very young children cannot be expected to give sustained attention to any one type of activity or topic to the degree possible for older children. Although individuals may show differences from the norm, the teacher of young children should expect to bring them into contact with a wide variety of activities and materials that accommodate their rapidly changing interests. Children in the intermediate grades are more likely to develop interests that are sustained over appreciably longer periods. Efforts to interest older children in reading in-depth about one particular topic, reading to pursue a hobby, or reading to obtain information of various treatments of a topic are likely to be effective.

Competence in Reading

It is difficult for an individual to become interested in anything that is more complex and more difficult than he or she is able to handle easily. Therefore, the nature of an individual's competence in reading is of prime significance when an attempt is being made to engage the learner's interests and develop favorable attitudes toward reading. Materials for independent reading must be selected with attention to readability. Attention must be given not only to the facility with which the learners might recognize words, but also to their abilities to deal with concepts involved in selections.

The manner in which instruction is given in formal classes for helping learners develop competencies in reading can affect their attitudes and interests in reading. Care must be taken to avoid use of procedures and materials that stimulate learner-resistance to reading, even if the development of affective behaviors happens not to be the prime concern of the moment. Procedures and materials that lack effectiveness for development of affective behaviors generally are lacking also in potential for development of cognitive behaviors.

Presently Held Interests

A learner's current interests can become bases for further development of interests or introduction of new ones. If a learner is already interested in sports, it is relatively easy to stimulate his or her interests in reading materials related to sports. Generally, when an individual has an established interest in anything, knowledge about that subject and pleasant associations with it are already present.

Interests and attitudes are developmental in nature. It is not reasonable to expect an individual suddenly to begin showing behaviors for which there have been no antecedent experiences. Many of the interests and attitudes held by individuals have their origin early in the person's development and in situations quite remote from the classroom. It is the teacher's responsibility to gain as much knowledge as possible about such interests and attitudes. In development of affective behaviors, as in other areas of development, it is often essential to begin at the learner's level and lead the individual gradually forward to personally appropriate levels of development.

Improving the Experiential Backgrounds of Learners

Interest and attitudes held by individuals are related to and influenced by the types of experiences they have had. The uniqueness of individuals makes it unlikely that two persons will have experienced identical phenomena. Individuals differ in their perceptions of their experiences, even though they may have common experiences. Thus, differences can be expected in interests and attitudes among individuals, although it appears that those individuals had identical previous experiences. Generalizations about an individual made on the basis of what is known of his past experiences should be made with caution.

Improving the experiential backgrounds of learners should be considered an integral part of any efforts made for improvement of their interests and attitudes toward reading. Several options are available to the classroom teacher for improving learners' backgrounds. Fostering positive social and intellectual climates in the classroom is a contribution to improvement of learners' backgrounds.

Improving the Social Climate

The social climate fostered in a classroom affects the quality of the learners' experiences. The nature of this climate is a major determinant of how learners perceive themselves in relation to the teacher and other members of the group. The prevailing social climate in a classroom will affect the learners' ability to work cooperatively with others, to share ideas, and to accept responsibilities.

The social climate is a reflection of the effect of a number of situational factors. An important influence on the social climate is the nature of interests and attitudes reflected by the teacher and sensed by the learners. A teacher who is highly interested in reading and reads a variety of selections to the class will increase the value learners assign to reading. A teacher who accepts and respects unique differences among the personalities of learners will stimulate like behavior in the class. The teacher's attitudes will likewise affect those of the class.

The teacher's active concern about the quality of the social climate that prevails in the classroom is another factor influencing the nature of the climate itself. The teacher who is concerned about fostering a positive social climate will utilize various techniques to determine the nature of the climate and to improve it. Use of sociometric techniques frequently can be helpful in this regard.* Such a concern on the teacher's part will become reflected in the learners as they become increasingly conscious of the importance of a positive climate. The teacher's concern about the nature of the social climate should be reflected in ways other than constantly reminding learners of their behaviors through verbal admonitions. The teacher should attempt to analyze and understand social relationships and patterns of acceptance and rejection shown by learners in the class.

Certain physical characteristics of the classroom can also have a positive or negative effect on the nature of the social climate. Attention should be given to attractiveness and comfort in the classroom setting. Arrangement and utilization of space can facilitate or inhibit freedom of movement and independent learning. Seating arrangements can encourage cooperation or competiveness. The presence or absence of varied centers of interest can inspire industry or boredom.

The social climate in a classroom does not exist in isolation from the intellectual climate. Social and intellectual climates in the classroom are interdependent and interrelated.

Improving the Intellectual Climate

The intellectual climate in a classroom is a reflection of attitudes toward, and efforts expended for, helping individuals learn and the

---

*For an explicit account of use of sociometric techniques in improving the social climate in the classroom, see Norman E. Gronlund, *Sociometry in the Classroom* (N.Y.: Harper and Row, 1959).

corresponding responses made by learners. Methods, procedures, materials, and other resources used for teaching greatly affect the intellectual climate.

The intellectual climate in a classroom can be marked by the efforts of learners who have been helped to recognize and accept responsibilities for learning. It can also be characterized by the efforts of learners who have been taught to accept learning as an externally imposed condition. There is a notable difference in the intellectual climate of a classroom where learners seek active involvement in learning and one where they wait passively or distractedly to be told when and what to learn.

Principles of accountability can be positive influences in determining an intellectual climate conducive to the well-being of all learners. Knowledge of needs, for example, not only can improve the teacher's efforts to meet them, but can help learners know and sense the relevancy of learning tasks. Knowledge of, and acceptance of, objectives permits a positive sense of direction for both the teacher and the learners. Knowing where one is headed is conducive to a feeling of security and reinforces individual initiative in the learning process. Individualization of instruction not only personalizes a learner's experiences in the classroom, but also can help him to assume a degree of independence and responsibility for achievement.

For a positive intellectual climate in the classroom, there should be appropriate balance between several elements: between real and vicarious experiences provided for the learners, between contact permitted with abstract ideas and concrete applications, between teacher-directed learning and independent learning, and — in reading particularly — among activities designed to help learners learn to read, read to learn, and read for enjoyment.

Relating Reading to Other Activities In and Out of School

If reading is to become a vital force in the life of any individual, it must be perceived by that individual as a valuable asset that can be used to enrich his experiences in other activities — both in and out of the classroom. Planned instruction in reading generally is aimed toward helping learners master basic competencies in reading. Refinement of these competencies depends on the uses an individual makes of reading. Learners should be helped to perceive the many functional and recreational uses of reading as means for accomplishment of their personal ends.

Avoiding Inaccurate Perceptions of the Meaning of Reading

From their earliest contact with school life, many learners perceive school as the place where they will learn to read. Although this type of anticipation by first graders may be gratifying to some parents and teachers, it is unfortunate if the child's concept of what reading is and where reading occurs becomes rigid at that point. From the outset, and onward, learners should be helped to see relationships between their efforts to learn how to read and applications of reading in other activities in and out of school.

Teachers should avoid use of statements and procedures that establish reading in the minds of learners merely as a subject to be learned during regular instructional periods. Regular instructional periods can be perceived as either those periods when direct instruction is given or those *free* periods when each learner is *required* to read independently. Establishing permanent reading groups on the basis of learners' ability or achievement and instructing those groups at the same time — and often in the same way — daily can help learners equate the procedure with reading itself. Failure to help learners become conscious of the use of reading in other areas of the curriculum also helps to establish the idea that reading is relegated to a particular class and period. It is unrealistic to assume that young children will make this relationship on their own. For example, at the end of one school day when time ran out because of preoccupation with many exciting activities related to completion of a unit in social studies, a concerned child reminded his teacher that the class had not had reading at all. The perplexed teacher could not understand this attitude, since — from the teacher's point of view — reading had been a principal activity for most of the day. Time and effort should be spent in helping learners develop a concept of what reading actually means.

Reading During Sharing Periods

Especially in the primary grades, many school days begin with a period during which learners are encouraged to share experiences or things of interest to themselves. Known by various names such as "sharing time" or "show and tell," the nature of these periods takes different forms in different classrooms. Sharing periods can be used to provide opportunities for learners who so desire to share with the class a favorite selection they have read. Defined objectives, teacher-learner planning, and creativity by teacher and learners can make results of reading worthy and attractive offerings for the sharing period.

Sharing periods can be scheduled at any time of the school day that serves the purposes in a particular classroom. These need not be relegated solely to use in the primary grades. With appropriate planning, sharing periods can be vehicles serving the use of the most sophisticated learners in the intermediate and upper grades. Ingenuity by the teacher can make the sharing period an opportunity for enlarging learners' concepts of the nature of reading and its uses.

Reading in the Content Areas

Teachers in elementary schools, whether in self-contained or open classrooms, have immediate opportunities for helping learners apply reading in other areas of the curriculum. Reading is a major tool for use in helping achieve objectives in mathematics, social studies, science, and other areas of the curriculum. Conversely, the content areas also afford various opportunities for development of reading competencies and for functional use of reading.

Learners need specific guidance, as a rule, in concept and vocabulary development, symbolic representation, and various other skills unique to each content area. According to Robert Karlin,

> Children have to learn to accommodate to a different style of writing, which is characterized by terseness, density of ideas, and inclusion of many unfamiliar and difficult concepts and vocabulary. In addition, they must learn to master another set of skills — reading-study skills — which enable them to read efficiently and solve problems associated with each subject area.[16]

Skills essential for competent use of reading in the content areas should be taught carefully and, if possible, in the context in which they are to be used. Only if a learner is competent in reading in the content areas will the learner be able to expand his or her concepts by reading texts and supplementary materials related to the areas. Without mastery of the basic skills required in reading in the content areas, it is unlikely that a learner can regard reading in those areas with enthusiasm and satisfaction.

Locational skills and study skills are included within the general categories of (1) locating information, (2) selection and evaluation of materials, (3) organizing information for retention and communication, (4) retaining information, and (5) communicating information and ideas to others.[17] Development of locational and study skills should be emphasized as part of regular instruction related to achievement of objectives in both the content areas and in reading. Learners should be made aware that these skills are those needed for common uses of reading in everyday affairs. Situations should be established to provide learners with practical experiences in using these skills in activities such as reading newspapers and magazines, reading to gain information related to the personal interests, using reference materials, or applying critical thinking to various issues and problems.

Independent Reading

In Chapter 4 of this book, attention was given to the problem and importance of helping learners achieve independence in reading. Independent reading is not only important for achieving objectives related directly to the reading program in the classroom, but it is also an important factor in helping learners perceive reading as a functional part of their lives in and out of school. Independence in reading is fostered by giving deliberate and organized attention to development of skills and attributes essential for self-direction. Self-direction involves use of the ability to define problems and engage in other steps of the problem-solving process. Self-direction also requires motivation and interest for pursuing activities and finding solutions to various problems. Many of the attitudes

---

[16] Robert Karlin, *Teaching Elementary Reading* (N. Y.: Harcourt Brace Jovanovich, 1971), p. 218.

[17] Robert Kranyik and Florence V. Shankman, *How to Teach Study Skills* (Englewood Cliffs, N. J.: Prentice-Hall, Teachers Practical Press, 1963).

deemed important in humanistic education are essential in an individual's development of inclinations and skills necessary for independent learning.

Homework Assignments

Homework assignments are often the subject of controversy in reading instruction. Sometimes the controversy involves the question of whether or not homework of any type should be assigned to learners. At other times, the controversy pertains to the nature of homework assignments that are appropriate. Whether or not homework assignments should be made depends on whether proposed assignments are essential in helping learners achieve objectives established as important for them. Questions related to the nature of reading homework assignments that should be made cannot be answered so succinctly. The type of homework assignments, if any, must be based, among other things, on the nature of work an individual is capable of doing on his own. Consideration should be given, also, to the relationship of the assignment to the learner's interests, needs, and pastimes. Reading requirements should be within the individual's independent reading level.

Many reports have been made regarding the large number of hours many children spend watching television. Homework assignments in reading that can be integrated with information or entertainment received by watching television can serve several purposes. If achievement of objectives required by an individual can be facilitated with help from television, an assignment that requires its use would then be appropriate. Efforts can be made to improve an individual's taste in selection of television shows by integrating an assignment with a particular program. Ability to use critical-thinking abilities sometimes can be assisted by having learners apply these skills to analysis of television commercials and other offerings.

Influence of the Teacher's Attitudes and Interests

Many of the factors essential in helping learners develop affective behaviors depend directly on the teacher. The teacher's attitudes and competencies are among the most powerful influences on the types of attitudes and interests that will be developed by learners. Attitudes should be distinguished from competencies, for these are not developed in the same ways. The teacher who recognizes the essential distinction between attitudes and competencies is in a position to improve personal performance with regard to each type of factor.

Although reduced to simple terms, a dictionary definition is useful in making the distinction between attitudes and competencies. An attitude is defined as a disposition, feeling, or position taken with regard to a person or thing.[18] A competency is a skill, an aspect of knowledge, or experience appropriate for performing

---

[18] *The Random House Dictionary of the English Language*, Unabridged edition (N. Y.: Random House, 1966), p. 96.

a task.[19] This distinction should be kept in mind, since many competencies described in teacher-training are, in fact, attitudes. Several specific attitudes that are potentially useful in establishing a positive classroom environment for development of affective behaviors are described in the following sections. Later in this chapter, desirable teacher competencies will be stated.

Enthusiasm
Enthusiasm for reading, for working with learners, and for teaching and learning should characterize the disposition of the teacher. Learners, under the influence of a teacher who shows enthusiasm for reading, are likely to develop favorable inclinations toward reading. It is not unusual for learners to imitate or emulate characteristics they perceive in the teacher.

Enthusiasm, however, does not emanate from an individual to an effective degree if it is not sincerely felt and unconsciously expressed. Enthusiasm cannot be simulated, effectively, for very long. An insincere attempt to show enthusiasm can easily be perceived by observers and particularly by children. Genuine enthusiasm by the teacher is reflected through what he or she says and does, though more is involved. What the teacher is also contributes to the total picture of personal enthusiasm.

Enthusiasm on the part of the teacher has potential for encouraging enthusiasm in learners' attitudes toward reading; however, it alone is not sufficient to change attitudes of learners in permanent and significant ways. Yet, it is mainly the teacher's enthusiasm for all aspects of teaching and learning that determines whether he will foster conditions in the classroom which will improve learners' attitudes. Leland Jacobs has described the effect felt when the teacher is "personally so enthusiastic about literature that he generates in others his sense of the values of reading. He so enjoys experiences in reading that he is anxious to lead others to similar pleasures."[20]

Some investigations have shown that teachers of reading often lack within themselves the attitudes and interests they attempt to help learners develop. Robert V. Duffey reported results from measuring the reading habits of a selected group of elementary teachers on two separate occasions. In each investigation, the reading habits of the teachers revealed little evidence that they either liked to read or engaged frequently in reading. In reference to results of these studies, a significant question was raised by Lloyd W. Kline, "How will teachers whose personal reading is a small, sometime thing generate enthusiasm for reading among young learners?"[21]

Empathy
Ability to identify with learners and to perceive the problems with which they are faced is essential for the teacher who seeks to bring about positive changes in learners' behaviors. Remembering what it is like to be

---

[19] *The Random House Dictionary of the English Language,* p. 300.

[20] Leland B. Jacobs, "The Individual and His World of Books," *Education* 74 (May, 1954), pp. 523–26.

[21] Robert V. Duffey, "What to Do?" cited in Lloyd W. Kline, "The Teacher as Reader," *The Reading Teacher* 27, No. 2 (November, 1973), pp. 132–33.

a learner helps to keep the teacher in touch with learners. If, as Chaucer stated, gladly would he teach and gladly learn, remembering what it is like to be a learner does not require a feat of memory. The teacher who is constantly seeking to improve his own knowledge and understanding is, in fact, a learner. Involvement in learning and its problems can increase the teacher's sensitivity to problems met by learners.

Recognizing the Importance of the Individual

The importance of individualizing instruction in order to achieve identifiable results in instruction was discussed in Chapter 4. Recognition of the importance of the individual is also a positive approach to the development of desirable affective behaviors.

Individuals tend to respond positively to recognition of their worth as important human beings. One of the earliest studies related to the significance of recognition on increasing the productivity of workers has implications for use in classroom situations. A study carried out at the Hawthorne Works of the Western Electric Company from 1927 to 1932 showed that recognition of the importance of individuals was the most significant factor in increasing their productivity.[22]

Recognition of the worth of an individual helps him or her to develop and maintain a healthy self-concept. Without a positive self-concept, an individual is unlikely to develop interest and motivation to engage personal participation in learning. Participation by the individual is an important factor in achievement of either cognitive or affective behaviors.

Valuing Differences Among Learners

Differences among learners should not only be accepted and recognized, but also valued. Valuing differences among individuals is apparent in opportunities the teacher makes available to each learner for contributing to the program. Unruh and Turner claim that "A great variety of specialties and talents provides security for a society because for any emergency that may arise there are resources and expertise to be applied.[23] Implementation of this idea in the classroom helps to make each individual aware of personal worth and dignity as well as that of others.

Specific Activities and Techniques for Stimulating Reading Interest

Achievement of objectives in the affective domain should be an on-going concern in all aspects of reading instruction. The prevailing

---

[22] George C. Homans, "The Western Electric Researches" in *Human Factors in Management*, S. D. Haslett, editor (N. Y.: Harper and Brothers, 1951), p. 15.

[23] Adolph Unruh and Harold E. Turner, *Supervision for Change and Innovation* (Boston: Houghton Mifflin, 1970), p. 79.

social and intellectual climates and the teacher's attitudes and competencies are meaningful influences in achieving significant changes in learners' affective behaviors. Use of varied activities and techniques, however, can contribute positively to achievement of short-term specific objectives. Several activities and techniques for enlivening the reading program are described or listed below.

1. *"Touch" or "Feel" Table*
   Objectives: Uses descriptive words. Associates words with objects.
   Materials: Extensive collection of common, everyday objects that appeal to the sense of touch. Examples: cottonballs, rubber bands, tennis ball, walnut, etc.
   Procedures: Place objects on table. Provide descriptive words, one to a card, to be used as references, if needed, by learners. As individuals, or in groups, learners use the table to:
                 (a) Explore an object
                 (b) Write a word or words to describe the object (Use prepared cards to obtain descriptive words, if needed.)
   Variations: Include objects that appeal to other senses and apply the same procedures stated above.

2. *"WANTED" Posters*
   Objective: Writes brief, humorous, descriptions.
   Materials: Pictures of characters from stories, the news, the comics, etc.
   Procedures: Child selects a picture. Paste it on a sheet of paper. Write a description of the character wanted. Example: WANTED: Superman, for flying without a license.

3. *"Caterpillar Pockets"*
   Objectives: Recognizes words. Identifies similar sounds. Notes likenesses and differences in words.
   Materials: (a) Large circles placed on a chart to resemble a caterpillar. Leave circles open at top to form a pocket. Label each circle to indicate words, blends, digraphs, etc.
                 (b) Cards on which are printed words, blends, digraphs, etc.
   Procedures: Shuffle cards. Child selects a card and identifies contents. Child places card in appropriate pocket. For example, "blast" used to identify a blend would be placed in the circle labeled "blends."

4. *Sequencing*
   Objectives: Notes sequence of ideas. Notes sequence of events.
   Materials: Experience stories, comic strips, etc.
   Procedures: Cut an experience chart into separate sentences. Child places the sentences into correct order. (To make this so that the child can check himself, prepare mimeographed copies of the original story.) When comic strips are used, cut each strip into frames and number the backs of the frames. Child places the frames in order. If the numbers on back of frames are in order when the activity is completed, the child can see that his work is correct.

5. *Giving Clear Directions*
   Objectives: States directions clearly. Follows directions accurately.
   Materials: Several strips of paper on which are stated different tasks.
   Procedures: Each child selects a slip of paper on which is stated a specific task. Each child writes directions for accomplishing the task stated on the

slip he has selected. Collect all directions. Distribute to class. Each child follows the new directions. If directions are not specific and clear, the tasks cannot be performed correctly.

6. *Puppets to Introduce Characters in a Story*

Objective:	Identifies characters in a story.
Materials:	Stick puppets to represent characters in a story.
Procedures:	A few days before starting a new story, introduce the characters. Discuss the character's name and a few of his characteristics. Permit children to "make friends" with the characters before reading the story.

7. *Phonics Musical Chairs*

Objective:	Identifies sounds represented by single graphemes or groups of graphemes.
Materials:	Chairs, each labeled with a grapheme or combination of graphemes. There should be one less chair than players. Music.
Procedures:	As music is played, children march around chairs. When the music stops each child sits in the nearest chair. Child without a chair is out of the game. Each child must think of a word that begins with the sounds indicated on his chair. If a child cannot think of a word, repeats a word, or uses a wrong word, he is out and the chair is removed. The game continues until there is a winner.
Variation:	Game can also be played by using ending sounds, vowel sounds, etc.

8. *Dramatic Expressions*

Objective:	Uses colorful words and synonyms.
Procedures:	Child is given an action word. For example "tell": he demonstrates more colorful synonyms of that word — "shout," "yell," "whisper," etc. Words may be used in a chart or in a story.

9. *Twenty Questions*

Objective:	Identifies objects in the classroom by their characteristics.
Procedures:	One child selects an object in the classroom and states its beginning letter. Children in the class ask questions about characteristics of the object. The child can answer only yes or no. After twenty questions have been asked, the answer is given. Discuss the object, write its name, etc., before going to the next.

Competencies Required of Teachers to Foster Development of Affective Behaviors

Generally, all competencies required of teachers for effective instruction contribute to the development of behaviors in the affective domain. Some competencies, however, should relate primarily to helping learners develop affective behaviors. Some of these are suggested below.

1. Makes provisions for learners to express feelings and perceptions acquired from reading through use of the arts.
2. Establishes opportunities for learners to express feelings and perceptions acquired from reading through oral expression.
3. Establishes opportunities for learners to express feelings and perceptions through creative writing.

4. Encourages learners in analyzing and utilizing various patterns of communication within the classroom.
5. Designs learning experiences to acquaint learners with types of good literature.
6. Selects books for the classroom that reflect interests of learners of pertinent age groups.
7. Selects books for the classroom that accommodate interests of individuals.
8. Uses techniques to determine the interests of individuals.
9. Provides real and vicarious experiences to help learners develop communication abilities.
10. Establishes attractive displays of books and other reading materials in the classroom.
11. Utilizes resources in the school and community for improving interests and attitudes of learners.
12. Provides periods of time in which individuals are permitted to read independently.
13. Formulates questions to encourage critical thinking.
14. Reads a variety of types of literature to the class.
15. Formulates questions to develop abilities to interpret ideas encountered through reading.
16. Provides various opportunities for group discussion of ideas encountered through reading.
17. Assesses the nature of social relationships in the class.
18. Uses techniques to improve the social climate in the classroom.
19. Uses techniques to develop permanent interests in reading.
20. Maintains effective human relationships with each person in the class.
21. Relates effectively with learners of various ethnic backgrounds.
22. Uses strategies to increase learners' appreciations of similarities and differences among persons of varying backgrounds.

SUMMARY

Development of interests, attitudes, and other affective behaviors lies in the major context of humanistic education. Ideals of humanistic education and the ultimate values sought in reading are related. Positive attitudes related to reading are influenced significantly by the prevailing social and intellectual climates in the classroom environment. Sporadic, discrete efforts cannot be relied upon to help individuals develop lasting and important attitudes toward reading. Efforts to achieve accountability in helping learners develop affective behaviors must be interwoven and continuous with those focused on development of cognitive skills and abilities.

In the classroom, significant influences on development of affective behaviors include attitudes and competencies of the teacher and the environment established for learning.

Review Questions

1. Describe some of the affective behaviors that must be developed if a learner is to develop competence in basic skills and abilities required for reading. **(1.1)***

---

*Boldface numbers in parentheses refer to the numbered behavioral objectives at the beginning of the chapter.

2. Can reading be taught effectively by focusing efforts of instruction solely on development of cognitive behaviors? Why? Why not? (**1.1**)

3. Describe specific ideals of humanistic education to which you believe reading can contribute directly. (**1.2**)

4. Explain how instructional procedures, designed primarily for development of cognitive skills and abilities, can contribute simultaneously to development of affective behaviors. (**1.3**)

5. What specific affective behaviors usually receive most emphasis during reading instruction? (**1.3**)

6. Describe ways in which a learner's environmental and experiential background contributes to development of his interests and attitudes. (**2.1**)

7. Why should plans for helping learners develop cognitive behaviors provide, at the same time, for development of affective behaviors? (**2.2**)

8. State a rational for holding, or not holding, a teacher accountable for learners' achievement of affective objectives. (**2.2**)

9. How do interests generally held by children in the primary grades differ from those generally held by children in intermediate grades? (**2.3**)

10. How does knowledge held by a teacher regarding general interests characteristic of children of a particular age group help in determining ways to improve a learner's interest in reading? (**2.3**)

11. Describe some specific techniques that can be used in the classroom for the purpose of increasing children's interests in reading. (**2.4**)

12. Describe some of the components of the social climate in a classroom that are directly related to the teacher's attitudes. (**3.1**)

13. Are teacher competencies, alone, sufficient for helping learners develop affective behaviors desirable in humanistic education? (**3.2**)

14. What specific competencies do you believe essential for a teacher if learners' affective behaviors are to be developed in desired directions? (**3.2**)

15. What factors related to readiness should be considered in the attempts to help learners develop new interests and increased interest in reading? (**4.1**)

16. Give examples of real experiences that can be provided in the classroom that will help increase learners' readiness for development of affective and cognitive behaviors. (**5.2**)

17. Why is it important to discuss real experiences if these are to be valuable for improving the effectiveness of reading? (**5.3**)

18. Using a brainstorming technique, list all the ways you can think of for using the community in which the school exists to improve reading instruction. (**5.4**)

19. What particular factors in a classroom situation serve to characterize the social climate that generally prevails? (**6.1**)

20. What are some particular teaching strategies that contribute to the nature of the social climate in the classroom? (**6.2**)

21. Are there differences between the types of factors that comprise the social and intellectual climates in the classroom? If so, how do these differ? (**7.1**)

22. Would you differentiate between procedures used for maintaining a positive social climate in the classroom and those used to improve the intellectual climate? If so, how? (**7.2**)

23. State some procedures you might use in helping a first grader develop a concept of the meaning of reading. **(8.1)** How would these procedures differ from those you would use in order to sensitize children in intermediate grades to the nature of reading? **(8.1)**

24. Describe some techniques that might be used to stimulate children's interests in reading current events. **(8.2)**

25. What television programs would you suggest to a sixth grader in the attempt to help him relate his television and reading interests? Why? **(8.3)**

26. Prepare a bibliography of books related to a content area of your choice for use in helping children improve their concepts related to that area. **(8.4)**

27. What differences do you see in independent reading and individualized reading? **(8.5)**

28. How do attitudes and competencies differ? **(9.1)**

29. What attitudes are important for a teacher who attempts to help learners develop desirable affective behaviors? **(9.2)**

30. What are some of the effects teachers' attitudes seem to have on those of learners? **(9.3)**

31. Describe some specific techniques that can be used to enliven the reading program. **(10.1)**

32. What seem to be competencies needed by a teacher for helping learners develop affective behaviors? **(11.0)**

Selected References

1. Bamman, Henry A., Mildred A. Dawson, and Robert J. Whitehead, *Oral Interpretation of Children's Literature*. Dubuque, Iowa: William C. Brown, 1964.

2. Benne, Kenneth O., and Bozidar Muntyan, *Human Relations and Curriculum Change*. N. Y.: Dryden Press, 1951.

3. Combs, Arthur W., *Educational Accountability: Beyond Behavioral Objectives*. Washington D. C.: Association for Supervision and Curriculum Development, 1972.

4. Crosby, Muriel, editor, *Reading Ladders for Human Relations*, Fourth edition. Washington, D. C.: American Council on Education, 1963.

5. Harris, Dale B., "How Children Learn Interests, Motives, and Attitudes," *49th Yearbook, Part I, National Society for the Study of Education*. Chicago: University of Chicago Press, 1950.

6. Huck, Charlotte, and Doris Kuhn, *Children's Literature in the Elementary School*. N. Y.: Holt, Rinehart and Winston, 1968.

7. Huus, Helen, editor, *Evaluating Books for Children and Young People* (Perspectives in Reading No. 10). Newark, Del.: International Reading Association, 1968.

8. Johns, Jerry L., "What Do Inner-City Children Prefer to Read?" *The Reading Teacher*, 26, No. 5 (February, 1973), pp. 462–67.

9. Karlin, Robert, *Teaching Elementary Reading*. N. Y.: Harcourt Brace Jovanovich, 1971.

10. Kranyik, Robert, and Florence V. Shankman, *How to Teach Study Skills*. Englewood Cliffs, N. J.: Prentice-Hall, Teachers Practical Press, 1963.

11. Krathwohl, David R., Benjamin S. Bloom, and Bertram B. Masia, *Taxonomy of Educational Objectives, Handbook II: Affective Domain.* N. Y.: David McKay Co., 1964.
12. Norvell, G. W., *What Boys and Girls Like to Read.* Morristown, N. J.: Silver-Burdett, 1968.
13. Raths, Louis E., Merrill Harmin, and Sidney B. Simon, *Values and Teaching.* Columbus, Ohio: Charles E. Merrill, 1966.
14. Rollins, Charlemae, *We Build Together.* Champaign, Ill.: National Council of Teachers of English, 1967.
15. Sebesta, Sam Leaton, editor, *Ivory, Apes, and Peacocks: The Literature Point of View* (Proceedings of the Twelfth Annual Convention, Vol. 12, Part II). Newark, Del.: International Reading Association, 1968.
16. Witty, P. A., A. M. Freeland, and E. Grotberg, *The Teaching of Reading: A Developmental Process.* Boston: D. C. Heath, 1966, Ch. 3.

6

Evaluation of Achievement in Reading

Evaluation is increased in importance and in dimensions in the light of educational accountability. Accountability in reading instruction requires evidence that learners acquire competence in reading commensurate with their potential. Evaluation is the means through which systematic collection, presentation, and reporting of this evidence is made possible.

Accountability in reading instruction requires that attention be given to pertinent aspects of evaluation before, during, and after instruction. Need assessment, as discussed in Chapter 2 of this book, is an aspect of evaluation that receives its greatest impetus prior to instruction. The present chapter focuses on the types of evaluation required for determining the degree to which learners have achieved objective. Evaluating for this purpose is emphasized after instruction is given. All evaluation practices, whether for purposes of need assessment or for determining the effectiveness of instruction, must be given some attention throughout the instructional process.

Behavioral Objectives

The content of Chapter 6 is presented in such a way that after reading it, an individual

1.0 Understands the meaning of evaluation in reading instruction

    1.1 Explains the meaning of the term "evaluation"

    1.2 Describes the process of evaluation

    1.3 Explains the function of objectives in evaluation of achievement

    1.4 Explains the interrelated nature of the processes of evaluation and instruction

    1.5 Applies important principles in evaluation of achievement in reading

2.0 Understands the role of measurement in accountability
    2.1 Describes characteristics of techniques of measurement
    2.2 Describes the types of results achieved by use of techniques of measurement
    2.3 Explains why results of measurement are needed in accountability for reading instruction
3.0 Knows major types of measurement instruments used in reading instruction
    3.1 Identifies characteristics of standardized tests
    3.2 Describes various types of test norms
    3.3 Explains uses of test norms
    3.4 Identifies criteria for selection of standardized tests
    3.5 Differentiates between "group" and "individual" reading tests
    3.6 Describes advantages and disadvantages of standardized group tests in reading
    3.7 Describes characteristics of basal-reader tests
    3.8 Explains uses of basal-reader tests
    3.9 Describes characteristics of "criterion-referenced" measures
4.0 Knows major sources of test information
    4.1 Identifies sources of information related to standardized tests
    4.2 Describes types of information available from various sources of test information
5.0 Understands uses of observational techniques in evaluation of reading achievement
    5.1 Identifies various types of observational techniques
    5.2 Describes uses of observational techniques
    5.3 Explains why observational techniques are required in comprehensive evaluation of achievement in reading
6.0 Recognizes types of competencies required of teachers for evaluation of achievement in reading

Meaning of Evaluation in Reading Instruction

From the standpoint of the classroom teacher seeking accountability in reading instruction, the meaning of evaluation is very specific. Evaluation can be defined as the process of determining and reporting the extent to which objectives have been achieved.[1] Stated another way, evaluation consists of determination of the extent to which learners' behaviors have changed as a result of instruction.

Implementation of this concept of evaluation frequently has been neglected in conventional practices in education. Classroom practices in evaluation often are too narrow to satisfy the demands of accountability. For instance, evaluation equated with measurement and its results is too limited to reveal the full range of learners' achievement in reading, when objectives for a program are defined appropriately.

A concept of evaluation that is too broad, on the other hand, can be equally as ineffective as one that is too narrow in producing evidence of accountability.

---

[1] Norman E. Gronlund, *Measurement and Evaluation in Teaching* (N. Y.: Macmillan, 1971), pp. 7–8.

Evaluation, conceived too broadly, cannot reveal specific and identifiable behaviors as evidence of effective instruction. Too broad a concept of evaluation is likely to place undue emphasis on subjective judgments. Accountability requires both objective and subjective evidence of learning. The meaning of evaluation that should be embraced by teachers of reading should encompass understanding of, and competency in the use of, a wide variety of both measurement and observational procedures. Measurement and other types of procedures for gathering evidence of achievement by learners should be seen in relation to the unique purposes each serves best in the total process of evaluation.

Evaluation as a Process

Evaluation in reading instruction can be called a process, rather than a discrete activity, because (1) it is continuous throughout and embedded within the larger process of instruction and (2) it consists of a series of clearly defined, interrelated steps or stages.

Evaluation tends to lose its potential for improving instructional results if it is viewed as an activity separate from regular instructional concerns. The process of evaluation is a subprocess of the total process of instruction. Evaluation of achievement is, therefore, an integral part of the instructional process. Placed in a graphic representation, the nature of evaluation in the instructional process can be visualized as follows:

Step 1
Objectives for
instruction are ⟶
defined and stated.

Step 2
Teaching strategies and
materials appropriate for ⟶
achieving the objectives
are applied.

Step 3
Evaluation procedures appropriate for determining learners' ⟶
progress toward the stated
objectives are applied.

Step 4
The results of
evaluation are interpreted. ⟶

Step 5
The results of evaluation are used
to improve further instruction
and achievement.

Evaluation plays a part in every step of the instructional process. That part of the instructional process noted in steps 1, 3, 4, and 5, in essence, constitutes the process of evaluation.

The Function of Objectives in Evaluation

Objectives constitute a much-needed basis by which the effectiveness of instruction and achievement can be determined. The question given paramount attention in evaluation is that which is directed to the extent to which learners have achieved objectives upon which instruction was focused. In absence of objectives, neither instruction nor evaluation can be expected to proceed effectively. Both instructional practices and evaluation practices depend upon direction provided by objectives.

The process of evaluation begins with the establishment of objectives. It reaches a crucial point as judgment is made of the degree to which objectives were achieved by learners. This point is crucial, because the results of evaluation are important determinants of subsequent objectives and instructional procedures. This concept of the meaning of evaluation makes no provision for meaningless practices, such as testing merely for the sake of testing.

Principles of Evaluation

The evaluation process in reading instruction becomes strengthened in proportion to the degree to which practices used are supported by valid principles. Valid and basic principles of evaluation stress comprehensiveness, continuity, and cooperation in evaluation practices.

Comprehensiveness in evaluation means that attention is given in evaluation to all aspects of instruction and results of instruction. Included among these aspects are the instructional systems and materials that are used, attitudes and competencies of the teacher, the organizational plan for instruction, and the learners' attainment of all objectives set for instruction. Each program of instruction has its own important and unique elements and a plan for evaluation would lack comprehensiveness if it did not provide for attention to all important elements.

Recognition of the principle of comprehensiveness in evaluation also means that a variety of procedures and materials will be required for effective evaluation. There is no one best method or material of evaluation for answering all questions that must be asked in determination of the effectiveness of instruction and achievement. For this reason, it is important that an extensive repertoire of procedures and materials of evaluation characterize a teacher's knowledge and competencies.

The principle of continuity in evaluation requires that evaluation be implemented as an on-going concern. There is no one period of time or point in the instructional process that is the only time or point to be set aside for purposes of evaluation. Continuity, as a principle of evaluation, is not being observed when evaluation is engaged in as an activity only at specified times during the school year. Evaluation must precede, accompany, and conclude the instructional process, if it is to be effective.

Observation of the principle of cooperation in evaluation means that all persons affected by it will be permitted to participate in it according to their capabilities and roles. All persons affected by evaluation do not and need not participate in the same ways and to the same degrees of involvement. The nature of the learners, the instructional situation, and persons to whom results must be reported are important factors in determining how the principle of cooperation in evaluation will be observed. As an example, merely to report information about his learning to a learner or to his parent does not satisfy the principle of cooperation in evaluation. The learner should be regarded as an active participant in determining the progress he has made toward objectives set for his achievement. The manner and extent to which learners can cooperate in evaluation depend on their ages, experiences, competencies, and attitudes.

The Role of Measurement in Accountability

The terms "measurement" and "evaluation" are used, at times, as if their meanings are synonymous. Although there are many relationships between measurement and evaluation, the meanings of these terms are not the same. Measurement serves a role in the larger framework of evaluation. Measurement, as required in the total process of evaluation, is important in establishing accountability in reading instruction, since the results of measurement of achievement in reading are quantitative in nature. Quantitative results provide information related to how many or how much of a particular behavior or behaviors have been achieved by learners. In education, quantitative information is gathered, principally, through the use of various types of tests that produce numerical scores as evidence of learning.[2] For instance, it can be reported that a learner recognizes the letters of the alphabet, all words in a selection, or that he answers all questions in a specified set correctly. It can be reported and evidence can be set forth to show that an individual advanced a reading-grade level as a result of instruction. These and many other similar types of behaviors related to cognitive skills and abilities, particularly, can be substantiated through the results of quantitative measures. These kinds of information often are needed in the process of evaluation.

Characteristics of Measurement Techniques

Techniques of measurement produce what is sometimes described as "hard" data. "Hard" data generally consist of test scores resulting from administration of various types of tests. While "hard" data are not always possible to attain, nor appropriate, as evidence of achievement of all objectives for which accountability should be sought, their impact on establishment of the effectiveness of instruction and learning is considerable. Pretest scores and posttest scores resultant from administration of carefully selected and valid tests are seldom questioned as important evidence of accountability.

Various types of tests constitute what are generally considered to be techniques of measurement. Included among techniques of measurement are standardized tests, commercial tests (not necessarily standardized) tests constructed by classroom teachers, and other classifications of tests. Within these broad categories of tests are other types of classifications. Tests may be norm-referenced or criterion-referenced. They may be oral or written. They may be designed for group or individual administration. They may pertain to broad areas of academic achievement or they may be focused specifically on competencies related to a particular area such as reading. Use of many different types of tests may be essential to evaluate adequately a learner's or learners' achievement in reading.

---

[2]Gronlund, *Measurement and Evaluation in Teaching*, p. 8.

Regardless of the way in which tests may be categorized, several characteristics combine to determine their quality for use in evaluation in a particular situation. These characteristics include (1) the purpose a test is expected to serve, (2) the validity of its results, (3) the reliability of its results, (4) its objectivity, and (5) the ease with which it can be used in a particular situation.

Classroom teachers faced with the prospect of selecting tests for measurement of learners' achievement in reading should be aware of the importance of test characteristics on the quality of information gathered for evaluation purposes. Furthermore, detailed knowledge regarding how test characteristics are determined is helpful in understanding this importance. Basic texts in evaluation should be consulted for this purpose. Several texts that offer detailed information related to test characteristics are included among the selected references at the conclusion of Chapter 6 of this book.

Each major characteristic to which attention should be given when instruments of measurement are considered, however, can be described briefly. The purpose of a test, for example, concerns whether the information sought is expected to show a learner's relative standing in a defined group or whether the information sought is to reveal his absolute achievement of a single behavior or a category of behaviors.

Validity of test results is determined by whether or not these actually serve the uses for which they are intended.[3] Uses for which test results often are sought include descriptions of specific achievement by a learner or what may be expected of a learner in terms of future performance. Results of a test for any use are valuable only insofar as these are truthful.

Reliability of test results indicates to the user whether or not results are consistent in the information from various administrations of the test. Test scores, rather than being reliable or consistent in general, are reliable in particular ways. Reliability of test results is usually determined in relation to one of the following: (1) reliability over different periods of time, (2) reliability in terms of different samples of questions, and (3) reliability according to ratings by different individuals. The uses expected of test results indicate that aspect of reliability which is pertinent and should, thus, be examined.

Scores from a test should be free from influences of bias, prejudice, or opinions of the scorer or scorers. The degree to which the same results of a test are obtained by various scorers reflects test objectivity. For example, the results of limited choice (objective) tests as compared with those of essay tests generally reflect a higher degree of objectivity.

The ease with which a test can be used in a particular situation depends on several practical considerations. These include how conveniently a test can be administered in terms of personnel, financial and other resources. Also important are considerations regarding how easily a test can be scored, interpreted and its results applied in a particular situation.

In addition to characteristics mentioned so far, attention should be given in test selection to several other factors that may be of concern because of the unique nature of the learner or learners being tested. Language development and the nature of concepts held by a particular learner or set of learners must be considered in determining the appropriateness of a test in a given situation. Again, uses of the

---

[3]Gronlund, *Measurement and Evaluation in Teaching*, p. 75.

test results will play a major role in determination of whether a test reflects cultural bias or other weaknesses that may invalidate its uses for particular learners.

Types of Results Obtainable From
Techniques of Measurement

Earlier in Chapter 6, mention was made of the quantitative nature of the results obtainable from test administration. While test results are quantitative and are usually expressed in numerical scores, scores may be of several different types. Generally, raw scores and several varieties of derived scores may constitute the quantitative evidence resultant from use of techniques of measurement.

A raw score is the number of points achieved by responding to a test when the test has been scored according to directions. Directions may indicate that one, five, or ten, etc. points are given for each correct answer. Thus, if one point is given for each correct answer according to scoring directions, a learner answering forty questions out of a possible fifty may be given a raw score of forty points. In relation to tests constructed and scored by teachers in classrooms, raw scores are useful, sometimes, for the purposes of the test. As a rule, however, raw scores are seriously limited in the nature of information these may make available. Consequently, various types of derived scores demand the attention of teachers involved in evaluation to any significant degree.

For many important uses of test results, particularly those related to standardized tests, a knowledge of the nature of derived scores is important to the classroom teacher. Gronlund defines a derived score as a "numerical report of test performance in terms of the pupil's relative position in a clearly defined reference group."[4] Several types of derived scores commonly essential in interpretation of the results of standardized tests are presented later in this chapter.

Need for Results of Measurement in
Accountability in Reading Instruction

The results of measurement are essential in establishing accountability in reading instruction. Because a large number of behaviors that indicate achievement in reading are highly concrete in nature, measurement techniques can provide data that are highly indisputable as evidence of existence of these behaviors. Appropriately gathered, interpreted, and reported, data produced by measurement reflect objectivity to the degree necessary for verifying behavioral changes in learners. Accountability often requires comparisons between one learner and other learners or between one group of learners and another group. Information regarding relative standing of an individual or of a group in reference to others can be gained through use of test data. Mathematics can be applied to test data thus making possible the construction of test profiles, norms, and the like, that are essential for making comparisons.

Measurement data permit easy communication of the results of instruction to others.[5] Such data require and make possible exact interpretation of meaning, an

---

[4]Gronlund, *Measurement and Evaluation in Teaching*, p. 373.

[5]Jum C. Nunnally, *Educational Measurement and Evaluation* (N. Y.: McGraw-Hill, 1972), p. 10.

exactness not possible when subjective terminology is used. Subjective terminology such as "very good," "fair," "satisfactory," and the like, are open to varied interpretations depending on an individual's experiences, perceptions, or biases. Measurement data tend to remove the subjectivity from evaluation of learner achievement, thus strengthening any claim for accountability.

Finally, measurement data are more economical and efficient than subjective evaluations conducted thoroughly enough to be dependable. The use of observational techniques and lengthy narrative descriptions of a learner's behavior generally are not feasible in typical classroom situations.

Major Tests Used in Measurement of Reading Achievement

Many different types of tests are available for measuring achievement in reading. The range of data resultant from different instruments of measurement is necessary to evaluate achievement by learners accurately. Among types of tests that are available and frequently used are (1) standardized tests; (2) various types of commercial tests, including those accompanying many basal reader instructional systems; (3) teacher-constructed tests; and (4) criterion-referenced measures.

Characteristics of Standardized Tests

Standardized tests are (1) designed to conform to pertinent required specifications, (2) administered initially to samples or groups of the population for whom they are designed, (3) administered, scored, and interpreted under specified conditions, and (4) inclusive of norms established on the basis of the performances of groups during initial administrations or tryouts of the test. Standardized tests of interest to persons involved in reading instruction include those designed to survey general achievement in reading and those designed to indicate strengths and weaknesses shown by a learner with respect to various areas of performance in reading.

Several features characterize the nature of a standardized test. These include (1) content presented in the form of a set of test items focused on measurement of a particular type of behavior, (2) precise directions for administering and scoring the test and, frequently, for interpreting the results of the test, and (3) norms pertinent to the type of test represented. In addiion, many standardized tests are available in equivalent or optional forms. Invariably, a test manual designed to accompany a particular standardized test comprises an important part of the basic materials required for effective use of the test.

The availability of precise directions for administering, scoring, and even interpreting the results of many tests make it possible for any teacher to use a standardized test with a high degree of competence. When directions are followed, such tests permit the gathering of information with generally acceptable levels of validity and reliability. Guidelines and other information often made available to users of a test simplify the process of interpretation of test scores. Many publishers of standardized tests provide optional scoring services that further facilitate efficiency and ease with which a test may be used.

Perhaps the most important characteristic of standardized tests is the norms provided. The term "test norm" refers to the typical or average performance of individuals in the groups upon whom the test was standardized. Individuals involved in the standardization process are expected to be representative of the types of individuals to whom the test can be administered appropriately.

Norms of standardized tests are useful for providing the basis for several comparisons often pertinent in evaluation of achievement in reading. According to Roger Farr, "Norms are descriptive of existing types of performance and are not to be regarded as standards or as desirable levels of attainment."[6] Comparisons made possible by the use of norms include (1) comparison of a learner's performance on a given test with the performances of other individuals whose characteristics are similar to those of the learner under consideration; (2) comparison of a learner's performance on each of two forms of the same test administered at different times; and (3) comparison of a learner's performance on two different tests focused on measurement of the same abilities or characteristics. All of these kinds of comparisons are needed at various times and for various reasons related to evaluation of learners' reading achievement.

Meanings of some of the most frequently encountered types of test norms and derived scores are as follows:

Age-Equivalent Scores: Norms based on chronological age indicative of the chronological age group in which an individual's raw score is average.

Grade-Equivalent Scores: Norms based on grade level in school indicative of the particular grade group in which an individual's raw score is average.

Percentile: A point in the distribution of test scores below which falls the percentage of test scores indicated by the given percentile. For instance, the fifteenth percentile shows the point or score below which 15 percent of the scores fall. "Percentile" makes no reference to the percent of correct answers an individual has achieved on a test.

Reading Age: An age-equivalent score assigned to the average score on a reading test for individuals at a given age.

Stanine: One of the steps in a nine-point scale of normalized standard scores. The stanine scale has values from one to nine, with a mean of five, and a standard deviation of two.

Criteria for Selection
of Standardized Tests

Standardized tests in reading do not meet all requirements for total evaluation of learners' achievement in reading. Nevertheless, their

---

[6] Roger Farr, *Reading: What Can be Measured?* (Newark, Del.: International Reading Association, 1969), p. 221.

uses are unique enough and important enough to justify careful attention to their selection. Some of the most important elements to be examined in determining the nature and suitability of a test in a particular situation include the following:

Title of the test
Author/Authors
Publisher
Date of publication
Purpose of the test
Instructional objectives toward which the test is focused
Grade/Age levels of learners for whom the test is designed
Types of norms available
Nature of the "norming" groups used in standardization of the test
Scoring methods (hand and/or machine)
Time required for administration
Types of alternative or optional forms available
Costs
Validity reported for test results (type/types)
Reliability reported for test results (type/types)
Special requirements for administration of the test
Adequacy of manual

In order to comprehend the information regarding elements included in the list above, the teacher must have knowledge and understanding of pertinent language and concepts used in test manuals. Some training in the area of measurement and evaluation is helpful to teachers in the quest for accountability. In lieu of formal study in measurement and evaluation, a teacher can accomplish much understanding through personal study of basic texts in the area of measurement and evaluation. Several important resources are indicated in the list of selected references at the end of this chapter.

Group Versus Individual Reading Tests

As apparent from the terms used in their designation, group tests are administered to groups of learners at a time while individual tests are administered on a one-to-one basis. Group or individual administration may characterize either survey or diagnostic tests in reading. Normally, group tests used in classroom situations require the use of paper and pencils for learner responses, although there are some exceptions. Individual tests may or may not require respondents to use paper and pencil and may or may not involve use of additional materials or apparatuses. Because of the one-to-one relationship between the teacher and the learner during administration of an individual test, important additional information about an individual's behavior may become available to the teacher during administration of the test. Thus, as a general rule, results of group tests tend to be less dependable as bases for major decisions regarding learners' achievement than are those of individual tests.

Benefits to be derived from administration of either a group or individual test for purposes of evaluation of reading achievement are relative to the degree to which the test corresponds with objectives sought in the instructional program. Because of this it is important to analyze a test in terms of the nature of its content for measuring the kinds of behaviors sought in instruction.

Time and skill often required in administration of an individual test and in interpretation of its results tend to limit its usefulness in classroom situations. In many instances, when individual testing is required for a learner, the teacher must refer the case to a specialist who may be in charge of testing in the school. The teacher, however, should be familiar with the nature of individual tests in order to make intelligent referrals and in order to utilize reports that may accompany a learner when he is returned for further instruction in the classroom.

Advantages and Limitations of Standardized Group Tests in Reading

Major advantages provided by use of group tests in reading can be summarized as follows:

1. Group tests provide a means for comparison of learners' general achievement in reading.
2. Results of group tests in reading generally are more reliable, more objective, and a more detailed measure of a learner's overall achievement in reading than are possible from use of more subjective measures.
3. When results of a group test in reading are used in comparison with a learner's results on a test of mental ability, information is available regarding whether the individual is working up to his potential.
4. Results of group tests in reading permit comparisons between individuals and between groups.
5. Through analysis of the content of some group tests in reading, detailed information can be gathered regarding specific skills and abilities important in reading.
6. Results of group tests in reading generally are sufficient as bases for initial organizational and instructional procedures during the beginning of an instructional program.

Disadvantages frequently identified in connection with uses of group tests in reading include the following:

1. According to Roger Farr, "The most serious deficiency in using standardized tests to diagnose reading achievement is the lack of discriminant validity (the validity of tests as measures of distinct skills or abilities) for the various subtests of reading."[7]
2. Subtests of many group tests in reading tend to be too short to provide dependable measures of specific skills of a learner.

Characteristics of Basal-Reader Tests

Frequently, tests are included among total instructional materials made available by publishers of basal reader series. Generally, these tests are not constructed according to standards as rigorous as those required in construction of standardized tests in reading. Nor have norms been established, as a rule, as a basic characteristic of these tests. Directions and conditions for administering the tests lack the rigid standards required in use of standardized tests.

In format, several similarities exist between basal-reader tests and standardized tests. Objective test items, such as multiple-choice, completion, and true-false items, are the major types of test items included in both types of tests. Content in both basal-reader tests and standardized tests in reading normally consists of that related to vocabulary, word-analysis skills, and basic comprehension skills.

---

[7] Farr, *Reading: What Can be Measured?* p. 82.

Basal-reader tests are of most importance as techniques of measurement in an instructional program where they are used in conjunction with accompanying basal-reader materials. Used in this way, generally, there is a close relationship between instructional objectives and evaluation of learners' skills and concepts achieved. Many of these tests are essentially criterion-referenced measures when used as part of the basal-reader materials of instruction. Basal-reader tests tend to be mastery tests, because all learners instructed through use of the accompanying instructional materials are expected to master the skills and concepts involved.

Uses of basal-reader tests can be varied according to purposes sought in a particular classroom. They can be used as pretests to determine elements in instruction that should be stressed during instruction. They are, likewise, useful as posttests to determine the extent to which learners have achieved the objectives of instruction.

Criterion-Referenced Measures

Comprehensive evaluation of all objectives achieved as a result of instruction in reading requires use of many different types of measurement. All purposes of evaluation cannot be served by reliance on the results of any one type or category of procedures.

Advent of the movement toward accountability has stimulated interest and activity related to criterion-referenced measures of achievement. Accountability makes exact knowledge of what behaviors are shown by a learner important both for determining next steps in the instructional program and for reporting results of instruction and learning. Criterion-referenced measures can serve both of these functions.

The nature of criterion-referenced measures can be distinguished by making a comparison between these and conventional mastery tests of achievement. In a mastery test, emphasis is on whether or not learners have acquired the exact behaviors called for in the test, rather than on how learners compare in their ability to respond correctly to requirements of the test. In this sense, a mastery test and a criterion-referenced test are alike. Criterion-referenced tests are absolute measures. Generally, their focus is upon simple dimensions of knowledge and skills learners are expected to master.

A criterion-referenced measure may consist of a test or a situation whose demands are related directly with specific objectives selected as the focus of instruction. An objective becomes the criterion against which performance or achievement of a learner can be judged. For those objectives whose achievement by learners can best be determined through actual task performance, a criterion-referenced test is desirable. Achievement of many objectives of reading instruction can be determined through use of criterion-referenced measures that require use of paper and pencil or answers given in an oral test format. In other cases, achievement of the objective can be determined best through use of an informal or observational technique. For example, achievement of an objective stated as "pronounces correctly all words in a selection" might best be determined as the learner is observed during oral reading of the selection, rather than through his responses to questions on a test.

Determination of whether a norm-referenced test or a criterion-referenced measure of some type should be used to gather information to be used as a basis for evaluation depends on the purposes to be served. Norm-referenced tests and criterion-referenced measures do not serve the same purposes in evaluation. Norm-referenced measures are needed when a learner's achievement must be compared with that of others. Criterion-referenced measures are essential when a learner's mastery or acquisition of certain behaviors is the purpose of evaluation. Hence, both types of measures are needed if a comprehensive approach is taken in evaluation of achievement.

Use of criterion-referenced measures permits direct implementation of evaluation as an integral part of the instructional process. Stated objectives for instruction easily become not only the focus for instruction, but also the focus of evaluation. Criterion-referenced measures help to make instruction and evaluation interrelated parts of the same process.

Recognition of some of the limitations of criterion-referenced measures helps to place their importance and uses into perspective. One limitation is the difficulty of procuring or constructing good criterion-referenced measures. The attempt to construct criterion-referenced measures for all objectives sought in reading instruction, in any effective program, would require a disproportionate use of the teacher's time. By their nature, criterion-referenced measures are limited to measurement of basic skills and concepts. Confining evaluation exclusively to these behaviors would leave achievement of many important objectives without evaluation. Furthermore, limiting an evaluation plan to inclusion of criterion-referenced measures only would leave serious gaps in information essential for determining the quality of learners' achievements. Results of criterion-referenced measures show only whether or not a given behavior is apparent, not the quality of that behavior. Results of criterion-referenced measures are absolute indicators of achievement. Comprehensive evaluation of achievement requires both absolute indications and also relative achievement of learners.

Sources of Test Information

Several sources are available for helping teachers obtain information related to major tests. These include Buros' *Mental Measurements Yearbooks*, Test Publishers' Catalogs, and professional journals in education.

Buros Mental Measurements Yearbooks

The Buros Mental Measurements Yearbooks are among the oldest and most important resources for evaluation of published tests. Several volumes comprise the complete set of the yearbooks, although the earlier volumes may be of little use to the teacher concerned with timely and relevant tests for use in a modern program of reading instruction. More recent volumes are likely to be of greatest use to the typical classroom teacher. Information is presented regarding costs of tests, the number of forms available, the time necessary to administer a test, validity, reliability, and the types of norms available for a test. In addition to this type of descriptive information, critical reviews are provided for each test. Each test is reviewed by two or more qualified reviewers who help to clarify strengths and weaknesses of the test. References to other sources of reviews provide still another opportunity for thorough evaluation of a test by a teacher who may not be skilled in test evaluation.

Of special interest to persons involved in reading instruction is a separate volume by Buros that focuses entirely on information and reviews related to tests of reading.[8] Information in this volume has been selected from volume one through five of the yearbooks and is more easily and directly obtained than from use of the larger and more comprehensive volumes.

Test Publishers' Catalogs

Publishers of tests will send their latest catalogs upon request to persons involved in selection of tests for use in instructional situations. Some publishers, in addition, provide free information related to techniques of testing, interpretation of test results, and methods of reporting results of tests. Included among these publishers are the following:

American Guidance Services, Inc.
Publishers Building
Circle Pines, Minnesota   55014

California Test Bureau
Del Monte Research Park
Monterey, California   93940

Cooperative Test Division
Educational Testing Service
Princeton, New Jersey   08540

Harcourt Brace Jovanovich, Inc.
757 Third Avenue
New York, N. Y.   10017

Houghton-Mifflin Company
2 Park Street
Boston, Massachusetts   02107

For a small fee test publishers generally provide specimen sets of tests that are of interest to teachers. A specimen set usually contains samples of all materials pertinent to a test, such as test manual, a test booklet, and scoring keys. Availability of specimen sets enables the teacher to evaluate the manual, test items, scoring procedures and the like in terms of their application and relevance in a particular instructional situation.

Professional Journals

Many professional journals of interest to teachers of reading are good sources for up-to-date information regarding tests, test ad-

---

[8]O. K. Buros, *Reading Tests and Reviews* (N. Y.: Gryphon Press, 1968).

ministration, interpretation of test results, and uses of test results. One example of these is *The Reading Teacher*, professional Journal of the International Reading Association. Test reviews and articles on testing are presented frequently in issues of the periodical.

Observational Techniques and Accountability in Reading Instruction

A teacher's accountability in reading instruction should be interpreted broadly enough to apply to all changes expected of learners as a result of learning experiences the teacher designs and implements in the classroom. Success in helping learners achieve objectives related to learning how to read is related to success in helping learners like and use reading. Instruments of measurement can be used to provide important information essential for accounting for many changes learners show in development of cognitive behaviors. Such instruments are not directly useful, however, for affirming existence of some cognitive and most affective behaviors also desirable. For many of these behaviors, observational techniques are needed. Information gained from use of observational techniques is needed, also, to verify and interpret as effectively as possible the results of many techniques of measurement.

The Nature of Observational Techniques

Observational techniques consist mainly of the means by which results of observations of learners' behaviors are recorded. Basically, the process of observation consists of carefully looking at some specific behavior, attribute, or product of learning according to a predetermined purpose. In order to report results of observation in a meaningful and organized way, some technique must be used. Some basic techniques of observation are:
1. Anecdotal records
2. Checklists
3. Rating scales
4. Interviews
5. Questionnaires

Anecdotal Records

The anecdotal record can be used to record observations of behavior made in specific situations. Within itself, the anecdotal record is not an instrument of evaluation. Contents of anecdotal records may be used as a basis for information needed in evaluation, however. To the degree that an anecdotal record contains pertinent information related to a purpose and is free from bias and prejudice, it can be a useful source of information that aids in evaluation of a learner's achievement.

An anecdote is a brief, concise, factual report of a specific behavior or incident related to the learner or learners under observation. The term "factual" is to be taken literally. An anecdote is a factual description and not an explanation or interpretation of the behavior or incident. Any explanation or interpretation of the meaning of the behavior or incident should be kept separated from the anecdote.[9] The term, "anecdotal record" can be applied to a single anecdote or to a series of anecdotes related to an individual.

An anecdote is useful for providing information related to achievement of objectives in reading instruction for which there is no better means of evaluation available. A teacher must use judgment based on the nature of the particular situation and that of particular objectives in order to determine whether an anecdote is the best means to be used for evaluation purposes. According to Gronland, "There is no advantage in using anecdotal records to obtain evidence of learning in areas where more objective and usable methods are available."[10]

Depending on the unique situation and the purpose of the observation, evaluation of the following types of behavior may require information that can be gathered by observation and recorded best as anecdotal records:
1. Listens attentively to oral reading of a poem.
2. Shares books read and enjoyed with others in the class.
3. Is open-minded during discussion of a story.
4. Shows initiative in expressing ideas related to a story.
5. Shares materials with others.

The form in which an anecdote may be recorded depends on the personal preference of the teacher. The anecdote, as a brief description, is usually written as a sentence or a brief paragraph. The description may be recorded on index cards or in a notebook organized for the purpose. For convenience and usability it is best to decide upon a particular method for recording anecdotes about individuals and be consistent in its use. Index cards arranged in a file box according to the names of the individuals in the class may be convenient for some teachers. Others may prefer organizing a notebook with a page assigned to each learner for use in recording pertinent descriptions. The sample anecdote in Figure 1 shows the significant parts that should be included.

Figure 1   Sample Anecdote

Name *Byers, Perry*

Date *4/19/75*   Place *Library*

Observation: Immediately upon entering the library, Terry selected several books. He spent the entire period leafing through, but not reading any of the books.

Interpretation: Terry is interested in reading, but has difficulty with word recognition.

Anecdotal records should be restricted to use in those situations and for those purposes for which they are suited. They permit some record of behavior of a

---

[9] Gronlund, *Measurement and Evaluation in Teaching*, p. 411.
[10] Gronlund, *Measurement and Evaluation in Teaching*, p. 413.

learner in an unstructured or natural situation. Although a learner's behavior may be spontaneous and unanticipated, frequently it may be important in revealing information about the learner that would not be gathered otherwise. Anecdotal records may be either positive or negative in nature and still may be useful in evaluation of a learner's behavior. Anecdotal records are useful, particularly, with young children who lack the skills to respond to more structured types of evaluation techniques.

Following the several guidelines listed below can improve the quality of anecdotal records as a source of information needed in comprehensive evaluation of achievement.

1. Maintain awareness of the objectives selected as focus for the observations.
2. Limit anecdotes to behaviors and incidents significant in terms of instructional objectives.
3. Conscientiously avoid prejudicial and biased statements.
4. If the behavior or incident is recorded immediately upon observation, it is more likely to be reported in a valid way.
5. Only one behavior or incident should be included in each anecdote.
6. The significance of anecdotes does not depend upon whether they are positive or negative or dramatic.
7. Interpretations regarding a learner's behavior should not be based on limited evidence. Evidence of many types should be examined before conclusions are drawn.
8. Conscientious attempts for accuracy and clear communication should be made in recording anecdotes. This is especially important when statements regarding learners are recorded on their permanent and cumulative school records.

Checklists

A checklist is an instrument that includes a number of traits or characteristics about an aspect of development or achievement that can be observed and indicated as being absolutely present or not. "Yes" or "no" answers (or check marks) generally are the only decisions that are provided for in checklists. Moreover, a checklist can be only as objective as the individual who records the information. The chief value of a checklist lies in its strength for keeping main points of observation in focus for the observer recording the information.

The checklist has many uses in evaluating reading instruction. It can be used as a means for observing a learner's reading behaviors in detail. It lends itself to the gathering of information related to a wide range of objectives, including those in the cognitive, affective, and psychomotor domains. It can be constructed so as to call attention to behaviors of a single type or to those representative of many different types. Teachers can construct their own checklists related directly to objectives sought in the particular situation. Any performance or behavior that can be stated in clear, descriptive terms can usually be included in a checklist.

Care should be shown in constructing a checklist or selecting a ready-made one to see that the specific traits, characteristics, or actions described are in unambiguous and unbiased terms. Use of terminology that indicates relativity and is subject to varied interpretations should be avoided. For instance, "Shows a weakness in pronunciation of short vowel sounds" can be interpreted variously by the person observing the behavior or by anyone to whom the information is given. Further information is necessary. "Pronounces short vowel sounds represented by 'a' " is clearer and more definitive. A checkmark or a yes/no answer can communicate the nature of the behavior called for in this item. The items in Figure 2, taken from a "Progress Report," are illustrative of characteristics open to numerous interpretations.

Figure 2   Portion of a Progress Report

Growth in Skills and Knowledge
Second Quarter

Reading	Yes	No	At times
Reads with understanding			
Reads well orally			
Shows growth in skills			
Enjoys reading			

Checklists for evaluation of behaviors related to reading instruction can be improved by observing guidelines such as the following:
1. Describe each behavior, action, characteristic in specific, unambiguous terms.
2. When it is necessary to include both positive and negative behaviors in the same checklist, divide the checklist into two parts: (Strengths–Weaknesses) or (Skills in which progress is adequate/inadequate).
3. Try to arrange behaviors, actions, or characteristics as sequentially as possible.

Rating Scales

Rating scales provide a more structured means for evaluating aspects of learners' behaviors than is possible through use of anecdotal records; they provide a more descriptive account than can be given in a checklist. A rating scale is a device by which can be shown the degree or extent to which defined characteristics or behaviors are shown. A rating scale can be constructed so that it can be used in evaluation of learners' behaviors or characteristics or so that it can be used with reference to situations or products of learning.

In appearance, rating scales and checklists are highly similar. In each, characteristics or other attribues subject to evaluation are made explicit. The checklist, however, allows only for an absolute yes or no as to the existence of an element, while the rating scale permits reaction to the relative amount or quality of an element that is under question. In either case, information gathered is only the reflection of the judgment of the observer.

Constructed and used properly, and interpreted only in terms of what it can report, a rating scale can be valuable in comprehensive evaluation of all important aspects of reading instruction. It is highly useful when judgments must be made about learners' interests, attitudes, work habits, initiative, cooperation, and the like. It serves to increase objectivity and preciseness of evaluation of the quality of products of learning such as book reports, creative expression in art, drama and music.

Rating scales improve the quality of evaluations often required in reading instruction in many ways. They help to focus observation toward particular ele-

Figure 3   Reading Behaviors Checklist

Name _____

	Yes	No
Readiness Skills		
Hears likenesses in words	—	—
Hears differences in words	—	—
Hears sounds at beginnings of words	—	—
Hears sounds at ends of words	—	—
Sees likenesses in letters	—	—
Sees differences in letters	—	—
Sees likenesses in words	—	—
Sees differences in words	—	—
Identifies letters of the alphabet	—	—
Listens to stories read	—	—
Provides endings for incomplete sentences	—	—
Has a basic sight vocabulary	—	—
Visually scrutinizes words	—	—
Notes details of words	—	—
Word-Recognition Skills		
Identifies words by their configuration	—	—
Identifies words by recognition of initial sounds	—	—
Pronounces phonic elements	—	—
Uses phonic elements to identify words	—	—
Notes endings of words (s, ed, ing, ly, est, 's)	—	—
Identifies root words	—	—
Identifies parts of compound words	—	—
Uses parts of compound words to identify new word	—	—
Identifies prefixes	—	—
Uses prefixes to identify new word	—	—
Identifies suffixes	—	—
Uses suffixes to aid word pronunciation	—	—
Identifies syllables	—	—
Uses syllables to aid word pronunciation	—	—
Uses context clues to aid work recognition	—	—
Comprehension skills		
Uses wide vocabulary in oral expression	—	—
Identifies main idea in a selection	—	—
Recalls details of a story	—	—
Recalls sequence of events in story	—	—
Identifies main characters in story	—	—
Summarizes main points in a selection	—	—
States inferences drawn from a selection	—	—
Attitudes Toward Reading		
Selects books voluntarily	—	—
Requests favorite stories	—	—
Asks questions related to his reading	—	—
Discusses ideas gained from reading	—	—
Expresses ideas gained from reading through creative art	—	—
Listens during oral reading	—	—

ments required in determination of whether certain objectives are achieved. All learners under consideration can be compared on the same set of behaviors or characteristics. Once a rating scale has been constructed it often can be used with many different individuals, groups, or products.

Characteristics or other factors toward which observation is to be focused must be specified on the scale. Either a number or a descriptive phrase can be used to identify the rating given to each element. Directions for a simple numerical scale, such as the sample shown in Figure 4, can clarify the meaning of each number included after each question. For instance, the number 3 can mean "always," 2 — "sometimes," and 1 — "seldom." The observer has only to circle or cross out the appropriate number to make his rating clear.

Figure 4   Sample of Behavior Rating Scale

1. To what extent does the learner volunteer to read orally?

                  3   2   1

2. Does the learner participate in discussion?

                  3   2   1

Interviews

The interview technique can be used for gathering information about an individual's cognitive and affective behaviors. Sometimes, results achieved from measurement of cognitive behaviors can be evaluated more effectively by engaging in a one-to-one relationship with the individual. For many affective behaviors, such as different types of attitudes, interests, or an individual's interest in reading, the interview provides a major and effective means of acquiring pertinent information.

Generally, the interview is implemented in an unstructured and informal manner. If the interview is unstructured, it does not proceed on the basis of previously determined questions, but depends on incidental cues for its direction. Even when it is unstructured, however, the interviewer should be guided by awareness of the objective or objectives under consideration. Otherwise, the interview can become meaningless as an evaluation procedure and conducive to highly subjective and biased conclusions on the part of the interviewer. Furthermore, improperly conducted, the interview can produce negative effects upon attitudes of the learner being interviewed.

A structured interview requires planning and prior determination of questions to be asked. These questions should be designed specifically to focus on determination of a learner's achievement of an objective or objectives. For structured interviews, the teacher can prepare a form containing the exact questions to be asked of all individuals to be interviewed. Records of the results of structured interviews lend themselves to better organization and a higher degree of objectivity than are possible when interviews are unstructured.

As an evaluation procedure, the interview should be used to gather information about a learner's achievement of objectives that cannot be gathered as effectively by use of other procedures.

Questionnaires

The questionnaire can be used to obtain much the same types of information that become available through use of the interview. There are at least two basic differences, however, between use of the questionnaire and interviews. Questionnaires represent a more organized approach in the evaluation of attitudes, interests, and the like, than is possible through interviews, and questionnaires can be used in group situations.

Questionnaires can be used as direct approaches to obtaining information about learners' achievement of objectives in either the cognitive or affective domains. Used in a direct manner, specific questions related to specific factors are presented to the learner for his direct answers. The learner is, thus, aware of the specific kind of information being sought when a direct questionnaire is used.

Questionnaires can also be constructed to provide information about behaviors on which the learner is unaware of being tested from the nature of the questions. Used in this way, the learner responds to a set of questions whose purposes are not apparent to him. On the basis of his responses, the questioner draws conclusions about behaviors other than those to which the questionnaire ostensibly refers.

Since questionnaires are presented in printed forms, they can be used only with individuals or groups of learners who are able to read. Generally, questionnaires are more useful during the intermediate or upper levels of the elementary school than they are at the primary level. At the primary level, questions must often be asked orally. Thus, if the method is used at this level, it is hardly distinguishable from the structured interview technique.

Competencies Required of Teachers

Competencies required of teachers for evaluation of the results of reading instruction generally include those required in need assessment, defining objectives, selecting and using various teaching strategies, and those indicating a command of the content of reading. Specific competencies related directly to evaluation of achievement include the following:

1. Skill in selecting procedures and materials suitable for gathering information related to the variety of objectives sought in reading instruction.
2. Skill in locating information needed in evaluation of procedures and materials to be used in the evaluation process.
3. Ability to design teaching and evaluation strategies that emphasize the integrated and interrelated relationships between instruction and evaluation.
4. Skill in selection of evaluation procedures and materials that are uniquely appropriate for use in evaluating achievement of specific objectives.
5. Knowledge of appropriate uses of standardized tests.
6. Ability to determine when norm-referenced or criterion-referenced measures are desirable for use in the evaluation process in a particular situation.
7. Ability to construct criterion-referenced measures appropriate for evaluation of learners' achievement of objectives in a particular instructional program.
8. Ability to distinguish between the need for use of formal or informal measures of achievement.
9. Skill in construction and use of various types of techniques for recording observations.

10. Ability to interpret the results of various types of evaluation procedures.
11. Knowledge of the types and uses of various derived scores.
12. Ability to involve learners in cooperative efforts for evaluation of their achievement of various types of objectives.
13. Ability to determine the types of records essential for maintaining awareness of learners' achievement.
14. Ability to report learners' achievement of objectives sought in an instructional program.

SUMMARY

Accountability in reading instruction is substantiated by evidence that learners under consideration in a program will achieve competence in reading in accordance with their potentialities. Evaluation is the process that makes possible this substantiation of instructional effectiveness.

Evaluation can be defined as a process whereby learners' achievement of objectives can be determined and reported. The meaning of evaluation should be interpreted broadly enough to include attention to objectives sought in all domains of learning. In evaluating achievement of objectives related to all domains of learning, a variety of measurement and observational techniques are needed.

To be most effective, evaluation must be perceived as a process supported by several major principles. As a process, evaluation is interwoven and interrelated with the instructional process. It is supported by principles that stipulate the need for comprehensiveness, continuity, and cooperation.

Review Questions

1. How is evaluation defined? **(1.1)** *
2. How does evaluation differ from measurement? **(1.1)**
3. Why is evaluation better described as a process rather than as a discrete activity? **(1.2)**
4. Explain how evaluation of learners' achievement in terms of objectives differs from conventional practices of administering tests, periodically, to cover subject matter topics? **(1.3)**
5. Show how the process of evaluation can be considered an interrelated part of the total process of instruction. **(1.4)**
6. Give examples that illustrate how the principles of comprehensiveness, continuity, and cooperation can be applied in evaluation of achievement in reading. **(1.5)**
7. Describe several characteristics that apply to instruments of measurement used in evaluation of achievement in reading. **(2.1)**
8. In what ways do results of measurement differ from results attained from the use of observational techniques? **(2.2)**

---

*Boldface numbers in parentheses refer to the numbered behavioral objectives at the beginning of the chapter.

9. Why are measurement results vital in educational accountability? (**2.3**)

10. What are some of the characteristics of standardized tests that should be taken into consideration when selections of measurement instruments must be made? (**3.1**)

11. Describe some of the types of test norms generally provided by standardized tests of reading achievement. (**3.2**)

12. What types of information generally are available from test norms? (**3.3**)

13. Make a list of criteria that should be considered in test selection. (**3.4**)

14. Besides the obvious difference indicated in the labels "group" and "individual," what are the major differences between these group and individual tests? (**3.5**)

15. What types of information needed in evaluation of reading achievement are best gathered through use of standardized tests? (**3.6**)

16. How do basal-reader tests differ from standardized group tests of reading achievement? (**3.7**)

17. What types of information may be expected from results of administering basal-reader tests? (**3.8**)

18. Describe "criterion-referenced" tests. What are essential differences between "criterion-referenced" and "norm-referenced" tests? (**3.9**)

19. Why are "criterion-referenced" tests especially needed in instructional situations in which accountability is sought? (**3.9**)

20. Make a list of some important sources of test information. (**4.1**)

21. Select two important sources of test information and describe the kind of information these make available. (**4.2**)

22. Why are observational techniques essential in a program of comprehensive evaluation of achievement in reading? (**5.1**)

23. What types of behaviors generally must be evaluated on the basis of information available only from use of observational techniques? (**5.2**)

24. In what ways can information attained from use of observational techniques aid in interpretation of results of measurement? (**5.3**)

25. Describe some of the competencies you believe are most important for teachers in evaluation of learners' achievement in reading. (**6.0**)

Selected References

1. Bleismer, Emery P., "Informal Teacher Testing in Reading," *The Reading Teacher,* 26 (December, 1972), 268–72.

2. Bloom, Benjamin S., J. Thomas Hastings, and George F. Madaus, *Handbook on Formative and Summative Evaluation of Student Learning.* N. Y.: McGraw-Hill, 1971.

3. Bracht, Glenn H., Kenneth D. Hopkins, and Julian C. Staley, *Perspectives in Educational and Psychological Measurement.* Englewood Cliffs, N. J.: Prentice-Hall, 1972.

4. Gronlund, Norman E., *Measurement and Evaluation in Teaching.* N. Y.: Macmillan, 1971.

5. ————, *Constructing Achievement Tests.* Englewood Cliffs, N. J.: Prentice-Hall, 1968.
6. Farr, Roger, *Reading: What Can be Measured?* Newark, Del.: International Reading Association, 1969.
7. Glaser, R., "Instructional Technology and the Measurement of Learning Outcomes: Some Questions," *American Psychologist,* 18 (1963), 519–21.
8. Lyman, Howard B., *Test Scores and What They Mean.* Englewood Cliffs, N. J.: Prentice-Hall, 1963.
9. Marshall, Jon Clark, and Lloyde Wesley Hales, *Essentials of Testing.* Reading, Mass.: Addison-Wesley, 1972.
10. Manuel, Herschel T., *Elementary Statistics for Teachers.* N. Y.: American Book, 1962.
11. Noll, Victor H., and Dale P. Scannell, *Introduction to Educational Measurement,* Third edition. Boston: Houghton Mifflin, 1972.
12. Noll, Victor H., Dale P. Scannell, and Rachel P. Noll, *Introductory Readings in Educational Measurement.* Boston: Houghton Mifflin, 1972.
13. Smith, Fred M., and Sam Adams, *Educational Measurement for the Classroom Teacher.* N. Y.: Harper and Brothers, 1966.
14. Wildavsky, Aaron, "A Program of Accountability for Elementary Schools" in *Readings on Teaching Reading,* S. L. Sebesta and C. J. Wallen, editors. Chicago: Science Research Associates, 1972.
15. Wood, Dorothy Adkins, *Test Construction.* Columbus, Ohio: Charles E. Merrill, 1961.

Basic Concepts and Skills In Reading

7 Developing Skills in Word Recognition

Reading instruction is unique among areas of instruction in the curriculum. Regular, formal instruction must be provided to ensure that learners develop skills and concepts essential in effective reading. At the same time, development in reading cannot proceed effectively if restricted exclusively to organized, formal periods of instruction. In addition, reading is essential in instruction and learning in all areas of the curriculum; it is essential also in many activities outside of school. In order to read effectively a learner must use reading in other areas of the curriculum and in pertinent activities outside of school.

Although reading is not considered a content area in and of itself, the reading teacher should be in command of certain content or subject matter. While teachers' manuals, guidebooks, curriculum guides, and the like, often include content for reading instruction, a teacher must possess the background knowledge that permits intelligent use of these materials. Reading content must be selected, organized, and emphasized according to the needs of particular learners in particular situations. Student practice in developing skills and concepts in reading should be based on sound research results. Thorough acquaintance with the content of reading instruction makes these and other desirable teaching behaviors possible. Chapters 7 and 8 are focused on that basic content required in reading instruction.

Behavioral Objectives

The content of Chapter 7 is presented in such a way that after reading it, an individual
- **1.0**   Understands the nature of the reading act
  - **1.1**   Identifies authoritative definitions of reading

1.2   Describes major components of the reading act
1.3   States a personal concept of the nature of reading
1.4   States reasons why a teacher of reading should clarify his personal concept of the nature of reading
1.5   States a rationale for helping each learner conceptualize the meaning of reading
2.0   Understands the importance of readiness for initial formal instruction in reading
    2.1   Explains the meaning of "reading readiness"
    2.2   Identifies factors related to initial readiness for reading
    2.3   Describes procedures used for development of initial reading readiness
3.0   Understands the importance of developmental readiness for reading
    3.1   Explains the meaning of "developmental readiness for reading"
    3.2   Identifies factors related to developmental reading readiness
    3.3   Explains relationships between initial reading readiness and readiness for reading at subsequent levels of instruction
    3.4   Describes procedures useful in helping learners develop and maintain readiness for reading as instruction proceeds
4.0   Recognizes areas of initial reading instruction related specifically to development of decoding skills in reading
    4.1   Describes concerns related to each of the following
        4.1.1   Sight vocabulary
        4.1.2   Initial decoding skills
5.0   Recognizes major approaches used in initial reading instruction
    5.1   Describes characteristics of "code-emphasis" approaches
    5.2   Describes characteristics of approaches in which meaning is emphasized as an initial concern
    5.3   Compares advantages and limitations of major approaches to reading instruction
    5.4   States a rationale for use of a selected approach to reading instruction
6.0   Understands the developmental nature of decoding skills in reading
    6.1   Explains relationships between each of the following elements:
        6.1.1   An initial basic sight vocabulary and continuing development of a sight vocabulary
        6.1.2   Initial and developmental decoding skills
    6.2   Categorizes basic decoding skills
    6.3   Explains why a variety of decoding skills should be mastered
7.0   Understands the role of phonics in reading
    7.1   Differentiates between "phonics" and "phonetics"
    7.2   Differentiates between analytic and synthetic approaches in phonics instruction
    7.3   Differentiates between inductive and deductive approaches in reading instruction
    7.4   Describes elements in phonics instruction
8.0   Understands uses of structural-analysis skills in decoding
    8.1   Explains the meaning of structural-analysis skills in reading
    8.2   Describes specific skills in structural analysis
9.0   Understands uses of contextual clues in decoding
    9.1   Explains the meaning of "contextual clues."
    9.2   Identifies various types of contextual clues
10.0   Understands influences of linguistics on reading instructional practices

10.1   Identifies linguistic cues that aid in development of decoding skills
10.2   Defines terminology related to linguistics and reading
11.0 Recognizes teacher-competencies essential for helping learners develop ability in word recognition

The Nature of Reading

The nature of reading can be compared to that of any phenomenon so pervasive and familiar that everyone takes it for granted. Although many persons read, it is obvious that few take the time to analyze the nature of reading. Many teachers and prospective teachers are hard pressed when faced with the prospect of defining reading.

Definitions of reading are presented in many professional texts used to prepare teachers to teach reading. In many others, knowledge of the nature of reading is taken for granted. When definitions of reading are included in texts, seldom are two found to be identical. Considering the significance of the teacher's concept of reading on the effectiveness and direction of his instructional practices, both the variability in definitions given and the lack of attention to the matter in many books are significant. As Arthur Heilman has remarked, "It is difficult to understand why there is no universally accepted definition of reading."[1]

Much evidence exists to attest to the difficulty in defining or describing the nature of reading. Some evidence is apparent in the large number of different definitions available. Other evidence stems from recognition of the complexity of reading and the numerous perspectives from which it can be viewed. Teachers should clarify their understandings of the nature of reading from the perspective of classroom instruction and for purposes of accountability.

Accountability also demands that teachers have an awareness of the practical implications of that understanding. The teacher's concept of reading is ultimately the one that will be operational in the classroom, since what the teacher believes about the nature of reading will affect all of his or her instructional practices. Need assessment, objectives, individualization of instruction, humanistic educational practices in reading instruction, and other procedures are crucially affected by the teacher's concept of reading.

The concept of reading held by a teacher should be based on the best that is known, authoritatively, about the nature of reading. An original conception of reading unrelated to the results of research or recognized experience would be of scant benefit in improving the effectiveness of instruction.

Authorities' Definitions of Reading

Reading has been described or defined in various ways by writers and researchers in reading and in fields closely allied with reading.

---

[1]Arthur W. Heilman, *Principles and Practices of Teaching Reading* (Columbus, Ohio: Charles E. Merrill, 1967), p. 140.

Many descriptions of reading highlight its comprehensiveness, its values, and its complexity. In 1940, W. S. Gray offered, in part, the following description of reading:

> The concept of reading presented in this section is broad and comprehensive. It conceives reading as a purposeful activity which may alter the outlook of the individual, deepen his understanding, aid in the reconstruction of experience, stimulate intellectual and emotional growth, modify behavior, and in these various ways, promote the development of rich and stable personalities.[2]

And according to Ruth Strang:

> Reading is many-sided. It is a visual task involving sensation and perception. Reading is a psychological process; it involves fusing symbols with their meanings to comprehend an author's thought. Reading is a complex and unique experience involving the organism as a whole. It is a pattern of activities which varies with the reader's purpose and the kind of material which he is reading. . . .[3]

Broad conceptions of reading such as those expressed by Gray and Strang describe values and satisfactions available through reading as well as the basic nature of the act of reading. Translating conceptions such as these into classroom instructional practices is not an easy or simple task for the teacher.

Robert Karlin distinguishes between the "reading act" which he describes as dealing with "surface activities and behaviors . . . . involving the decoding of language symbols and understanding what meanings they convey" and the "reading process" that involves "understanding of the succession of actions which occur to make the reading act possible."[4] This distinction between the reading act and the reading process can be useful to teachers, for it helps to place elements of reading development into a perspective practical for classroom situations.

Consideration of each of the operations included in a "model of the reading process" presented by Smith and Harris also indicates those specific areas of reading toward which instructional efforts can be focused.[5] Of ten operations included in the model, only two are observable: the first operation, in which the reader encounters the visual stimulus, and the last operation, in which — at times — the response to reading is visible. Teachers should attempt to understand internal operations involved in reading; although, in a practical sense, it is through learners' observable behavior that accountability can be established.

---

[2]William S. Gray, "Reading and Factors Influencing Reading Efficiency." Chapter 2 in *Reading in General Education* (Washington, D. C.: American Council on Education, 1940), p. 50.

[3]Ruth Strang, "The Nature of Reading." In *Problems in the Improvement of Reading*, Ruth Strang, Constance McCullough, and Arthur Traxler, editors (N.Y.: McGraw-Hill, 1955), p. 62.

[4]Robert Karlin, *Teaching Elementary Reading* (N. Y.: Harcourt Brace Jovanovich, 1971), p. 17.

[5]Larry A. Harris and Carl B. Smith, *Reading Instruction Through Diagnostic Teaching* (N. Y.: Holt, Rinehart, and Winston, 1972), p. 9.

Reading has been described simply as "the meaningful interpretation of visual symbols."[6] It has been referred to as "part of the process of human communication in which thoughts are transmitted through the medium of the printed word."[7] It has been called "a mental process involving the interpretation of signs perceived by the sense organs."[8] It has been described as a process consisting of "receiving thought through printed and written symbols . . . comprehending the expression by a writer of a book or article. . . . understanding of a message — printed or written — of the sender."[9]

Despite differences in choices of words and in the aspects of reading emphasized in these descriptions of reading, certain elements are common in all of the expressions. Reading, generally, is described as involving (1) recognition and identification of printed or written symbols and (2) perception of and understanding of the meaning of the selection. Stated another way, reading involves the ability to decode (recognize and interpret speech sounds represented by graphic symbols used in the writing system) and the ability to understand the meaning conveyed. Several levels of meaning might be understood according to the potential and purpose of the reader. Two aspects of reading, decoding and acquiring meaning, are basic in the concerns of classroom instruction in reading.

Having clear ideas of what the process of reading involves provides the teacher with built-in guidelines for instructional practices. This helps to prevent the use of practices that may be mutually contradictory or invalidating. Thus, as preparation for providing a sound program, the teacher should consider the nature of the personal concept he or she actually holds regarding the meaning of reading.

Several teachers and prospective teachers, when asked to verbalize their concepts of reading, offered statements such as the following:

1. "Reading is an experience to broaden one's knowledge and improve his abilities to communicate."
2. "Reading is the ability to (1) translate symbols into sounds; (2) comprehend meanings of words; and (3) generalize the overall theme, message, or idea communicated in a selection."
3. "Reading is the ability to understand what one sees."
4. "Reading is an experience that opens up the gateway of living."
5. "Reading is translation of printed or written symbols in order to understand and interpret meanings intended by the author."
6. "Reading is the process of decoding printed or written symbols in order to understand and interpret meanings intended by the author."

Consideration of one's personal concept regarding the nature of reading is a prerequisite for effective reading instruction. The teacher of reading is not likely to enter the classroom armed with a textbook on teaching reading or with a

---

[6] Albert J. Harris, *How to Increase Reading Ability,* Fourth edition, revised (N. Y.: David McKay Co., 1961), p. 8.

[7] Gertrude Hildreth, *Teaching Reading* (N. Y.: Holt, Rinehart and Winston, 1958), p. 2.

[8] Carl J. Wallen, *Competency in Teaching Reading* (Chicago: Science Research Associates, 1972), p. 7.

[9] James A. Fitzgerald and Patricia G. Fitzgerald, *Teaching Reading and the Language Arts* (Milwaukee: Bruce Publishing, 1965), p. 84.

memorized definition or description of reading. In the final analysis, the teacher's own understanding of the nature of reading will guide and affect instructional practices. Examination of the preceding list of descriptions of the meaning of reading suggests that the majority of these would present grave problems if attempts were made to translate them into guidelines for instructional practices. In addition to defining a personal conception of reading, then, every teacher of reading should clarify a concept of reading that is useful in guiding practices in classroom instruction and is reflective of the best that is known regarding the actual nature of reading.

What is actually known about the nature of reading shows it to be a complex process. Reading does not consist of one specific ability or skill but involves a complex of many interrelated and interacting skills and abilities. Any aspect of reading depends on the simultaneous use of numerous skills and subskills. Both the abilities to decode symbols and to determine meaning are significant in reading. Within each of these aspects of reading, numerous skills, abilities, and concepts are included.

Reading is a symbolic process. Abilities to deal with symbols used in both language and writing are basic requirements in reading. The writing system makes use of graphic or visual symbols representing speech sounds which, in turn, represent meaning. Further, reading can be called both a thinking and a mechanical process. For instructional purposes, decoding or word recognition can be called a mechanical process, while understanding meaning can be called a thinking process. For the purpose of clarifying and developing skills required to perform the two aspects of reading, these processes may be considered separately. In actual reading, the processes occur simultaneously and cannot be separated.

Readiness for Initial Reading Instruction

Instruction in reading proceeds more effectively and more efficiently if consideration is given to the types of skills, abilities, and concepts related to reading that a learner is ready to develop. Readiness is considered to be crucially important in initial formal reading instruction.

Readiness is a crucial concern at the outset of formal instruction in reading both because of the number of factors influencing it and due to the influence it has on a learner's subsequent achievement in reading. During later stages of development in reading, readiness continues a factor to be considered, but it is less crucial. The number of factors becomes fewer as a result of previous achievement and the greater maturity of the reader.

Meaning of Reading Readiness

Readiness means, simply, that all personal factors and factors applicable to the task at hand are in favorable states for enabling the individual to receive and respond to stimuli related to the new learning. Readiness is helpful in facilitating learning regardless of the age of the learner and the nature of the learning task. A composite of physical, mental, social, emotional, and environmental factors[10] are recognized as being influential on an individual's readiness for learning. Because of the nature of reading and the demands it makes on the individual, reading readiness has received much attention.

Attention was first drawn to the subject of readiness for reading instruction in the Report of the National Committee on Reading in 1925.[11] Interpretation of the contents of this report led to concern about the appropriate *time* for teaching a learner to read. Many persons embraced the view that readiness was chiefly a maturational concern. As a consequence, practices of waiting for the natural maturation of learners to make them ready for reading instruction became prevalent. Results of a study by Morphett and Washburne tended to establish the practice of requiring learners to have a mental age of six years and five months as a prerequisite for reading.[12]

Modern conceptions of the nature and role of reading readiness reflect many changes from those views held predominantly during early years of attention to the concept. As additional knowledge has been gained, new implications regarding readiness have come into being. Objectives of modern programs of reading instruction reflect these changes. The concern for reading readiness now focuses on specific factors rather than on global aspects of an individual's development. Most learners are regarded as being ready for some — if not all — aspects of reading instruction. It is also felt that weaknesses in many areas of an individual's readiness for reading can be strengthened by appropriate structured experiences, rather than by depending on the passage of time.

Individual differences in reading readiness are now recognized, whereas all learners of a particular age were once expected to show mainly the same characteristics. Many learners are ready for formal instruction in reading prior to entrance into school. Recognition is given to the fact that many experiences in which many children engage prior to school attendance contribute to development of readiness to read.[13]

In many schools, the development of readiness for formal instruction in reading is expected to be an integral part of initial instruction in reading, rather than a prerequisite for it. Activities designed to help individuals develop readiness for reading include many such as the following:

1. Participation in classroom and school routines.
2. Activities designed to increase listening ability.
3. Activities designed to increase participation in oral expression.

---

[10] William H. Burton, *Reading in Child Development* (Indianapolis: Bobbs-Merrill, 1959), p. 194.

Gertrude B. Hildreth, *Readiness for School Beginners* (Yonkers, N. Y.: World Book, 1950).

[11] *Report of the National Committee on Reading* Twenty-Fourth Yearbook of the National Society for the Study of Education, Part I (Chicago: University of Chicago Press, 1925).

[12] Mabel Morphett and Carleton Washburne, "When Should Children Begin to Read?" *Elementary School Journal*, 31 (March, 1931), pp. 496–503.

[13] W. Schramm and E. Parker, *Television in the Lives of Our Children* (Palo Alto, Ca.: Stanford University Press, 1961).

4. Activities designed to increase interest in reading.
5. Activities designed to improve learners' conceptual level.
6. Activities designed to improve the ability to make fine visual and auditory discriminations as required in the act of reading.

Factors Related to Reading Readiness

While research results are inconclusive with regard to the specific amount of influence a specific factor has upon an individual's readiness for reading instruction, several factors have been specified as having significance in the aggregation of factors determining reading readiness.

Intelligence

Intelligence is recognized as a factor in all learning. An absolute level of intelligence, however, has not been identified as a prerequisite for success in beginning reading. Results from an earlier study that established, for many years, a specific mental age as a requirement for reading are no longer considered to be dependable.[14] Results from subsequent studies have tended to emphasize the importance of other factors and conditions pertinent to an individual's success in learning to read.[15]

Attitude Toward Reading

Early in their beginning reading, learners vary widely in their attitudes toward the task. Some learners approach the prospect of learning to read with great desire and anticipation, while others may show no strong feeling either for or against reading. Still, there may be others who view reading as a frightening or even distasteful experience. All of these and other attitudes will have an effect upon learners' success in learning to read and upon the activities that should be provided for their development of readiness. For some learners, it is important to provide experiences that will sustain and nourish the favorable attitudes that are already present upon school entrance. For others, efforts must be made to encourage an interest in reading. In some cases, fear and suspicion held by learners toward reading must be overcome and replaced with feelings of confidence and motivation.

The Learner's Concept of Reading

It is believed by some authorities that part of readiness to read depends upon the learner's concept of the meaning of reading.[16] It is

---

[14] Morphett and Washburne, "When Should Children Begin to Read?" pp. 496–503.

[15] Dolores Durkin, "A Study of Children Who Learned to Read Prior to First Grade," *California Journal of Educational Research*, 10 (May, 1959), pp. 109–13.

[16] R. V. Allen, "Concept Development of Young Children in Reading Instruction," Twenty-Fourth Yearbook, Claremont College Reading Conference (Claremont, Ca., 1959), pp. 12–21.

helpful if a learner understands that the printed materials he or she is confronted with contain messages similar to those the learner is accustomed to giving and receiving from others in speech. The learner must be helped to realize that the meaning of messages in print can be interpreted on the basis of personal experiences once the necessary associations have been made between the symbols used in print and the language sounds with which the learner is already familiar. Proponents of some approaches to reading instruction stress the importance of helping learners develop the concept of reading as "speech written down."

Ability to Listen

For a number of reasons, a learner's ability to listen is an important factor in readiness for reading. Arthur W. Heilman noted that listening is closely related to several aspects of reading, including expansion of concepts, reading with proper intonation patterns, participating in oral reading, and development of sound work habits.[17] Other relationships between listening and reading have been pointed out by Paul S. Anderson, who indicated that both the processes of listening and reading require readiness for accomplishment. Factors influencing both processes include the learner's mental ability, vocabulary development, ability to follow a sequence of ideas, and interest in language. Both processes require perception of single words, although the units in each are phrases, sentences, and paragraphs.[18]

The results of a study by Ralph Kellogg stressed the primacy of listening skills among the four language skills of listening, speaking, reading, and writing. Kellogg's research helped to call attention to the importance of experience in hearing sounds of language and relating these to objects and actions previously experienced on learning to speak, to read, and to write.[19] A study by Len Lasnik referred to common factors in all language arts as vocabulary, auditory discrimination, and organization of ideas. According to Lasnik, "Physiologically and psychologically, listening comes first and thus undergirds the whole language arts program."[20]

It is essential to determine individual differences in ability to listen among young children, despite the tendency to take ability to listen for granted. Anderson has observed that there is as wide a difference in ability to listen as there is in any other area of development.[21] Some learners are more oriented toward auditory learning styles while others favor other sensory modes. Determining these differences and providing experiences essential in improving learners' abilities to listen are major concerns during initial reading readiness.

---

[17] Arthur W. Heilman, *Principles and Practices of Teaching Reading*, p. 56.

[18] Paul S. Anderson, *Language Skills in Elementary Education*, Second edition (N. Y.: Macmillan, 1972), p. 72.

[19] Ralph E. Kellogg, *A Study of the Effect of a First Grade Listening Instructional Program Upon Achievement in Listening and Reading.* Cooperative Research Project 6–8489 (San Diego, Ca., Department of Education, San Diego County, 1966), p. 25.

[20] Len L. Lasnik, *Programs in Oral Communication* (Hayward, Ca.: Department of Education, Alameda County, 1969).

[21] Paul S. Anderson, *Language Skills in Elementary Education*, p. 72.

Language Development

Much of an individual's progress in learning to read depends on language development.[22] Evidence of language development is apparent in the facility an individual shows in both speaking and listening. Thus, the ability to express oneself in sentences and to comprehend those spoken by others is one indication of readiness for learning to read. Language development is closely related to other important factors in development, such as intelligence and opportunities for verbalization in the learner's experiential background. As might be expected, then, notable differences can be found in language development among children in beginning reading. Being aware of these differences among a group of learners and providing experiences essential for development of language abilities are major concerns in modern programs of reading readiness.

Auditory Discrimination

Auditory discrimination refers to the ability to distinguish between closely related speech sounds heard in words. It includes the ability to blend speech sounds represented by various letters used in the construction of words. Auditory discrimination involves other abilities also, such as auditory acuity (keenness or sharpness of hearing), understanding, and retention.[23] Research results show that a learner's ability to discriminate between closely related speech sounds can be improved by training.[24] Many important activities provided for learners during initial reading readiness are focused on development of auditory discrimination ability.

Visual Discrimination

Reading requires the ability to distinguish between printed or written words. Visual discrimination ability relates directly to this task and is an important concern during initial reading readiness and during initial instruction in reading. In reading, visual discrimination is the term used to refer to the ability of a learner to distinguish likenesses and differences between and among letters and/or words that tend to be closely related in form.

Visual acuity refers to acuteness or clarity in vision. Being able to see clearly obviously is essential for making discriminations required in reading, but it is not a guarantee of the learner's ability to distinguish between and among closely related visual forms.

During reading readiness, attention is given to the ability of a learner to perceive likenesses and differences among letters of the alphabet. At the same time, it is

[22] Esther Milner, "A Study of the Relationship Between Reading Readiness in Grade One School Children and Patterns of Parent-Child Interaction," *Child Development*, 22 (1951), pp. 95–112.

[23] Joseph M. Wepman, "Auditory Discrimination, Speech and Reading," *The Elementary School Journal*, 60 (March, 1960), pp. 325–33.

[24] Donald Durrell and Helen Murphy, "Reading in Grade One," *Journal of Education*, 146 (December, 1962), pp. 14–18.

Nicholas Silvaroli and W. H. Wheelock, "An Investigation of Auditory Training for Beginning Readers," *The Reading Teacher*, 20 (December, 1966), pp. 247–51.

recognized that reading does not consist merely in the recognition of isolated letters. Ability to recognize letter forms achieves its importance from its contribution to ability to recognize words as required in the act of reading.

Barrett reviewed the literature on relationships between visual discrimination and reading and found that research results show that the ability to perceive differences among *words* is more important in reading than is the ability to differentiate among letters.[25]

Questions often are raised by prospective teachers and by teachers regarding whether or not it is important to teach learners recognition of letters of the alphabet by name. In his analysis of the process of reading, Charles Fries stresses importance of teaching children to recognize letter symbols and their names. According to Fries, "Building up the habits of seeing written forms in the significant direction sequence the writing system uses is one of the first tasks of learning to read — one that should be accomplished during the readiness program."[26]

Results of several studies also have emphasized the importance of teaching the learner to recognize and name letters of the alphabet as a prerequisite of learning to read. On the basis of several studies conducted under his direction at Boston University, Donald Durrell concluded that knowledge of letter forms is significantly related to ability to discriminate between words.[27] Bond and Dykstra drew similar conclusions from results of the First Grade Studies. Knowledge of letter names, these researchers claimed, was the best predictor of success in beginning reading.[28]

Helping learners develop skills in visual discrimination is a major task required of teachers during reading readiness and during initial instruction in reading. Several studies have produced evidence that training in visual discrimination helps learners improve abilities in recognizing letters and word forms. Results of research have shown, also, that activities designed to help children discriminate between non-word forms generally are not productive in developing strengths needed in reading.[29]

Recognition of letters and knowledge of letter names have not been shown to be causal factors in success in learning to read.[30] Nor has it been shown, conclusively, that children who lack this knowledge do not experience success in learning to read. There also are results of studies to suggest that children who have no prior knowledge of letter names and sounds also succeed in beginning

---

[25] Thomas C. Barrett, "The Relationship between Measures of Pre-Reading Visual Discrimination and First-Grade Reading Achievement: A Review of the Literature," *Reading Research Quarterly*, 1 (Fall, 1965), pp. 51–76.

[26] Charles C. Fries, *Linguistics and Reading* (N. Y.: Holt, Rinehart, and Winston, 1963), p. 123.

[27] Donald D. Durrell and Helen A. Murphy, "Reading Readiness," *Journal of Education*, 146 (December, 1963), p. 5.

[28] Guy L. Bond and Robert Dykstra, Coordinating Center for First-Grade Reading Instruction Programs, *Final Report*, U. S. Department of Health, Education, and Welfare, Project No. X001 (Minneapolis: University of Minnesota, 1967).

[29] A. Nicholson, "Background Abilities Related to Reading Success in First Grade." Unpublished Doctoral Dissertation, Boston University, 1957.

[30] S. Muehl, "The Effects of Letter-Name Knowledge on Learning to Read a Word List in Kindergarten Children," *Journal of Educational Psychology*, 53 (August, 1962), pp. 181–86.

reading. In one of these studies, Linehan compared the achievement of 314 children who had been taught letter names and sounds with the achievement of 300 children to whom these had not been taught. No significant difference was found in the reading achievement of the children in the study at the end of their first year in school.[31]

Typical Activities Used in Development of Initial Reading Readiness

Activities designed for development of reading-readiness abilities are essential for many children prior to and during initial formal instruction in reading. As stated earlier, reading readiness periods are not considered to be periods during which children wait passively for sufficient maturation to begin learning to read. Research related to the development of many essential factors suggests the importance of training in making a difference in a learner's development of reading readiness. Various activities can be used to improve development of a learner's ability related to various factors important in initial reading readiness.

Improving Attitudes Toward Reading

To help reluctant, apprehensive, or apathetic learners improve attitudes toward reading, activities such as the following are often used.
1. Oral reading by the teacher
2. Relating learners' experiences with those of story characters
3. Telling stories and illustrating these by using various types of props:
   a. The flannel board
   b. Puppets
   c. Teacher-learner constructed "movies"
4. Calling attention to stories or poems by attractive bulletin board displays, preferably with built-in provisions for learner participation
5. Using recorded stories and music to provide experiences in listening
6. Creating "experience stories" with learners' participation
7. Engaging learners in discussion and interpretation of pictures
8. Permitting learners to supply missing endings to stories
9. Arranging attractive displays of picture books; encouraging learners to discuss favorite books

Improving Learners' Concepts of Reading

Little can be accomplished in attempting to help learners develop a concept of what it means to read by telling them what reading is. Much can be accomplished, however, by utilizing indirect means such as the

---

[31] E. B. Linehan, "Early Instruction in Letter Names and Sounds as Related to Success in Beginning Reading." Unpublished Doctoral Dissertation, Boston University, 1957.

following to lead learners to their own understanding of the meaning of reading.
1. Constructing and reading experience stories (individual and group work)
2. Oral reading by the teacher, followed by discussion with learners
3. Oral reading to the class, followed by activities encouraging learners to illustrate parts of the story
4. Using "listening posts" in the classroom: let children use earphones and listen as a recorded story is read and encourage learners to follow illustrations and words in the book as the story is read
5. Provide various experiences in which learners are led to recognize relationships between printed words and phrases and the spoken words
6. Provide associations between a learner and his name; objects and their names; furnishings and areas in the classroom with appropriate labels
7. Have learners "read" pictures; tell what is happening in the picture; discuss characters in the picture
8. Use techniques, such as construction of "helpers'" charts, calendars, weather charts, and the like, to call attention to meanings of printed expressions.

Developing Language Ability
Both concepts and varied opportunities for oral use of language are required in development of language ability. Numerous real and vicarious experiences should be provided for building concepts and for using these in oral expression of various types.
1. Provide real experiences and relate aspects of these with appropriate words, phrases, sentences
2. Follow real experiences with appropriate discussion
3. Construct and use experience stories in discussion
4. Use techniques that emphasize dramatic expression; acting out nursery rhymes, stories, familiar events, favorite characters
5. Use experiences designed to emphasize sensory awareness: "tasting" parties, "feeling boxes," listening games, followed always by appropriate discussion
6. Ask questions related to ideas and activities with which children are familiar and to which they can respond freely
7. Play games requiring learners to follow oral directions

Developing Skills in Visual Discrimination
Training in visual discrimination can be accomplished through use of various activities that require learners to make increasingly finer and finer discriminations. Activities such as the following often are used as part of the program designed to improve learners' abilities to make the kinds of discriminations required in the act of reading.
1. Present charts or other materials to learners on which appear rows of uppercase letters all of which are the same except in one instance. Instruct learners to identify the one letter in each row that is different from the others. Begin by using a letter that differs grossly from others in a particular row. Move gradually to use of a "different" letter that tends to be very similar to others in the row.

$$\begin{array}{cccccc} D & D & D & D & D & Y & \quad (Y) \\ A & A & A & A & B & A & \quad (B) \\ E & E & F & E & E & E & \quad (F) \end{array}$$

2. Again, using charts or other appropriate materials, present words or phrases in the same manner as above.

BOY, BOY, TREE, BOY   (TREE)

AM, AM, AM, AS, AM   (AS)

AM, AM, AN, AM, AM   (AN)

RUN TO THE STORE. ⎫

BRING THE BOOK. ⎬   (BRING THE BOOK.)

RUN TO THE STORE. ⎭

SIT DOWN. STAND UP. SIT DOWN.   (STAND UP)

3. Circle the word that is different in each row.

go: go, go, run

see: to, see, to

4. Mark an "X" over each word in the row that begins the same as the first word in the row.

		X	X						
Made	Four	Mine	Me	After	The	See	To	Am	

	X		X		X				
Boy	Be	Toy	Bow	Wow	By	See	Me	You	So

	X		X				X		
See	Show	Yes	So	Too	This	Coat	Some	To	

5. Draw a line from the word in the first list that begins the same as the word in the second list.

boy   they

baby   box

tree   by

see   so

Improving Experiential Background of Learners

The experiential backgrounds that learners bring to formal reading instruction can be augmented through experiences provided during the initial readiness period. Basically, experiences useful in the improvement of background needed for reading will emphasize variety and reality as learners are repeatedly exposed to ideas they are being helped to develop. Generally, trips, experiences with different types of realia, use of audiovisual aids, and other media can be used to focus learners' attention toward and increase their interest in particular concepts desirable for improving the quality of their reading experiences. In order to maximize the effectiveness of any experiences to which learners are brought for improvement of backgrounds needed for reading, the purpose of the experience must be clarified. Deliberate efforts must be made to build and utilize vocabulary related to the experiences. Provisions must be made for continuity of experiences and recognition of relationships between them if they are to be effective in improving concepts held by learners.

Developing Auditory Discrimination Abilities

Generally, in order to improve learners' abilities to make auditory discriminations of speech sounds essential in recognition of relationships between symbols used in the writing system and speech, activities should focus on these relationships. Learners should be repeatedly and consistently engaged in situations that require them to make finer and finer discriminations between closely related sounds.

1. Use activities that help children hear and identify rhyming sounds:
   a. Pronounce a series of words, all of which rhyme except one. Children identify the word that is different.

   > ring, sing, bring, give, wing
   > red, bed, fed, led, true

   b. Pronounce several pairs of words, all of which rhyme with each other except one pair. Children identify odd pair.

   > ring, sing   ball, call
   > bring, thing   fall, hall
   > lead, speed   chair, hair

   c. Recite two-line rhymes. Omit the last word in the second line. Children supply the missing word.

   > It is a pretty day.
   > Let us go outside to _____.

   d. Recite nursery rhymes. Have children supply the missing last line.

   > Little Bo Peep has lost her sheep
   > And can't tell where to find them.
   > Leave them alone, and they will come home
   > _____

2. Have children identify words that begin with the same sound.
   a. Pronounce a series of words that begin with the same sound. Include one word that is different. Children identify word that is different.

   > baby, bone, bat, bird, table
   > sit, so, shall, show, took, sign

   b. Pronounce a series of words that begin with the same sound. Children supply other words that begin with the same sound.
   c. Group pictures of objects that begin with the same sound. Include a picture of an object whose name begins with a different sound. Children identify object that begins with a different sound.
3. Identify words that end with the same sound.
   a. Pronounce a series of words that end with the same sound, except in the case of one word. Children identify the word ending with the odd sound.

   > pet, bit, sit, sand
   > moon, spoon, turn, up

4. Identify words that vary in length.
   a. Pronounce a series of two-syllable words. Include a one-syllable word and have learners identify the odd word.

Developmental Readiness for Reading

As learners develop higher levels of competence in reading, the need for attention to readiness does not end. Just as initial readiness influences an individual's chances for gaining from formal instruction in reading, developmental readiness affects the efficiency and effectiveness with which higher skills and more difficult concepts will be achieved. Several factors of readiness continue to be important at subsequent levels of a learner's development.

Needs unique to an individual suggest clues to what types of experiences he or she may need in order to build readiness for a phase of reading instruction. Generally, however, attention must be given to an individual's (1) sight vocabulary, (2) flexibility and competence in the use of decoding skills, (3) conceptual development, (4) ability to handle complex styles of writing, (5) study skills, and (6) attitudes, interests, and motivations.

Continuous Development of a Sight Vocabulary

Often when reference is made to development of a sight vocabulary, the meaning refers to the few words a beginner is expected to recognize by sight before he is faced with development of word-analysis skills. Too little attention is given to the continued importance of a sight vocabulary as a learner proceeds in development in reading, the nature of an individual's sight vocabulary affects the competency, efficiency, and rate of his reading.

Concern for development of an adequate sight vocabulary at levels subsequent to initial formal instruction in reading must focus on far more than whether the reader has acquired recognition of a few structure words or basic words frequently used in narrative writing. From the intermediate grades onward, a wide variety of types of materials must be read by learners. An adequate sight vocabulary for learners at these levels must consist of recognition of words from many — often widely divergent — sources. Words related to various content areas of the curriculum, periodicals, and supplementary instructional materials are only a few of the sources learners are faced with. Reading for these learners will not be effective if an inordinate amount of time and effort must be devoted to word analysis.

Flexibility and Ease in the Use of Decoding Skills

In initial reading readiness, efforts are made to help learners develop many skills, including those related to auditory and visual discrimination. Development of these abilities helps to establish a learner's readiness for more sophisticated skills of decoding. Readiness for reading materials required as learners progress through the schools includes development of abilities to select and use the skills of decoding that are appropriate to whatever reading task is at hand. Increasing complexity characterizes the styles of writing and nature of words learners confront. Figurative language, various types of illustrations, charts, diagrams, maps, graphs — all increase demands on the reader for flexible use of many different methods of decoding.

Readiness for Development of Study Skills

Readiness for use of various study skills often depends on mastery of particular subskills related to a major skill. For example, use of the dictionary requires mastery of the ability to alphabetize and understand alphabetization. Selection of a pertinent meaning of a word from a group of various meanings provided in a dictionary requires appropriate use of the context in which the word appears in the materials being read. Making sure that learners develop mastery of subskills related to major skills is an aspect of developmental readiness of concern to teachers of reading.

Continued Growth of Concepts

Learners in the schools must deal with content that is growing more and more complex in terms of number and types of concepts encountered. Real as well as vicarious experiences must be provided continuously and their results discussed and related to concerns pertinent to the learners, so that meaning is achieved from reading. As developmental readiness, rather than initial readiness, becomes the concern, an increased amount of vicarious experience becomes essential in helping learners develop and maintain readiness for their reading experiences. Not only are older and more experienced readers able to profit by vicarious experience, but their broadened requirements, concerns, and perspectives make it essential.

Emphasis in Initial Development of Word-Recognition Skills

Reading involves use of both decoding skills and the abilities to think or to understand the meaning conveyed or implied by printed words, phrases, sentences, or other meaningful units of written or printed expression. Those skills used directly in translation of the printed code into its speech counterparts are known as decoding or word-recognition skills. Skills and abilities in understanding the meaning of printed or written expressions and selections are categorized as skills or abilities of comprehension. Since reading is more than preoccupation with translation of the printed code into speech sounds or words, skills of decoding cannot be separated, realistically, from those required in searching for and achieving meaning. At the same time, meaning cannot be acquired from reading unless the printed code is broken and its references understood. In a broad sense, decoding involves both (1) conversion of printed symbols into speech sounds represented and (2) perception and understanding of the meanings represented by speech sounds in the patterns of expressions in which they are used.

For analysis only, decoding skills may be separated from those required for comprehension of meaning. For the same purpose, skills of decoding emphasized in beginning reading instruction may be considered separately from those emphasized during subsequent stages of reading instruction. Decoding skills in reading cannot be graded as such, but they can be considered developmental in nature. Skills in decoding taught to beginners in reading differ from those emphasized in later instruction only in terms of aspects emphasized, not in kind. Skills introduced during initial instruction in reading later become more refined and more complex in ways they are used.

Areas of emphasis in initial development of decoding skills relate to skills of concern during initial reading readiness and to those emphasized during subsequent stages of reading instruction. Among areas of decoding skills emphasized during initial reading instruction are (1) development of sight words, (2) recognition of phonic elements and patterns, (3) use of contextual clues, and (4) development of structural analysis skills.

Recognition of Words by Sight

Helping learners develop a basic vocabulary of words whose forms are recognized merely by sight is a basic concern during initial reading instruction. This term *sight words* refers to a basic stock of words recognized by the reader instantaneously and automatically without use of word-analysis skills as an aid to recognition. Automatic and rapid recognition of words is required for all efficient and effective reading. Acquisition of a stock of sight words is especially advantageous for the beginning reader.

Among advantages in development of a basic stock of sight words by a beginning reader are several fairly obvious ones. The learner can be helped to develop, simultaneously, a concept of what reading actually means. Having command of some sight words gives the learner confidence brought on by a sense of early accomplishment and often has motivational value for further learning. Sight words provide a basis for subsequent development of skills in word analysis essential for decoding words unfamiliar in print later encountered in reading.

Several principles should be observed in efforts to help young learners develop the ability to recognize words in print. Words introduced for the purpose should be words whose meanings are understood by the learner. Only the printed form of each word may be unfamiliar. These are words the learner himself has used and understood when they have been used by others. Words stressed in development of sight vocabulary generally are those found in widely used word lists and in the unique vocabularies of a particular group of learners.

Varied types of techniques are used to present the printed forms of words to learners and to relate these to their speech counterparts and meanings. Generally, the printed froms of words are presented in some form of meaningful context. Such contexts for presenting words include phrases, sentences, paragraphs, pictures, experience charts, oral discussion, and the like.

Among techniques useful in helping learners develop a stock of basic sight words are those requiring (1) careful scrutiny of the word, (2) association of the printed form of the word with the object or idea it represents, (3) visual memory of words, and (4) relating words to actual experiences of the learners. All of these techniques are interrelated and interdependent. Most of these are used simultaneously or in mutually reinforcing ways in order to increase learners' familiarity with the printed forms of words.

Through the same types of activities utilized to help in development of a basic sight vocabulary, many other skills essential in reading can be emphasized. Left-to-right orientation to the page, to a chart, or to a chalkboard presentation of reading selections, for example, can be emphasized as the teacher demonstrates the principle in work with the learners.

Some specific techniques that can aid in development of ability to recognize words by sight include the following:

1. Label objects in the classroom — such as doors, window, chalkboard, easel — making sure that learners recognize the relationship between the printed form of the name and the spoken word.
2. Focus a learner's attention on the printed form of his name and the printed forms of the names of others in the class. Place each child's name on a tagboard strip so that he has ready reference to it for the many uses he may wish to make of it.
3. Utilize children's experiences and their oral expression in construction of experience stories. Be sure each learner sees the relationship between his oral expression and its graphic representation. Provide many opportunities for learners to read the story, talk about it, use the sentences and words in many different ways.

> *Our Trip to the Zoo*
> Yesterday we went to the zoo.
> We saw all kinds of animals.
> The elephants were very big.
> The giraffes were very tall.
> We had fun at the zoo.
> Gerald's mother went to the zoo, too.*

4. Cut out the sentences in an experience story. Have children put these in order.
5. Reconstruct an experience story from words and phrases cut out of the original chart.
6. Keep bulletin board displays timely and relevant to daily news in the class, the weather, birthdays, holidays, and other events important in the lives of learners in the class.
7. Provide sensory experiences; relate children's reactions with appropriate words.
8. Use lists of words on charts or in other places conveniently available to learners to be used as needed in their own written expression.
9. Encourage learners to "tell" stories through their own original drawings or other art illustrations and through dictating one-sentence stories to be printed by the teacher.
10. Consistently focus children's attention on structure words and their uses in various forms of written expression.
11. Have learners collect pictures and construct picture dictionaries.
12. Present words through various multisensory approaches in order to accommodate various learning styles preferred by learners in the group.
13. Call attention to unique features of shapes of words.
14. Provide experiences that permit learners to classify or categorize objects and pictures and their names.
15. Devise and use word games; play commercially available word games.
16. Be consistent in providing numerous and varied experiences that bring learners into contact with words and their meanings.

Phonic Elements and Patterns

Foundations are laid for helping learners develop abilities for using phonics as a decoding aid during initial reading readiness activities and initial instruction in reading. Auditory and visual discrimination

---

*Experience story taken from a chart in a first-grade classroom.

abilities and skills are related directly to skills required in phonics analysis. Many of the same techniques used to make learners conscious of similarities and differences in printed words and in the sounds of speech elements during the readiness period are continued during initial formal instruction in reading. Efforts to sensitize learners to the use of phonic elements and patterns usually accompany efforts to develop a basic sight vocabulary.

Phonic elements and patterns can be described as those letters (graphemes) and combinations of letters representative of speech sounds and used to aid in word-recognition. Phonic elements stressed during initial instruction in reading include consonants and various types of consonant combinations — such as blends and digraphs — and vowels and vowel combinations — such as digraphs and diphthongs.

Specific techniques for introducing learners to use of phonic elements and patterns as initial skills in decoding are included in manuals and guides designed to accompany use of core materials for the teaching of reading. Each school or school system generally provides the teacher with basic or core materials related to the particular approach to reading selected for use in a specific situation. In many cases, techniques described in manuals or guides are followed closely by teachers using that approach adopted in the school. There is no basic content or specific set of teaching strategies that can be recommended for use by all teachers in all instructional situations. Generally, however, introduction and development of skills related to phonic elements and patterns in reading instruction should be based on guidelines such as those discussed in the remainder of this section.

Inductive methods are usually preferable to deductive ones for introducing learners to the use of phonic elements and patterns as word-recognition aids. Inductive methods stress giving learners a variety of experiences in the use of a skill and helping them to realize a generalization as a result of the experiences. Deductive methods, on the other hand, stress first the learning of a generalization followed by examples of that generalization in practice. For example, an inductive approach taken to helping learners recognize similarities in words beginning with the same consonant requires (1) presenting learners with several examples of words that begin with the same sound:

<table>
<tr><td>boy</td><td>boat</td></tr>
<tr><td>be</td><td>been</td></tr>
<tr><td>by</td><td>bow</td></tr>
</table>

and (2) encouraging learners to discover that all the words in the list begin with the letter "b," and, thus, all begin alike—with the speech sound represented by "b."

A deductive approach to teaching use of the same element would begin by first helping learners become aware of the speech sound represented by "b," after which attention would be focused on examples of words that begin with the sound.

Early during phonics instruction, learners are helped to utilize the skill known as phonic element substitution. Phonic element substitution involves (1) substituting initial elements of words in order to form new words of the remaining parts, or (2) forming new words by changing the remainder of a word rather than its beginning element. For example,

1. When a given word is known and the correct sounds associated with other consonants that can be applied, new words can be formed by merely changing the initial element:

dog	ball	day
bog	call	bay
cog	fall	lay
fog	hall	say

2. Or, in the opposite type of substitution, other words can be formed by holding the initial phonic element constant and changing the endings of the word.

fun	fill
fan	fall
fin	fell

Phonics instruction can be initiated by focusing first on either consonants and the sounds these represent or on vowels and the sounds to which they refer. In the majority of instructional systems used in classroom instruction, attention is first given to consonants. Heilman states several reasons for this:

1. A large number of words in beginning reading begin with consonants.
2. Beginning phonic analysis with beginning sounds of words encourages the practice of reading from left-to-right and focuses the learner's attention on the first part of the word. Both of these practices are essential in effective reading.
3. Sounds represented by consonants are more consistent than those represented by vowels.[32]

Auditory Blending

Auditory blending involves synthesizing separate sounds in a word into the total sound of the whole word. Auditory blending becomes extremely important when a synthetic approach to phonics instruction is used. (Synthetic approaches are deductive in nature and require teaching letters and the sounds these represent first and then synthesizing the sounds into words. Analytic methods are inductive, requiring the learner first to analyze groups of words in order to determine phonic elements that are common to all the words under consideration.) For instance, auditory blending becomes a necessity when each part of the word "cat" is "sounded out"—"cuh," "aah," "tuh." These sounds must be synthesized or blended before the word "cat" is pronounced.

Contextual Clues

The use of contextual clues in decoding is introduced to learners during initial reading instruction. Using contextual clues involves arriving at the pronunciation of a word on the basis of the meaning of the selection in which the word exists. Beginners in reading can be helped to identify the printed form of words with which they have had previous experience, but for which recognition is not automatic and instantaneous, by calling their attention to contextual clues. Contextual clues may be found in printed verbal materials, oral expression, pictorial materials, actual experience, and the like.

Generally, learners are taught to use contextual clues at the same time they are taught to use other methods of decoding. Contextual clues, used alone, have many

---

[32] Arthur Heilman, *Phonics in Proper Perspective* (Columbus, Ohio: Charles E. Merrill, 1964), p. 15.

limitations for word recognition. The relations of learners' previous experiences with those under consideration in a reading selection are critical determinants of the successful use of contextual clues for decoding purposes. In initial instruction in the use of contextual clues, techniques are used to encourage learners to listen for clues to word meanings in spoken sentences, in the verbal context of printed words, in pictures used along with presentation of a word, and in exercises to teach learners to recognize antonyms and synonyms.

Structural Analysis Skills in Beginning Reading

Recognizing a word by analyzing its parts is known as structural analysis. Beginners in reading can be helped to note structural changes in words early during initial instruction in reading. Some of these skills emphasized in initial reading instruction include (1) helping children to notice what happens to the pronunciation and meaning of words when inflectional endings such as "s," "es," "ed," and "ing" are added; (2) noting and understanding how compound words are formed; and (3) scrutinizing the parts of a compound word in order to recognize the whole word. Skills in structural analysis generally are taught simultaneously with the teaching of skills in phonic analysis.

Approaches to Initial Reading Instruction

There is widespread agreement that an important aspect of initial reading instruction involves helping learners begin development of use of decoding skills. There is less agreement regarding the best type of approach for helping learners develop the kinds of skills and abilities needed in reading. The basic question, often raised, concerns whether an approach that emphasizes meaning in reading or one that emphasizes breaking the printed code should be used during initial reading instruction. Many research efforts have been directed toward discovery of evidence which would clearly indicate the proper emphasis for beginning instruction in reading.

In 1967, Jeanne Chall concluded on the basis of her analysis of research in reading from 1912 to 1965 that a code-emphasis approach in which direct and intensive efforts are focused early on decoding produces better results from reading instruction than approaches which place primary emphasis on meaning. According to Chall, "The evidence indicates that better results in terms of reading for meaning are achieved with the programs that emphasize code at the start than with programs that stress meaning at the beginning."[33] Chall stated further, "My recommendation for a methods change does not apply to all pupils. Some pupils may have a unique or uncommon way of learning. Insisting on one method for all may complicate things further."[34]

Rather than settling the debate, the results reported by Chall served to stimulate further attention to the relative importance of code-emphasis and meaning-

---

[33] Jeanne Chall, *Learning to Read: The Great Debate* (N. Y.: McGraw-Hill, 1967), p. 307.
[34] Chall, *Learning to Read: The Great Debate*, p. 309.

emphasis approaches in initial reading instruction. Purposes of the nationwide First Grade Reading Study sponsored by the United States Office of Education included that of determining which of numerous approaches to initial reading instruction produces better results in reading achievement at the end of first grade. Results of the study seemed to favor approaches that stress code-emphasis for beginning reading instruction. The final report included the statement: "From the evidence reported concerning the use of phonics in teaching children to read earlier, there can be little doubt that phonics should be an important part of the reading program. However, there is disagreement on the type of phonic approach which should be used and on the amount of phonics which should be included in the reading program."[35]

Results from these and other major studies focused on the issue have not resolved the matter conclusively. Some uncertainty still exists regarding whether emphasis in beginning reading should be on deciphering the code or on understanding meaning through a whole-word approach as a first concern during initial reading instruction. Approaches favoring a code-emphasis during initial reading instruction have proliferated, however, and many traditional basal-reader approaches that once emphasized attention to whole words and to meaning have undergone changes that reflect increased balance between code-emphasis and meaning aspects of reading.

Agreement does exist among authorities that no one approach can be considered best for all learners in all situations at all times. Many factors about the particular learners involved must be considered in determining an effective approach for initial reading instruction. The nature and needs of particular learners must be taken into consideration in determining how emphasis in beginning reading should be placed. In practice, whether a meaning or a code-emphasis approach is utilized, attention must be given to both the decoding and meaning aspects of reading.

The Developmental Nature of Reading Skills

Acquiring skills in reading is a developmental process for an individual. While there is no definite point at which an individual's development in reading suddenly changes from one level to another, it is true that competence in major skills often depends upon achievement of related subskills. For example, instantaneous recognition of sight words requires the ability to make appropriate visual discriminations. Ability to use skills of phonics for decoding depends upon ability to make appropriate auditory discriminations. Skill in critical reading begins first with ability to understand the literal meaning of a selection.

---

[35] Guy L. Bond and Robert Dykstra, *Final Report Project No. X 001* (Washington, D. C.: Bureau of Research, Office of Education, U. S. Department of Health, Education, and Welfare, 1967), p. 41.

Reading is a complex process involving many interrelated subskills and skills rather than consisting of use of one general ability. Competence in any aspect of reading whether that of decoding or comprehension depends on acquisition of many different basic skills upon which skills at higher levels depend.

The developmental nature of reading should be considered from the standpoint of the individual rather than from the standpoint of requirements for a particular grade level in school. The arbitrary grade-level assignments of the schools along with materials established, traditionally, for use at particular grade levels have caused expectations that particular skills and concepts are to be taught at particular levels or grades in the schools. This conception is augmented, as well, by some texts used in the preparation of teachers, in which skills in reading are categorized according to grade levels. In view of this, learners at a particular grade level often are expected to do the work relegated to that grade level, rather than that which may be suitable to their levels of achievement.

Skills learners are expected to acquire as evidence of initial readiness for reading instruction are related integrally to those in which development is sought during initial reading instruction. Basic skills emphasized during initial reading instruction are the same as those of concern at subsequent levels of instruction. As learners develop maturity and experience, emphasis on complexity of skills—not on the nature of the skills—changes.

Basic Word-Recognition Skills

Although numerous skills are involved, basic skills in word recognition can be categorized into four major types. Such a categorization is useful for it gives the teacher a framework in which to place the numerous skills involved, rather than trying to think of every specific skill.

Major categories of word-recognition skills include (1) configuration, (2) phonics analysis, (3) structural analysis, and (4) use of the context. For the purpose of analysis, each of these categories of skills can be considered separately. In practice, a learner must be helped to develop flexibility in use of the skills, and ability to use these simultaneously, if necessary, in the act of reading.

Recognizing Words by Their Configuration

Although limited in applicability, configuration can be identified as a category of skills used in word recognition. Configuration, as a category of word-recognition skills, includes those skills essential for closely scrutinizing a word and recognizing it by its shape and appearance. Since differences in the shapes of many words are frequently very slight, configuration clues cannot be depended upon in many cases. Several specific skills of configuration can be described.

1. Scrutinizing a word carefully in order to become familiar with its general shape; outlining the shape of the word for emphasis

    dog   mother   father

2. Observing striking characteristics of a word

   m a t t e r   tt   (double letters)
   l o o k   oo

3. Observing the length of a word

   g r a n d f a t h e r   b a b y

4. Observing that two or more words comprise a single word

   farm   yard   farmyard
   toy   land   toyland

Recognizing a word by its configuration involves associating the word with a particular shape or a set of special features. Many times a word is recognized by associating it with other types of stimuli. Other types of stimuli may consist of a concrete object, a sensory impression, an idea, and the like. Anytime a word is recognized by relating it to a stimulus, some type of association technique is being used. Many teaching techniques for strengthening learners' memories for particular words are based on association. Some of these include:

1. Using games that require the learner to match a word with an object, a picture, etc.
2. Identifying objects in the classroom by labels
3. Associating a word with a sensory impression such as taste, touch, etc.
4. Matching a word with its counterpart in an experience story

Recognizing Words by Applying Phonics Skills

Skills involving the use of phonics are of major importance in word recognition. So important do some teachers regard phonics that, inadvertently, they tend to equate phonics analysis with the actual act of reading. Lacking clear understanding of either the role or nature of phonics, many others tend to neglect appropriate attention to these skills.

The way in which the terms "phonics" and "phonetics" often are used interchangeably in the literature and by teachers suggests that an understanding of the role of phonics in reading necessitates, first of all, clarification of the meanings of these terms.

Differentiation between the meanings of "phonics" and "phonetics" helps to clarify the nature of the content included in each. Charles Fries has suggested that the term phonics is used to "represent the various sets of teaching practices that aim to develop the pupil's ability to sound out a word."[36] According to Arthur Heilman, " 'phonics' refers to a facet of reading instruction teaching speech sounds of letters and groups of letters in words."[37] These definitions emphasize the role of phonics as a part of phonetics selected to help develop reading ability. Focusing attention on the content of phonics as only that part of phonetics of particular interest in reading instruction simplifies the teacher's task. Phonetics, according to Fries "is a set of techniques by which to identify and describe, in absolute terms, all the differences of sound features that occur in any language."[38] Dealing with phonetics in a classroom situation in which reading instruction is of primary interest would be a formidable task. Clearly, the content and practices related to phonics are not synonymous with those of phonetics.

---

[36] Fries, *Linguistics and Reading*, p. 141.

[37] Heilman, *Phonics in Proper Perspective*, p. 2.

[38] Fries, *Linguistics and Reading*, p. 150.

Application of phonics skills is only one of several ways by which printed words can be decoded. Skills of phonics can be applied to many, but not to all, problems in decoding. Some words are more effectively and efficiently analyzed for purposes of recognition by skills other than those involving the use of phonics.

Generally, the content of phonics consists of (1) phonics skills, (2) the sequence in which these are developed, and (3) generalizations related to uses of phonics.

Phonics skills involve relating letters and combinations of letters to the speech sounds these represent. Twenty-six letters comprise the English alphabet. Used singly or in combinations these represent more than forty sounds in the English language. Sensitizing learners to these relationships and helping them acquire skills essential for using the relationships in the process of word recognition is a major task in reading instruction. Since there are many inconsistencies and irregularities in the correspondence between the alphabet and the speech sounds represented, the task is not simple.

Specifically, phonics skills include relating single consonants, combinations of consonants, single vowels, and combinations of vowels to the sounds represented. Instructional procedures focus on helping learners apply skills in recognition of:

1. Single consonants and the sounds represented (consonants in initial, final, and medial positions in words)
2. Consonant blends and the sounds represented (two or three consonants blended so that each is heard in the sound produced — e.g., st, gr, br, str, tch, etc.)
3. Consonant digraphs and the sounds represented (two consonant sounds blended to produce a completely new sound different from that represented by either of the two consonants involved — e.g., sh, wh, th, or nk, ng, ck, qu, etc.)
4. Consonant irregularities
5. Silent consonants
6. Short and long vowels and the sounds represented
7. Vowel digraphs and the sounds represented (two vowels representing one speech sound — e.g., ee, oo, ai, oa, ei, etc.)
8. Vowel diphthongs and the sounds represented (two vowels almost blended to represent one speech sound — e.g., oi, oy, ou, ow, etc.)
9. Short and long vowels modified by certain consonants
10. Silent vowels
11. Syllabication

Sequence in which phonics skills should be developed has not been determined authoritatively. Clearly, however, certain skills related to phonics must be developed prior to development of others. For instance, skills in auditory and visual discrimination must precede development of higher skills which depend on these abilities. Ideally, the sequence of skills that should be taught to an individual would depend on the unique needs and abilities of that individual. Practically, sequence for the development of phonics skills for learners in a particular situation is often suggested by, and dependent on, the nature of the instructional program in use in that situation. While the teacher in the classroom generally must arrive at a sequence on the basis of knowledge of the learners and the materials in use in the particular situation, the following is offered as representative of many suggestions made for sequence of development of phonics skills:

1. Development of auditory and visual discrimination ability
2. Teaching of consonants and the sounds represented (consonants that represent only one sound generally are taught first)

3. Consonant blends (a) at the beginning of words, (b) at the ends of words, and (c) in the medial position in words
4. Consonant digraphs
5. Short vowel sounds (usually in trigraphs — e.g., bat, bet, bit, etc.)
6. Long vowel sounds (b<u>a</u>ke, b<u>i</u>te, etc.)
7. Silent letters (<u>k</u>nife, <u>w</u>rite, <u>g</u>nat, <u>h</u>our, etc.)
8. Vowels modified when followed by r, l, u, etc. (e.g., ar, er, or, etc.; al, all, aw, au, etc.)
9. Vowel digraphs
10. Diphthongs
11. Syllabication

Syllabication is the process of analyzing a word by dividing it into its pronounceable units. A syllable is a pronounceable unit consisting of a group of letters containing a sounded vowel, or a sounded vowel alone. While syllabication involves phonics skills, it involves structural analysis skills as well.

As a word-recognition skill, syllabication includes both analysis of a word into its pronounceable units and blending or synthesizing the units to produce the correct pronunciation of the word. Correct pronunciation of a word also involves knowledge and skill related to the correct placement of emphasis or accent. Several generalizations govern the correct division of a word and synthesis of the parts to produce the pronunciation of the complete word correctly accented.

In beginning reading instruction, learners are helped to understand syllabication through informal techniques designed to increase their consciousness of the sounded parts of words. Beginning readers are gradually led to the realization that a word has as many syllables as it has sounded vowels. Students practice identification of the number of sounds heard in a word as it is pronounced. They are then led to recognize the relationships between the printed form of a word and the number of syllables heard in the word. Care must be taken to avoid leading children to think that for every vowel seen in a word there is a syllable or sounded part. Of course, beginners in reading should have mastered recognition of the relationships between vowels and consonants and the sounds these represent before they are expected to deal with syllabication in a formal sense.

Numerous generalizations relate to the correct division of words into syllables, yet a relatively few govern ordinary usage of the skill. Mastery of the following generalizations can enable a learner to solve many problems associated with recognition of a word on the basis of its syllables.

1. *Generally, a word includes as many syllables as there are vowel sounds heard in the word.* The number of vowel sounds heard in a word is not necessarily the same as the number of vowels seen in the printed form of the word. ("bat" — one sound heard, one-syllable word; "receive" — two vowel sounds heard, although four vowels are seen in the printed word).
2. *When two consonants occur together in a word, division of the word is usually between the two consonants.*

cattle	cat	tle
pencil	pen	cil
butter	but	ter
little	lit	tle

3. *A word containing a single consonant occurring between two vowels is usually divided between the first vowel and the consonant.*

around	a	round
before	be	fore
because	be	cause

4. *Consonant digraphs and consonant blends are not divided.*

feather	fea(th)	er
rocket	ro(ck)	et
singer	si(ng)	er

5. *Words containing "le" preceded by a consonant generally divide in such a way that the consonant goes with "le."*

fable	fa	ble
noble	no	ble
startle	star	tle
ladle	la	dle
fiddle	fid	dle

6. *Prefixes and suffixes constitute syllables either before or after the root word and so are not divided.*

preview	pre	view	
review	re	view	
unclear	un	clear	
clearly	clear	ly	
softly	soft	ly	
unlikely	un	like	ly

Phonics generalizations comprise a third major category of phonics content to which attention must be given during instruction. Generalizations related to phonics uses are guidelines, subject to varying degrees of utility in many cases. Results of several studies have highlighted the varying degrees of utility of various phonic generalizations. One of the earliest studies concerned with the utility of phonics generalizations was that by Theodore Clymer.[39] Clymer selected forty-five generalizations and counted the number of examples that could be found in the word lists of several widely used primary-level basal reading series. Wide variation was found both in the number and types of generalizations applicable to words used in the basal readers examined. Emans examined the usefulness of phonics generalizations in materials used beyond the third grade.[40] Focusing on the same concern, Bailey examined materials used throughout the elementary grades.[41] Results of each of these studies showed that wide variation exists in the degrees to which phonics generalizations are useful in helping learners deal with instructional materials used in elementary schools.

Some phonics generalizations found by all three of the above-mentioned investigators to have 100 percent utility included the following:

1. When "c" precedes "o" or "a" in a word, the "c" is the sound of "k" (as in coal, care, cast, cart).

---

[39] Theodore Clymer, "The Utility of Phonics Generalizations in the Primary Grades," *The Reading Teacher*, 16 (January, 1963), pp. 252–58.

[40] Robert Emans, "The Usefulness of Phonics Generalizations Above the Third Grade," *The Reading Teacher*, 20 (February, 1967), pp. 419–25.

[41] Mildred Hart Bailey, "The Utility of Phonics Generalizations in Grades One Through Six," *The Reading Teacher*, 20 (February, 1967), pp. 413–18.

2. When "c" and "h" occur together in a word, they produce one sound (change, chime, chair).
3. When "ght" appear together in a word, the "gh" is silent (night, caught, sight).
4. When a word begins with "kn," the "k" is silent (knight, knife).
5. When a word begins wtih "wr" the "w" is silent (wrist, wrinkle, write).
6. When "tion" appears as the last syllable in a word, it is unaccented (notion, station).
7. As a final syllable in a word, "ture" is unaccented (puncture, furniture, future, nature).

Among phonic generalizations found by all three researchers to have high utility (although not 100 percent) are the following:
1. A vowel occurring in the middle of a one-syllable word usually is short (bad, bed, bid, lot, cup).
2. In words in which vowel digraphs occur, the first vowel usually is long and the second vowel is silent (maid, each, boat, fruit).
3. In words where double "e" occurs, the lone "e" sound is heard (beet, feet, meet).
4. In words where "ay" occurs, the "y" is silent and the sound represented by long "a" is heard (day, gray, spray, tray, say).
5. When two of the same consonants occur together, the sound of only one is heard (bull, drill, sill, fill, buff, butt).
6. The sound of "c" when followed by "e" or "i" is likely to be "s" (cell, cite, ceiling, city).

Some of the phonics generalizations found by each of the investigators cited to have little usefulness, relatively, included the following:
1. When "y" or "ey" occurs in a last syllable that is unaccented, the long sound represented by "e" is heard (money, turkey).
2. When "y" is used as a vowel in words, it sometimes represents the same sound as that referred to by "i" (by, ally, sty).

Knowledge of phonics generalizations is useful in helping teachers determine those upon which emphasis should be placed during instruction. Learners should be led inductively to knowledge of those that are significant in improving their techniques of word recognition.

Guidelines for Phonics Instruction

Instructional practices related to phonics should be based on several important guidelines. Among these are the following:
1. Make sure that each learner expected to learn and use phonics skills has developed essential skills and abilities related to auditory and visual discriminations. If an individual cannot differentiate between closely related speech sounds and identify symbols of written expression related to these sounds, he will be unable to profit from instruction in phonics.
2. Teach phonics as *one*, but not the *only*, means for aiding word recognition. Phonics analysis should be regarded as a tool, among other tools, that can be used to facilitate word recognition.
3. Emphasize only those specific skills and generalizations related to phonics that are useful for developing independence in word recognition.
4. Teach essential phonics generalizations functionally, not as isolated elements to be learned for their own sake.

5. Avoid emphasizing phonics analysis to the extent the learners involved develop the erroneous concept that reading and phonics analysis are the same.
6. Use knowledge about particular learners — including their needs, competencies in reading, learning styles, and the like, as a basis for selecting phonics content to be stressed in their programs of instruction.
7. Undergird instructional practices in phonics with a thorough knowledge of the content of phonics. Many sources are available for the purpose of helping teachers develop detailed knowledge of basic content in phonics.*

Skills in Structural Analysis

Structural analysis pertains to examination of the structure of a word and using the result of the analysis to determine the pronunciation and/or meaning of the word. Skills in this category are not to be confused with those categorized as skills used in recognition of a word by its configuration. Structural analysis involves examination of the inherent structure of a word, while skills of configuration focus only on the external shape or special features of the word. The skills of configuration and those of structural analysis differ in the nature of skills required to perform each and in their relative importance as aids to decoding.

Structural analysis requires analysis of the meaningful units of a word. Meaningful units of a word are those parts influencing not only the pronunciation, but the meaning of the word as well. Meaningful units include root words, prefixes, suffixes, inflectional endings, compounding of words and other variants and derivatives of a word.

Both phonics and structural-analysis skills are needed among the skills of a competent reader. Learners who favor a learning style that places stress on the visual modality may tend toward use of the structural-analysis skills in preference to those of phonics. Those whose learning styles are more auditory may tend to favor use of phonics skills. Regardless of the learning style favored, the nature of many words will require use of both types of skills to achieve word recognition.

Specific Content Related to Structural Analysis

The content of structural-analysis instruction includes many specific skills, generalizations, as well as some knowledge regarding possible sequence of the development of the skills involved. Some of the basic skills involved are (1) recognition of root words, (2) identification of affixes, their nature and meanings, (3) recognition and understanding of the meanings of inflectional endings, (4) recognition and understanding of the concept of compound words, and (5) recognition and understanding of the concept of contractions.

1. *Recognition of root words* (base words unchanged by affixes or inflectional endings).
2. *Identification of affixes, their nature, and meanings* (Affixes include (1) the prefix, a meaningful unit attached at the beginning of a word, and (2) the suffix, a mean-

---

*For examples, see Heilman, *Phonics in Proper Perspective*, and Wilson and Hall, *Programmed Word Attack for Teachers* listed in "Selected References" at the end of this chapter.

ingful unit attached at the end of a word. In either case, the affix affects the meaning of the words.)

Prefix	*Meaning*	*Example*
a-	in, at	alive
	on	asleep
be-	to make	befriend
bi-	double	bicycle
de-	out of, away	detour
tele-	afar	television
un-	not, opposite	unhappy
fore-	before	foreleg

Suffix	*Meaning*	*Example*
-able	capable of	breakable
-age	act of, cost of	passage postage
-ful	full of	helpful
-ness	state of being	happiness
-less	free from, lacking	worthless

3. *Recognition and understanding of inflectional endings and their meanings* Inflectional endings are attached at the ends of root words and indicate grammatical changes related to case, gender, mood, voice, number, tense, and person. For example:

case	boy	(nominative)
	boy's	(possessive)
tense	receive	(present)
	received	(past)
number	boy	(singular)
	boys	(plural)

4. *Recognition of compound words and understanding of the concept of compounding* Compound words consist of two or more words combined to form one word. The meaning of the word formed may be derived from a combination of the meanings of the words included, or it may be an original one different from that of either of the words used singly. For example:

farmyard, broadcast, underhand

Words already recognizable by a learner when they are encountered separately may appear to be unfamilar when combined to form a new word, until the learner is made aware of the concept of compounding.

5. *Recognition of contractions and understanding of their meanings* A contraction is an abbreviated form of two words combined to form one word. One or more letters omitted from the words involved are replaced with an apostrophe. For example,

does not doesn't

can not can't

Numerous specific skills are included in the general category of structural analysis skills. Those that should be emphasized in a particular program of instruction should be determined on the basis of the needs and characteristics of the learners.

Sequence for Developing
Structural-Analysis Skills

A specific scheme of order for development of skills related to structural analysis has not been rigidly and finally determined. Only guidelines can be offered, because taking into consideration the nature of particular learners is important. Generally, simpler skills should be developed prior to attempts at the development of more complex skills. For example, recognition of root words would have to precede effective work with prefixes and suffixes. Several guidelines, rather than specific directives, can be followed in determining an appropriate sequence for skill development in structural analysis for the purpose of word recognition.

1. Skills related to structural analysis should be sought deliberately and according to specific plans for their inclusion in the program of instruction. Although many skills of structural analysis may be "discovered" naturally by learners, their importance in reading is sufficient to merit deliberate — rather then incidental — attention in the program.
2. Words that are already in the speaking and meaning vocabularies of learners should form the basis of early work in structural analysis.
3. Words in the "sight vocabularies" of beginners in reading are useful for introducing basic and simple concepts and skills related to structural analysis.
4. New words to be analyzed, structurally, should be presented in an appropriate context, rather than as isolated units, as a general rule. Use of the context can be helpful in determining pronunciation and meanings of a word. The context serves, as well, as a means for checking the accuracy of recognition of a word by structural analysis. Furthermore, the use of context in conjunction with use of the skills of structural analysis helps to develop the concept that many different skills of word recognition can be used and are needed in effective reading.
5. Practices that encourage learners to find "little words" in "big words" should be used with caution. In the word "grandfather," for instance, numerous "little words" can be found, none of which contribute to the pronunciation or meaning of the word — "an," "fat," "and," "her," etc.
6. Learners should be helped to develop flexibility in use of skills in word recognition. Practices in instruction should not result in development of dependence on any one skill or type of skill as the only means of decoding. Learners should be taught how to use many skills and to use the most suitable and efficient means at their disposal for word recognition.
7. Generalizations govern use of inflectional endings, formation of compound words, attachment of affixes and other skills in structural analysis. Learners should be led to formulate and recognize pertinent generalizations after experiences with many examples of their applications.

Using the Context as a Means
of Word Recognition

Examination of a passage where an unrecognized word occurs in order to determine the pronunciation or meaning of the word requires skills in the use of contextual clues. Contextual clues can be used by a reader at any level of development. Those clues available and useful to a beginner in reading, however, are more limited and simpler than those that are useful to experienced readers. This is true only because advanced readers are more familiar with use of the technique, but also because they have wider experience. Experience related to what is being read is crucial in determining the effectiveness with which an individual can use contextual clues as aids to word recognition.

Use of contextual clues does not refer to one general skill but to several specific skills. Attention has been called to several types of contextual clues: of "definitions," in which the sentence in which the unknown word appears defines the unknown word; "experience," when the reader "discovers" the unknown word on the basis of his personal experience; "comparison," where the reader finds relationships between the unknown word and other pertinent words in the sentence; "synonym," where one relies on a synonym of the unknown word; "familiar-expression," in which knowledge of figurative language, idiomatic expressions, and the like is used to determine the unknown word; and "summary," in which the unknown word can be seen to summarize major ideas in the selection.[42]

Learners should be taught to use contextual clues for solving those problems in decoding that are not readily solved by use of skills of other types. Using contextual clues is not a matter of wildly guessing what a word might be. Learners should be taught to use other skills of word recognition to check the results they have achieved by using contextual clues for determining a word.

Linguistics' Influences on Development of Skills in Word Recognition

During the 1960s, ideas and practices advocated by several linguists first began to make a significant impact on reading instruction. Subsequently, the influence of linguistic science has continued to be a factor in reading instructional practices. This influence has permeated several specific concerns in reading instruction, including practices for developing techniques of word recognition.

Notable among linguistics researchers from whose works have stemmed implications for the teaching of reading were Leonard Bloomfield, Charles C. Fries, and Clarence L. Barnhart. In 1942, Bloomfield first advanced ideas to the effect that reading instruction should be structured and sequential, and that it should focus chiefly, on relationships between the basic sounds of language and the symbols used in their representation.[43] Later, Barnhart prepared and published materials based, largely, on the ideas advanced by Bloomfield.[44] Among these ideas were the following:

1. Language is primarily speech. Reading instruction should be based on the oral language acquired by the child during his preschool days.

---

[42] Constance McCullough, "Recognition of Context Clues in Reading," *Elementary English Review*, 22 (January, 1945), pp. 1–5.

Harris and Smith, *Reading Instruction Through Diagnostic Teaching*, p. 227.

[43] Leonard Bloomfield, "Linguistics and Reading," *Elementary English Review*, 19 (April, 1942), pp. 125–30; (May, 1942), pp. 183–86.

[44] Leonard Bloomfield and Clarence L. Barnhart, *Let's Read: A Linguistic Approach* (Detroit, Mich.: Wayne State University Press, 1961).

2. Word recognition should be taught according to sound patterns. Stress should be placed on the relationship between the sound of a word as spoken and the way it is written.

3. Reading instruction should start with phonic elements and simple words. Words should be presented in consistent, sequential patterns.

4. Simplest phonic elements are the short vowel sounds. Beginners in reading should be taught mastery of these and mastery of their graphic representations.

5. Long vowel sounds should be taught following mastery of short vowel sounds.

6. A large number of words that fit the CVC (consonant-vowel-consonant) pattern should be taught. After this, words consisting of the CVCV pattern should be taught.

7. Irregular sounds and patterns should be presented to the learner subsequent to mastery of regular patterns.

8. In beginning reading, the learner's immediate task is to break the code. English has an alphabetical writing system whose code can be easily broken if known and understood.

9. Language is systematic. It employs contrasting patterns that represent differences in meaning.

10. Emphasis during the readiness period should be placed on having children learn the alphabet, both upper- and lower-case letters. They should learn the names of the letters and the formation of graphemes (graphic symbols of the letters).

With some slight differences, related mainly to teaching procedures, Charles C. Fries advocated ideas similar to those stressed by Bloomfield and Barnhart. According to Fries, the beginning reader should not be asked to identify irregular words prior to mastery of those conforming to regular patterns. Reading instruction should begin with the simplest speech patterns which are also the most frequently encountered spelling patterns in the English language. Two major spelling patterns, CVC and CVCV, should be emphasized in beginning reading. Stress should be placed on the contrastive features of words—for example, fad, fade, or man, fan. Knowledge of the alphabet is an important aspect of reading readiness. Learners should develop high-speed responses to the written word through practice with regular phoneme-grapheme patterns.[45]

From the research and writings of linguists have come several changes and additions to terminology used to describe reading and practices in reading instruction. For instance, many of the following terms are now well-entrenched in the vocabulary related to reading and reading instruction:

Phoneme: Defined as the functional unit of speech sound, phoneme has become important to the relationships between speech sounds and their graphic representation. For instance, /b/ represents the speech sound or phoneme while b without the vertical lines is a graphic representation of the sound.

Code: The term "code" is used to indicate the written or printed representation of language (oral); written or printed material consists of a code that must be "broken," if read.

Decode: The term "decode" is used to describe the process of word recognition on the basis of sound-symbol correspondencies.

---

[45] Charles C. Fries, *Linguistics and Reading* (N. Y.: Holt, Rinehart and Winston, 1962).

Allophones: Allophones are subclasses of sounds comprising phonemes. (Speech sounds in words often depend upon their position in the word, rather than upon a specific sound that is always the same regardless of position as /p/ in "put" and in "upon.")

Minimal pairs: Two words that differ from each other by only one phoneme are known as "minimal pairs" as for example, can, man; rat, cat.

Method of contrast: A method for identification of phonemes by comparing and contrasting minimal pairs.

Many approaches to beginning reading implement ideas promoted by linguists in emphatic and direct ways. These are identified as linguistic approaches to reading. Several examples of these approaches are identified in Appendix B of this text.

Several implications for development of skills needed for word recognition are the result of ideas and practices advocated by linguists who have taken an active interest in reading instruction. These include placing emphasis on recognition of regular patterns in speech and in the graphic representations of these patterns. It is expected that knowledge of these patterns can be transferred to words that are met later and are unknown. Rasmussen and Goldberg have described the major way in which word recognition is viewed by many linguists, "Word attack, then, is developed by linguistic groupings. If the child can recognize the spelling pattern in a word that he has never seen before, and if he can group it with words that have the same pattern of sound and spelling relationships, then he can read the never-before-encountered word."[46]

Linguists also have advocated that specific efforts are focused on helping learners understand the nature of language as a means for improving their abilities to use decoding skills.

Competencies Required of Teachers for Developing Word-Recognition Abilities and Skills

1. Ability to read effectively.
2. Recognition of the interrelationships among all the language arts — listening, speaking, reading, and writing.
3. Ability to implement knowledge of the interrelationships among the language arts.
4. Understanding of the influences of language development or development of reading ability.
5. Understanding of the influences of an individual's speech patterns and habits on development of word-recognition ability.
6. Understanding of the reading process.
7. Understanding of those aspects of the reading process in which an individual's behavior can be observed directly.
8. Ability to focus instruction on specific aspects of development in reading without ignoring their relationships to the total process of reading.
9. Knowledge of the major categories of word-recognition skills and the types of specific skills that can be grouped in each category.

---

[46] Donald Rasmussen and Lynn Goldberg, *Teacher's Handbook*, SRA Series (Chicago: Science Research Associates, 1965), p. 5.

10. Ability to use techniques to encourage learners to develop flexibility in the use of word-recognition skills.
11. Ability to use techniques to encourage learners to understand and apply various types of skills to their problems in recognizing words.
12. Ability to determine an appropriate sequence in development of word-recognition skills for a particular learner or group of learners.
13. Understanding of the nature of reading readiness.
14. Ability to implement major ideas related to reading readiness for beginners in reading and for learners at various developmental levels in reading.
15. Understanding of relationships between initial reading readiness and developmental readiness for reading.
16. Understanding of the continuity that characterizes the nature of word-recognition skills from one level of development in reading to another.
17. Ability to design learning experiences appropriate for helping learners develop specific skills in word recognition.
18. Understanding of how all aspects of reading instruction contribute to effective development of specific skills in word recognition and ability to implement this understanding in specific practices.

SUMMARY

Chapter 7 presents an overview of the categories of skills used in word recognition. Skills in word recognition are the same, essentially, at all levels of development in reading. Skills that beginning readers are helped to develop are the same as those developed at subsequent levels. Differences in the nature of skills encountered at various levels of development pertain to complexity and emphasis rather than to kinds of skills.

Specific skills in word recognition that should be developed by learners in a particular classroom situation must be decided, in a major sense, on the basis of the needs and abilities of the learners and the nature of the approach used in instruction. The classroom teacher should be aware of the types of skills required in word recognition and the general sequences in which these are developed so that appropriate skills and an appropriate order for their development can be emphasized in the particular program under consideration.

Major categories of skills used in word recognition are those of (1) configuration, (2) phonics, (3) structural analysis, and (4) context. Skills in these major categories represent various levels or degrees of utility. For instance, skills categorized as skills of configuration are extremely limited in terms of applicability, while uses of phonics skills are numerous and pervasive. Yet, a competent reader acquires mastery of all major types of word-recognition skills and uses these flexibly as needed in his reading.

Contributions made by linguists to reading instruction include provision for (1) a more structured approach to development of skills in word recognition and (2) a deeper understanding of relationships between language and its written or printed representation.

Among competencies needed by teachers for helping learners develop proficiency in skills of word recognition are those involving knowledge of (1) the nature of the process of reading, (2) the role of readiness in reading, (3) specific word-recognition skills and (4) proficiency in the use of techniques for helping learners develop these skills.

Review Questions

1. Discuss the nature of definitions of reading offered by authorities in reading in terms of (a) similarities among definitions offered, (b) outstanding differences that may be found among definitions, and (c) implementation of definitions in classroom instructional practices in reading. **(1.1)**

2. State a rationale for having teachers of reading acquire familiarity with authoritative definitions of reading. **(1.1)**

3. Describe major components of the act of reading. **(1.2)**

4. What specific relationships can be determined between word-recognition and comprehension skills and abilities? **(1.2)**

5. State your personal definition of reading. **(1.3)**

6. Give illustrations to show how your concept of the nature of reading might affect aspects of instruction such as
   a. Procedures for developing reading readiness
   b. Selection of instructional materials
   c. Particular skills to be emphasized
   d. Selection of supplementary reading materials
   e. Selection of instructional aids
   (1.4)

7. In what ways might the teacher's concept of the nature of reading influence his attitudes and efforts toward helping learners recognize the nature of reading? **(1.4)**

8. Why should learners be helped to conceptualize the nature of reading? **(1.5)**

9. Describe characteristics of learners that should be taken into consideration in determining their ability to understand the nature of reading. **(1.5)**

10. How does the concept of reading readiness relate to the general meaning of readiness for learning? **(2.1)**

11. In what ways does "initial readiness for reading" relate to "developmental readiness for reading"? **(2.1)** **(3.1)**

12. Describe several major factors that, together, account for the nature and degree of readiness an individual may show for formal reading instruction. **(2.2)**

13. List several factors related to reading readiness. For each factor listed, describe the types of experiences generally provided to strengthen a learner's ability related to that factor. **(2.3)**

14. Describe factors of concern in developmental reading readiness that would not pertain to those of concern during initial reading readiness. **(3.2)**

15. What relationships can be seen between initial reading readiness and developmental readiness? **(3.3)**

16. In general, describe some of the procedures that should be used to improve readiness regardless of the level of a learner's development. **(3.4)**

17. Explain the meaning of a basic sight vocabulary. (**5.1.1.**)

18. What relationships can be seen between a basic sight vocabulary of concern during initial reading instruction and a sight vocabulary required for competent reading at any level of development? (**5.1.1**)

19. List specific decoding skills that should be stressed during initial instruction in reading. (**5.1.2**)

20. Compare characteristics generally shown in an approach to reading instruction that emphasizes decoding as a primary concern with those generally shown in approaches to initial instruction that place major emphasis on the acquisition of meaning. (**6.1**) (**6.2**)

21. Discuss relative advantages and limitations of code-emphasis approaches to initial reading instruction compared with those of "meaning" emphasis approaches. (**6.3**)

22. Based on your own experiences and familiarity with ideas in literature related to reading instruction, which type of approach do you believe to be most advantageous for giving learners a sound start in reading? State your reasons. (**6.4**)

23. In what specific ways can decoding or word-recognition skills be considered developmental in nature? (**7.0**)

24. What relationships exist between development of a basic sight vocabulary in initial reading instruction and continuous development of a sight vocabulary during all levels of development in reading? (**7.1.1**)

25. What are some similiarities and differences between initial skills taught in word recognition and those on which emphasis is placed throughout all levels of development in reading? (**7.1.2**)

26. Into what major categories can specific skills in word recognition be grouped? (**7.3**)

27. Within each major category of basic word-recognition skills, list several specific skills upon which reading instructional practices should focus. (**7.3**)

28. Why should an individual be knowledgeable about and competent in the use of a wide variety of word-recognition skills? (**7.4**)

29. What is the major role of phonics in development of competence in reading? (**8.0**)

30. What implications are there for selection of content to be used in instruction if the meanings of the terms "phonics" and "phonetics" are taken literally? (**8.1**)

31. What are the differences in using an analytic approach to phonics instruction compared with the use of a synthetic approach? (**8.2**)

32. What relationships can be seen between analytic approaches and inductive approaches in phonics instruction? What relationships can be seen between synthetic and deductive approaches? (**8.2**) (**8.3**)

33. Describe the general nature of each of the following:
    a. Phonics skills
    b. Sequence of development of phonics skills
    c. Phonics generalizations
    (**8.4**)

34. What is the general meaning of structural-analysis skills in word recognition? (**9.0**)

35. Make an outline of some of the major skills in structural-analysis and include several specific skills related to each major skill listed. (**9.1**)   (**9.2**)

36. Explain the use of contextual clues as aids to word recognition. (**10.1**)
37. List several specific types of contextual clues with which learners should become acquainted. (**10.2**)
38. Identify several specific ways in which the concerns of several linguists have influenced modern reading instruction. (**11.0**)
39. What specific linguistic cues are useful in development of skills in decoding? (**11.1**)

Selected References

1. Ames, Wilbur S., "The Development of a Classification Scheme of Contextual Aids," *Reading Research Quarterly*, 2 (Fall, 1966), 57–82.
2. Bagford, Jack, *Phonics: Its Role in Teaching Reading.* Iowa City: University of Iowa Press, 1967.
3. Bamman, Henry A., Mildred A. Dawson, and James J. McGovern, *Fundamentals of Basic Reading Instruction,* Third edition. N. Y.: David McKay Co., 1973.
4. Bloomfield, Leonard, "Linguistics and Reading," *Elementary English Review,* 19 (April, 1942), 125–30; (May, 1942): 183–86.
5. Bloomfield, Leonard, and Clarence L. Barnhart, *Let's Read: A Linguistic Approach.* Detroit, Michigan: Wayne State University, 1961.
6. Bond, Guy L., and Robert Dykstra, *Final Report, Project No. X001.* Washington, D. C.: Bureau of Research, Office of Education, U. S. Department of Health, Education, and Welfare, 1967.
7. Bush, Wilma Jo, and Marion Taylor Giles, *Aids to Psycholinguistic Teaching.* Columbus, Ohio: Charles E. Merrill, 1969.
8. Chall, Jeanne, *Learning to Read: The Great Debate.* N. Y.: McGraw-Hill, 1967.
9. Durkin, Dolores, *Teaching Them to Read.* Boston: Allyn and Bacon, 1974.
10. Fries, Charles C., *Linguistics and Reading.* N. Y.: Holt, Rinehart and Winston, 1963.
11. Frostig, Marianne, and David Horne, *The Frostig Program for the Development of Visual Perception.* Chicago: Follett Educational Corp., 1964.
12. Goodman, Kenneth S., "The Linguistics of Reading," *Elementary School Journal,* 64 (April, 1964), 355–61.
13. Hafner, Lawrence E., and Hayden B. Jolly, *Patterns of Teaching Reading in the Elementary School.* N. Y.: Macmillan, 1972.
14. Harris, Albert J., *How to Increase Reading Ability.* N. Y.: David McKay Co., 1961.
15. Harris, Larry A., and Carl B. Smith, *Reading Instruction Through Diagnostic Teaching.* N. Y.: Holt, Rinehart and Winston, 1972.
16. Heilman, Arthur W., *Phonics in Proper Perspective.* Columbus, Ohio: Charles E. Merrill, 1968.
17. Heilman, Arthur W., *Principles and Practices of Teaching Reading.* Columbus, Ohio: Charles E. Merrill, 1967.
18. Henderson, Ellen C., *Phonics in Learning to Read: A Handbook for Teachers.* Boston: Exposition Press, 1967.
19. Herrick, Virgil E., and Marcella Nerbovig, *Using Experience Charts with Children.* Columbus, Ohio: Charles E. Merrill, 1964.

20. Ilg, Frances L., and Louise B. Ames, *School Readiness*. N. Y.: Harper and Row, 1965.

21. Karlin, Robert, editor, *Perspectives on Elementary Reading*. Boston: Harcourt Brace Jovanovich, 1973.

22. Lamb, Pose, *Linguistics in Proper Prespective*. Columbus, Ohio: Charles E. Merrill, 1967.

23. LeFevre, Carl A., *Linguistics and the Teaching of Reading*. N. Y.: McGraw-Hill, 1964.

24. McCullough, Constance M., "Context Aids in Reading," *Reading Teacher*, 11 (April, 1958): 225–29.

25. Muehl, S., "The Effects of Letter-Name Knowledge on Learning to Read a Word List in Kindergarten Children," *Journal of Educational Psychology*, 53 (August, 1962), 181–86.

26. Rasmussen, Donald, and Lynn Goldberg, *Teacher's Handbook for the SRA Reading Series*. Chicago: Science Research Associates, 1965.

27. Savage, John F., *Linguistics for Teachers*. Chicago: Science Research Associates, 1973.

28. Silvaroli, Nicholas, and W. H. Wheelock, "An Investigation of Auditory Training for Beginning Readers," *Reading Teacher*, 20 (December, 1966), 247–55.

29. Simpson, Dorothy M., *Learning to Learn*. Columbus, Ohio: Charles E. Merrill, 1968.

30. Soffieti, James P., "Why Children Fail to Read: A Linguistic Analysis," *Harvard Educational Review*, 25 (Spring, 1955), 63–84.

31. Spache, George D., and Evelyn B. Spache, *Reading in the Elementary School*. Boston: Allyn and Bacon, 1973.

32. Vandever, Thomas R., *The Contribution of Phoneme-Grapheme Consistency and Cue Emphasis to Decoding in First Graders*. Nashville, Tenn.: George Peabody College for Teachers, Institute on Mental Health Retardation and Intellectual Development, 1971.

33. Wallen, Carl J., *Competency in Teaching Reading*. Chicago: Science Research Associates, 1972.

34. Wallen, Carl J., *Word Attack Skills in Reading*. Columbus, Ohio: Charles E. Merrill, 1969.

35. Wardhaugh, Ronald, "Syl-lab-i-ca-tion," *Elementary English*, 43 (November, 1966), 785–88.

36. Wilson, Robert M., and Mary Anne Hall, *Programmed Word Attack for Teachers*. Columbus, Ohio: Charles E. Merrill, 1968.

8

Skills and Abilities in Reading Comprehension

The ultimate test of the teacher's accountability in reading instruction is whether learners develop skills and abilities essential in reading instruction. Need assessment, objectives of instruction, individualization of instruction, humanistic education through reading, evaluation, and command of the content of reading by teachers are all for the purpose of helping learners achieve effectiveness in reading. There is general agreement by most authorities in reading that effectiveness in reading consists of reading comprehension. An understanding of the meaning of reading comprehension and knowledge of factors involved in it or influential in its development are proper concerns for teachers seeking accountability in reading.

Behavioral Objectives

The content of Chapter 8 is presented in such a way that after reading it, an individual
1.0 Understands the meaning of reading comprehension
    1.1 Explains why reading comprehension is difficult to define
    1.2 Cites authoritative definitions of reading comprehension
    1.3 States an operational definition of reading comprehension
    1.4 Describes relationships between reading comprehension and thinking abilities
2.0 Recognizes factors related to development of comprehension abilities
    2.1 Categorizes factors related to comprehension
    2.2 Describes factors inherent in the individual
    2.3 Describes factors related to the environment in which reading occurs
    2.4 Describes factors inherent in the material being read

2.5 Identifies factors amenable to control by the teacher
3.0 Understands that various levels of comprehension can be achieved
  3.1 Explains the nature of each level of comprehension
  3.2 Explains relationships among various levels of comprehension
  3.3 Describes the teacher's role in helping learners acquire various levels of comprehension
4.0 Knows specific skills that learners should develop in reading comprehension
  4.1 Identifies skills essential in reading comprehension
  4.2 Categorizes skills in reading comprehension
  4.3 Explains types of evidence that can be gathered to show learners' development of skills of reading comprehension
  4.4 Differentiates between skills essential in reading narrative materials and those required for reading in the content areas
5.0 Knows various types of instructional procedures essential in helping learners develop skills in reading comprehension
  5.1 Differentiates between the roles of silent and oral reading in development of reading comprehension
  5.2 Describes procedures in "guided" reading
  5.3 Explains uses of questioning strategies in development of comprehension
6.0 Recognizes skills indirectly influential in development of reading comprehension
  6.1 Identifies study skills
  6.2 Identifies skills essential in locating information
  6.3 Describes relationships between study skills and comprehension
  6.4 Describes relationships between skills of location and comprehension skills
7.0 Identifies teacher competencies essential for helping learners develop skills of reading comprehension

The Nature of Reading Comprehension

For several reasons, the precise nature of reading comprehension defies concise and exact description. Reading comprehension can be described in a variety of ways — none of which are unanimously accepted. One reason for this lack of agreement is that reading comprehension consists of internal behaviors that negate direct observation by an onlooker. It is recognized as being related to an individual's thinking abilities, yet thinking abilities themselves lack a single, universally accepted description. Despite this difficulty in describing reading comprehension fully and finally, each teacher must arrive at a definition that is operational in guiding instructional practices in the immediate situation. An operational definition of reading comprehension is essential to achievement of accountability for helping each learner develop reading competence.

Definitions of Reading Comprehension

Reading comprehension is described in various ways by authorities in reading. Spache and Spache claim that no basic definition exists for reading comprehension and proceed to describe it as involving a decoding process and a thinking process. These authors cite the influence of those who prepare instruments for the measurement of reading comprehension on the way it is sometimes perceived.[1]

Harris and Smith refer to comprehension as "the label usually applied to acquiring meaning from reading."[2] Yet, these authors admit that confusion exists regarding what it means to acquire meaning from reading.

Many authorities point to the numerous skills involved in reading comprehension rather than emphasizing an exact description of its nature. According to Harris and Sipay, "Reading comprehension is a complex process involving many different types of higher level thinking skills."[3] One of the most exhaustive lists of skills of comprehension has been presented by Walter B. Barbe. Barbe has analyzed reading comprehension according to the specific skills and abilities involved in it and has categorized these according to each grade level of the elementary school.[4]

Dolores Durkin stresses the need for a definition of comprehension that permits "observational outcomes." Durkin defines reading comprehension as "the fulfillment of a particular purpose through the use of appropriate material that is read in a particular way."[5]

Despite the semantic and philosophical differences often apparent among various definitions of reading comprehension, most experts agree that the concept relates to the reader's understanding of and reaction to the meaning of a particular reading selection.

Many persons hold that reading itself is synonymous with and dependent upon meaning acquired or realized by a reader as a result of the act. In the absence of any relationship to meaning, most authorities agree that the reading act is not complete. To debate the issue of whether an individual has read if he has merely decoded symbols, or whether the act of reading must also involve meaning, is inconsequential to the teacher involved in effective reading instruction. Clearly, both aspects of reading combine to constitute basic concerns in reading instruction. Learners must achieve comprehension as an integral part of reading, if accountability in reading instruction is to be achieved. The decoding skills and skills of comprehension are inseparable in the actual process of reading; thus, both facets of reading must be given appropriate balance in reading instruction.

An Operational Definition of Reading Comprehension

The process of acquiring meaning from a reading selection occurs within an individual and, hence, is not observable. As a result,

---

[1] George D. Spache and Evelyn B. Spache, *Reading in the Elementary School* (Boston: Allyn and Bacon, 1973), pp. 543–52.

[2] Larry A. Harris and Carl B. Smith, *Reading Instruction Through Diagnostic Teaching* (N. Y.: Holt, Rinehart and Winston, 1972), p. 239.

[3] Albert J. Harris and Edward R. Sipay, *Effective Teaching of Reading*, Second edition (N. Y.: David McKay Co., 1971), p. 274.

[4] Walter B. Barbe, *Educator's Guide to Personalized Reading Instruction* (Englewood Cliffs, N. J.: Prentice-Hall, 1961).

[5] Dolores Durkin, *Teaching Them to Read*, Second edition (Boston: Allyn and Bacon, 1974), p. 399.

comprehension of meaning by an individual must be described in terms of the person's responses. These responses may be answers to questions or behavior of some other kind. Teachers often design questions for assessing learners' comprehension, or they design other situations for the purpose. In this way, reading comprehension may be said to be whatever the teacher in charge of instruction determines it to be. What a teacher reports as a learner's comprehension often depends on the concept of comprehension held by the teacher.

Accountability cannot be claimed on the basis of behavior that cannot be observed or determined in some definitive way. In order to achieve accountability for comprehension skills the teacher must arrive at a meaning of the term that can be implemented in the instructional situation. It is important that the teacher define reading comprehension to clarify the specific skills he or she is attempting to help learners develop. This opinion is shared by certain authorities—among them Kerfoot, who has called attention to the "problem of inconsistency in both theoretical base and descriptive terminology" and has suggested that researchers and practitioners should try to define reading comprehension in terms of specific tasks.[6]

An operational definition of reading comprehension must include provisions for attention to specific skills and abilities essential for understanding an author's intended meaning. It should include, as well, attention to skills and abilities essential for interpreting and even applying meanings developed as a result of reading.

Defining reading comprehension operationally will require not one area, but several areas of concern. Since the nature of reading comprehension may vary according to the purposes held for reading and according to the nature of the materials being read, any operational definition of reading comprehension must provide for a degree of flexibility. For instructional purposes, reading comprehension must be defined with provisions for various, specific behaviors a learner is expected to show as a result of instruction.

Relationships Between Reading
Comprehension and Thinking Skills

Several researchers have called attention to relationships between skills involved in reading comprehension and those related to thinking. Many models of skills related to thinking have been equated with those involved in reading comprehension. One of the widely known models of thinking is that offered by Benjamin S. Bloom. In Bloom's model, levels of thinking are presented in hierarchical fashion, from least complex to most complex, as (1) memory, (2) translation, (3) interpretation, (4) application, (5) analysis, (6) synthesis, and (7) evaluation.[7] Skills in reading comprehension can be equated with the levels of thinking in Bloom's model. The levels of memory and translation are synonymous with skills essential in revealing the individual's understanding

---

[6]J. F. Kerfoot, "Problems and Research Considerations in Reading Comprehension" in *Developing Reading Comprehension Including Critical Reading*, Mildred Dawson, editor (Newark, Del.: International Reading Association, 1968), pp. 38–44.

[7]Benjamin S. Bloom, editor, *Taxonomy of Educational Objectives: Handbook I, Cognitive Domain* (N. Y.: David McKay Co., 1964).

of the meaning of a selection only in terms of facts and information remembered from what is read. Memory of what is read may be expressed in the words of the author or translated into the reader's own terminology. Interpretation, as defined in the third level of Bloom's model, relates to the level of reading comprehension in which the reader can not only report the author's meaning, but can also determine its significance. Application as described in Bloom's model can be equated with the level of reading comprehension in which the reader uses or applies ideas developed as a result of reading. Analysis, synthesis, and evaluation can be equated with the levels of reading comprehension that are expressed in critical and creative reactions by the reader.

In much the same way, J. P. Guilford's model of thinking can be compared to the various types and levels of reading comprehension. Guilford's model of thinking includes the levels of (1) cognition, recognition of information, (2) memory, retention of information, (3) divergent production, logical creative ideas, (4) convergent production, conclusive, inductive thinking, (5) evaluation, critical thinking.[8]

Donald P. Cleland has analyzed the thinking processes involved in reading as: (1) perception, meaningful response to graphic symbols including words, phrases, sentences, paragraphs, and longer selections; (2) apperception, relating new materials to one's own background of experience; (3) abstraction, including selection, perception, concepts and images; (4) appraisal, estimating the value of processes; (5) ideation, including inductive reasoning, generalizing opinions, conclusions, judgments, critical reasoning, problem-solving, and creative thinking; and (6) application, the use made of the ideas acquired by reading.[9]

These models help to explain how reading comprehension may be affected by a learner's thinking abilities. A mature individual, capable of and skillful in performance of higher levels of thinking, can be assumed to be capable of acquiring reading comprehension commensurate with his thinking powers, provided other essential factors are present. The type of material to be read, the kinds of purposes sought through reading, and the competence of the reader in the decoding aspects of reading are among other factors that may affect the degree to which a reader may experience his highest potential in reading comprehension.

Factors Related to Reading Comprehension

Factors related to reading comprehension include thinking skills and abilities such as those presented in many models of thinking, some of which are mentioned above. Several other factors are important in determining a reader's comprehension. Awareness of these factors can be useful in determining the nature of instructional materials and procedures that may be beneficial in a particular instructional situation.

---

[8] J. P. Guilford, "Frontiers in Thinking that Teachers Should Know About," *The Reading Teacher*, 13 (February, 1960), pp. 176–82.

[9] Donald P. Cleland, "A Construct of Comprehension in Reading and Inquiry," *Conference Proceedings*, 10 (Newark, Del.: International Reading Association, 1965), pp. 59–64.

Factors related to reading comprehension can be categorized according to (1) those stemming from the reader himself, (2) those stemming from the environment in which reading occurs, and (3) those related to the nature of the material being read. Examination of categories of factors influential in reading comprehension can reveal those factors that can be affected through instructional procedures and attitudes by the teacher.

Factors Inherent in the Individual

Factors affecting reading comprehension include the individual's intelligence, his experiential background, his language development, and several emotional factors including his self-concept, his interests, and his attitudes toward reading.

Thinking skills are related to an individual's intelligence. While no specific level of intelligence can be indicated as a minimum required for reading, it is obvious that intelligence is a determinant of the level and nature of comprehension an individual acquires through reading. Intelligence affects an individual's ability to concentrate on reading, to remember and retain what has been read, and to apply higher levels of thinking in order to interpret, evaluate, analyze or apply what has been read.

An individual's experiential background helps to determine the nature and level of meaning he may be able to attain through reading. It is through varied experiences that concepts are acquired. When an individual has acquired many well-developed concepts, he has a positive background to bring to the task of reading.

Among language skills important in reading comprehension are those essential for labeling concepts to be used in the process of thinking, and those essential for understanding various units of meaning in verbal communication, whether it is oral or written. Words, phrases, sentences, and the like comprise various units of language. An understanding of these factors is essential in understanding language reproduced in written or printed form. According to Harris and Smith, "Children who do not understand the structure of their language can neither listen to nor read English with understanding."[10] The results of several studies, including that by Ruddell,[11] have shown that reading comprehension is influenced by the learner's language patterns. Pratt has identified as two fundamental linguisitic skills essential in reading comprehension (1) knowledge of what a symbol stands for and (2) understanding of the grammatical relations inherent in a message.[12] Dialectal differences in the language used by an author and that used by a reader may also constitute a barrier to the reader's comprehension.

A person's emotional state may also affect his potential for reading comprehension. A negative self-concept, distractibility, and impatience, for example, may affect comprehension adversely.[13] An individual who regards himself favorably,

---

[10] Harris and Smith, *Reading Instruction Through Diagnostic Teaching*, p. 268.

[11] R. B. Ruddell, "The Effect of Oral and Written Patterns of Language on Reading Comprehension," *The Reading Teacher*, 18 (1965), pp. 270–75.

[12] Edward Pratt, "Reading as a Thinking Process," *Vistas in Reading*, Conference Proceedings, 11, Part 1, (Newark, Del.: International Reading Association, 1966), pp. 52–55.

[13] Ruth Strang, "Explorations of the Reading Process," *Reading Research Quarterly*, 2 (Spring, 1967), pp. 33–45.

has an active interest in reading, and likes to read usually will experience an effective level of reading comprehension provided other significant factors are also favorable.

Factors Related to the Reading Environment

The environment of reading instructions and of learners' voluntary reading constitutes an area from which may arise several factors influential upon reading comprehension. Physical factors such as lighting, seating arrangements, the proximity and availability of books and other reading materials, and the general comfort afforded readers are obvious factors in the reading environment that may affect learners' comprehension.

Not so obvious, but still of significance, are factors related to the environment that include the teacher's attitudes toward reading and toward learners and learning. Also influential may be other learners' attitudes. In short, the intellectual and social atmospheres fostered in the classroom may influence learners' reading comprehension either positively or negatively.

Instructional practices contribute to the classroom environment for reading instruction and for reading. Many of these practices can directly influence learners' reading comprehension. Instructional efforts designed to help learners perceive purposes for reading,[14] develop flexibility in reading rate, read widely, and utilize auxiliary skills—such as study skills and skills of location—facilitate learners' achievement of meaning in reading.

Rate of reading has not been found to have a significantly high relationship to a reader's comprehension. The skill with which an individual can adjust his rate of reading to the nature of his purposes for reading and the type of material being read, however, have been found to be factors in comprehension. Rankin summarized the results of several studies focused on relationships between rate of reading and comprehension and concluded that, "It appears that the confounding of rate and comprehension in measurement is, at least in part, responsible for some of the earlier findings that 'fast readers are good readers.' Other studies of the relationship between rate and 'power of comprehension' find only a slight relationship."[15]

What seems to be important is the rate at which a reader accomplishes his purposes for reading. A learner is expected to read at whatever constitutes an appropriate rate for the purpose he or she assigns to the reading.[16] For example, certain narrative or story materials are read for different purposes than are reading materials related to study in a content area of the curriculum and thus require a

---

[14] Helen K. Smith, "Research in Reading for Different Purposes" in *Changing Concepts of Instruction*, J. A. Figurel, editor (Newark, Del.: International Reading Association, 1961), pp. 119–22.

E. H. Henderson, "A Study of Individually Formulated Purposes for Reading," *Journal of Educational Research*, 58 (1965), pp. 438–41.

[15] E. F. Rankin, "The Relation Between Reading Rate and Comprehension" in *Problems, Programs, and Projects in College-Adult Reading*, E. P. Bleismer and R. C. Staiger, editors (National Reading Conference Yearbook, 1962), pp. 1–5.

[16] W. D. Sheldon and L. W. Carillo, "The Flexibility of Reading Rate," *Journal of Educational Psychology*, 43 (1952), pp. 37–45.

A. S. McDonald, "Research for the Classroom: Rate and Reading Flexibility," *Journal of Reading*, 8 (1965), pp. 187–91.

different rate. It is perhaps accurate to conclude that learners should be encouraged to read at a rate essential to development of their best comprehension for a particular type of reading. Freedom from tension and pressure for fast reading can only be conducive to improvement of comprehension for most readers.

Availability of a large number and variety of reading materials in the classroom environment contributes positively to development of learners' comprehension abilities. Instruction should be offered in how to read to achieve different purposes and with appropriate adjustment of rate in many different types of materials. Learners can practice using skills developed during instructional periods if there are opportunities in the environment for use of the skills. Opportunities consist of availability of materials suitable for accommodating needs and interests of all individuals involved in a program.

The use of other skills, that—for convenience—may be termed auxiliary skills, can be beneficial in helping learners achieve reading comprehension. Skills categorized as location skills and study skills tend to increase the efficiency with which an individual can locate and use information, thereby enlarging opportunities for achievement of reading comprehension.

Factors Related to Materials Read

Several factors affecting comprehension are inherent in the nature of the materials being read. Some of the most important of these factors are (1) the readability of the material, (2) the style and structure of writing, (3) the density of concepts included and (4) the rate at which these are encountered by the reader.

Readability pertains to the degree of ease with which material can be read by the individual. Obviously, what constitutes a desirable level of readability for one individual is not necessarily the same for another. To some extent, readability of materials relates to differences among individuals including their vocabularies, the nature of their concepts, the nature of their sight vocabularies, and their competencies in the use of word-recognition skills. Reading material that reflects the kind of readability that permits an individual to read with no problems in decoding or in familiarity with concepts involved is more conducive to comprehension than that which reflects a high degree of difficulty for him.

Structure and style of writing refer to the basic form of the material and its mode of presentation. Reading material in a narrative structure and in a lively easy-to-understand style presents a less challenging task in comprehension for most individuals than material of a technical nature.

Reading materials related to the various content areas—such as mathematics, science, or history, for example—are more difficult to comprehend for many individuals than are story-type materials. One of the major reasons for the increased difficulty in comparison with narrative materials is the density of concepts and the degree of unfamiliarity these hold for many readers. Often concepts occur in such rapid succession that the reader's problems of assimiliation become increased.

Sometimes, visual aids included as part of materials in the content areas facilitate comprehension. But this is not always the case. Unless a reader has command of certain study skills, locational skills, and the like, visual aids appearing in the text may increase his problems of comprehension.

Factors Related to Comprehension and Amenable to the Influence of the Teacher

This section has called attention to several specific factors in comprehension that can be influenced directly by the teacher. As a result of the instructional procedures used or the attitudes shown by the teacher, the influence of several factors on comprehension can either be increased or decreased. Still other factors related to comprehension may be influenced indirectly. There are some areas, however, over which any control or influence by the teacher is minimal or nonexistent.

While the teacher's influence on a learner's intelligence may be minimal or even nonexistent, a teacher's attitudes and instructional procedures can aid in development of thinking skills. The teacher can demonstrate to learners the use of many thinking skills involved in reading comprehension. He or she can also employ instructional procedures and materials essential for helping learners use their abilities to reason, recognize a sequence of ideas, recognize organizational patterns, and the like. Through questions, study guides, and other techniques, teachers can guide learners' thinking as they read.

Factors stemming from learners' experiential backgrounds can be modified and augmented where necessary through several instructional procedures. Real and vicarious experiences can be provided in and out of the classroom, and these can be related appropriately to the development of learners' meaning vocabularies. For example, trips can be taken to places of interest in the community, or films can be shown in the classroom in order to improve learner's vocabularies. In all instances, however, techniques that call for association of language with activities must be employed.

Several types of emotional factors affecting reading comprehension have been shown to be subject, to a large extent, to the influence of the teacher. Davidson and Lang reported, as a result of their research, that learners' self-concepts are influenced by their perceptions of how their teachers feel toward them, their perceptions of themselves, their perceptions of academic achievement and of classroom behavior.[17] Teachers' feelings about learners are communicated to learners through nuances, nonverbal behaviors and the like, even when overt evidence may be concealed. Feelings of learner-acceptance and approval by the teacher tend to stimulate similar feelings in learners. Positive feelings about the teacher and about themselves affect comprehension positively. According to Hamerchek, there is a positive correlation between high intellectual and achievement self-images and reading, mental, and educational ages.[18]

---

[17] H. H. Davidson and G. Lang, "Children's Perceptions of Their Teacher's Feelings Toward Them Related to Self-Perception, School Achievement, and Behavior" in *The Self in Growth, Teaching and Learning*, Don E. Hamerchek, editor (Englewood Cliffs, N. J.: Prentice-Hall, 1965), pp. 424–39.

[18] Don E. Hamerchek, "A Study of the Relationship Between Certain Measures of Growth and the Self-Images of Elementary School Children," *Unpublished PhD. Dissertation* (Ann Arbor, Mich.: University of Michigan, 1960), p. 210.

Many physical factors in the classroom environment cannot be changed substantially by the teacher. Size of the room, facilities permitting various types of groupings, lighting, and the like generally must be utilized much as they are by the teacher. Yet, the instructional procedures used can decrease the importance of many physical features of a classroom. The teacher's attitudes and the types of intellectual and social climates fostered in the classroom are all under major influence by the teacher. So, too, are many important factors related to materials used in instruction. Through an understanding of the nature of comprehension and the nature of available materials, the teacher often can make many modifications to improve learners' comprehension. Effects of readability of materials, style and structure of writing, nature and number of concepts encountered by learners can be modified through planning and mode of employment by the teacher.

Levels of Comprehension

Just as thinking takes place at various levels—somewhat hierarchical, but often overlapping and interdependent—so, too, does reading comprehension. Several researchers and writers in the field of reading are agreed that reading comprehension occurs at different levels of cognition.[19] These levels have been labeled somewhat variously by different persons, but many use the term "literal," "interpretive or inferential," and "applied" to distinguish the levels. DeBoer and Dallmann have explained these levels as involving (1) reading the lines, (2) reading between the lines, and (3) reading beyond the lines.[20]

The Nature of Specific Levels of Comprehension

Each level of comprehension can be described or distinguished according to types of behaviors shown by an individual as responses based on reading.

The literal level of comprehension is the level achieved by a reader when he or she is aware of the information or ideas imparted in a particular selection. At the literal level of comprehension, a reader shows in his responses that he understands what an author has said, although he may not have achieved an understanding of the significance of what was stated.

At the level of comprehension labeled variously as inferential or interpretive, the reader shows in his responses that not only does he know what the author has

---

[19] Phillip Shaw, "Achieving Personal Maturity Through Reading and By Recognizing and Constructing Meaning" in *Developing Comprehension Including Critical Reading*, Mildred A. Dawson, editor, pp. 55–57.

Harris and Smith, *Reading Instruction Through Diagnostic Teaching*, pp. 246–48.

Helen M. Robinson, "The Major Aspects of Reading" in *Reading: Seventy-Five Years of Progress* (Chicago: University of Chicago Press, 1966).

[20] John J. DeBoer and Martha Dallmann, *The Teaching of Reading* (N. Y.: Holt, Rinehart and Winston, 1970), p. 174.

stated, but also that he derives meanings from relationships among the author's statements. The reader can derive implied meanings or interpret meanings related to the message. Although the meanings achieved by a reader at the inferential or interpretive level of comprehension derive from personal experiences and perceptions, these are based on and confined to the information or ideas encountered in the selection.

At the applied level of comprehension, the reader uses knowledge of what the author has stated (literal level) and understanding of the significance of what was stated (interpretive level) and makes some type of application of the understandings and new ideas thus acquired. Application may be in terms of increased understanding of an idea previously encountered, recognition of new ideas, or in ability to utilize new ideas in unique ways, and the like. The applied level of comprehension includes behaviors expected as a result of critical reading and/or creative reading.

Relationships Among Levels of Comprehension

To an extent, all levels of comprehension are interrelated and interdependent. The only level that can be said to exist independently of another level is that of literal comprehension. Doubtlessly, even at the literal level of comprehension, there exists some influence from behaviors expected at the interpretive level. Meanings given by a reader to words, phrases, sentences, and the like, stem from the reader's background of experiences and perceptions rather than from the author's. As a reader determines what an author has stated—even at the literal level of comprehension—personal abilities to infer and interpret meaning are operative.

The interpretive level of comprehension requires that the reader sees relationships among facts, information, or ideas shared by an author. The reader must achieve meaning not only from what the author has actually stated, but in terms of what the statements, taken together, mean, or might mean. Obviously, interpretation of a statement or statements, or awareness of what these may imply, requires prior understanding at the literal level. Similarly, at the point at which a reader can apply results of the reading in creative and critical ways, he or she must first have achieved the literal and interpretive levels of comprehension.

Within each level of comprehension, achievement of individuals varies for many reasons. For example, the degree of excellence or precision achieved at any level of comprehension varies according to individual differences in cognitive and affective skills and abilities.

Teacher's Role in Helping Learners Acquire
Abilities and Skills in Reading Comprehension

The teacher has a direct role to play in determining the nature and level of reading comprehension learners under his charge will acquire. If only surface and superficial understanding of what is read is required, learners will reflect that requirement. Bruce Joyce, among other people, has called attention to the tendency of learners to value what they perceive as being valued by their teacher. According to Joyce, young children often are able to "lapse into senseless verbalisms when the words they use are not completely understood."[21] The teacher's role in increasing reading comprehension by learners involves the use of instructional strategies that emphasize meaning as the outcome of reading. Emphasis on meaning applies whether words or larger units of expression are under consideration. Larger units of expression include phrases, sentences, paragraphs, or a series of related paragraphs in longer selections.

Specific Skills in Reading Comprehension

Just stating that reading comprehension involves the ability to recognize and respond meaningfully to forms of written expression lacks the specificity needed to provide guidance for teachers seeking accountability in reading instruction. Similarly, accountability requires more than a general statement that reading comprehension involves understanding by the reader of what is read. "Understanding" refers to an internal process and condition that may be described variously by different persons. More specific terms that bear essentially the same meanings for different persons must be used for instructional purposes in describing reading comprehension. The specific skills or behaviors by which reading comprehension can be determined include, but are not exhausted by, the following:

1. Identification of the main idea in a selection
2. Identification of the significant details supporting the main idea in a selection
3. Restatement of the major ideas or events in a selection
4. Summarization of the major ideas in a selection
5. Identification of sequence (of events or of ideas)
6. Comparing or contrasting ideas (or events) in a selection with related ones in another selection (or with experiences from one's own background)
7. Drawing conclusions based on what was read
8. Making generalizations supported by facts or information read
9. Recognizing organizational patterns in the structure of a selection in order to conceptualize or report on the author's meanings
10. Identifying the author's purpose
11. Evaluating the author's expressed or implied purpose in relationship to what the author actually has communicated, according to the reader's understanding
12. Interpreting the meanings of expressions involving use of figurative language

Skill Categories in Reading Comprehension

Extensive lists of skills in reading comprehension are available from numerous sources.* Lists of skills appear not only in professional

---

[21] Bruce R. Joyce, *Strategies for Elementary Social Science Education* (Chicago: Science Research Associates, 1965), p. 103.

*See, for example, Dolores Durkin, *Teaching Them to Read*, pp. 396–97; Walter B. Barbe, *Educator's Guide to Personalized Reading*, pp. 152–205; George D. Spache and Evelyn B. Spache, *Reading in the Elementary School*, pp. 543–45.

texts for the preparation of teachers in reading instruction, but in curriculum guides, manuals accompanying basic curriculum materials for formal instruction in reading, and the like. Long lists of skills, however, must be categorized if these are to serve effectively for the guidance of instruction in reading.

One way of categorizing skills of comprehension in order to design instruction is to place them in a scheme based on those required at the various levels of comprehension. Some skills are essential for achieving literal comprehension of a selection. Additional and more complex skills are needed for achieving comprehension at the interpretive or applied levels. Once a teacher has knowledge of the strengths and weaknesses of learners in a particular group and a categorization of skills to be developed, instructional procedures can be focused on essential skills.

Skills essential for achieving literal comprehension, for example, include the following:

1. Identification of appropriate meanings for words as they appear in a selection
2. Following directions
3. Recalling sequence of events or ideas
4. Finding answers to specific questions
5. Observing symbolic cues to meaning (other than words), such as punctuation
6. Summarizing main ideas in a selection
7. Identification of significant details
8. Associating the text with pertinent illustrations
9. Following the plot sequence
10. Identifying key words or ideas

Skills essential for interpreting the meaning of a selection or deriving inferential meaning include skills such as the following:

1. Drawing logical conclusions
2. Predicting outcomes
3. Describing relationships
4. Suggesting another title for a story
5. Interpreting the meaning of figurative language
6. Identifying implied traits of a character

At the applied level of comprehension, additional skills such as the following may be essential:

1. Determining relative value of ideas
2. Comparing or contrasting ideas found in one selection with those found in another and deriving new ideas
3. Creating an original idea (or another product) as a result of experiences encountered in reading
4. Using ideas developed in reading to solve a defined problem
5. Expressing judgment regarding the merit of an idea or ideas

Evidence of Comprehension

Specific evidence of an individual's reading comprehension can be detected in a number of ways. One of the most direct ways is through use of questions to evoke the reader's responses. Questions for determining the nature and extent of an individual's comprehension are relied upon heavily by both teachers and test-makers. The nature and levels of questions asked to determine comprehension establish the nature and level of comprehension that can be determined.

While questions are recognized as important in helping learners develop and reveal achievement of skills in reading comprehension, questions are not the only means by which this can be done. Reasoner calls attention to this fact in his appeal that "other means be found for this reading-skill assessment, if one truly expects to learn about children's comprehension.[22]

If a teacher is clear about the objective or behavior sought as a result of reading, other situations besides those involving questions and answers can be established for assessing comprehension. An individual may reveal a facet of his reading comprehension through his initiative, creativity, or critical reaction in ways that may not be preconceived or set forth by the teacher. Whether or not this occurs depends more on the nature of the conditions in which reading occurs than it does on specific questions asked by the teacher.

Instruction in reading should proceed on the basis of defined objectives set to guide but not to restrict the limits of comprehension to be achieved by a learner. The learner should be permitted freedom and opportunity to explore his thinking or comprehension in ways unique to himself. This is especially pertinent to development of affective behaviors and higher levels of comprehension. Learners should be taught to ask their own questions of their reading in materials that they are particularly interested in and particularly sensitive to.

Comprehension Skills for
Reading Different Materials

Some differentiation, but not complete differentiation, may be made between skills required in comprehension of narrative materials and those required in comprehension of materials written for the content areas of the curriculum. Certain skills are basic in reading comprehension regardless of the nature of the materials being read. Several years ago, a review of the evidence then available related to comprehension skills and their use in reading materials of various types led Traxler and Townsend to the conclusion that there is a great deal in common between reading, in general, and reading in a particular content area.[23] More recently, after analyzing numerous skills required in reading as suggested by "many authors of professional texts on reading, many curriculum guides on reading instruction in the content areas, and many journal articles,"[24] Herber suggested that his examination casts "serious doubts that each subject area has the considerable number of skills unique to itself, as has been supposed. Examination of these lists leads to the conclusion that uniqueness lies in semantics rather than in skills: different authors use different names for the same process."[25]

---

[22] Charles F. Reasoner, *Where the Readers Are* (N. Y.: Dell Publishing, 1972), p. 14.

[23] Arthur E. Traxler and Agatha Townsend, *Another Five Years of Research in Reading: Summary and Bibliography* (New York: Educational Records Bureau, 1946), p. 21.

[24] Harold L. Herber, *Teaching Reading in Content Areas* (Englewood Cliffs, N. J.: Prentice-Hall, 1970), p. 121.

[25] Herber, *Teaching Reading in Content Areas*, p. 121.

Certain skills are basic in all levels of comprehension and in comprehension of all types of materials. Bond and Wagner state "Comprehension is made up of a number of abilities, including skills in recognizing words and their meanings, in grouping words as thought units, and in giving proper emphasis to the thought units so that the sentences may be understood. Moreover, it is the ability to ascertain the relationship between the sentences that enables the reader to understand the paragraph."[26] These skills are required whether reading is done in narrative-type materials or in materials designed for the content areas. While recognizing that some skills are more relevant to one area than to another, Karlin contends that "all of the reading skills that children use in reading narrative materials are needed to read factual materials."[27]

Comprehension of factual materials related to content areas of the curriculum generally requires the reader to utilize basic skills required in comprehension plus skills involved in (1) adjustment to the style of writing characteristic of each content area, (2) reacting to new words and to familiar words used in unique contexts, and (3) reacting to content characterized by conciseness and rapid presentation of numerous concepts.

Helping learners acquire comprehension in reading in content areas does not require that a teacher attempt to develop a completely new set of skills for each area. In the elementary school in which a teacher often must not only teach reading as reading, but must also teach reading in the content areas, such a task would be formidable. Helping learners read effectively in the content areas does require that they be taught to use the basic skills of comprehension flexibly and apply additional and unique skills as required in each area. Additional and unique skills in each content area generally include vocabulary, organizational patterns, symbolic representation, and illustrative materials unique to the area.

Instructional Procedures for Development of Comprehension

Procedures used in reading instruction affect learners' development of comprehension skills. Prominent among general procedures with which the teacher must be concerned are those that relate to the use of (1) oral reading, (2) guided reading, and (3) questioning strategies.

Oral Reading and Comprehension

In a major sense, reading is an individual and silent activity. Silent reading is emphasized throughout the elementary school to a far

---

[26] Guy L. Bond and Eva Bond Wagner, *Teaching the Child to Read* (N. Y.: Macmillan, 1966), p. 176.

[27] Roberta Karlin, *Teaching Elementary Reading* (N. Y.: Harcourt Brace Jovanovich, 1971), p. 218.

greater extent than is oral reading. For instructional purposes, oral reading is used more frequently and more widely during the primary grades than during the intermediate and upper grades. Except for reading in audience situations and reading for diagnostic or assessment purposes, both reading that is done for instructional purposes and that voluntarily engaged in for personal reasons generally are silent.

Except for the skills required in decoding the printed word, oral reading skills are similar to those required for effective speaking. In both oral reading and speaking, the individual must be in command of correct pronunciation of words, meanings of words, and knowledge of thought units and the pauses these require. Oral reading generally requires interpretation of the author's message. Without adequate comprehension, effective interpretation of the author's meaning is not likely to occur. According to Bamman and others, "One good way to check comprehension and to determine whether a pupil really understands and appreciates the situation in reading materials is to have him read aloud. The way he emphasizes critical ideas determines how well he is thinking."[28]

A program of reading instruction should provide learners with experiences in oral reading in audience situations. Several different forms of oral reading can be used to provide these experiences. At times, individuals should be provided opportunities to share selections for informing others. At other times, individuals should be given the chance to share their enjoyment and appreciation of a selection for enjoyment and appreciation by others. In each case, preparation is required both by the individual reading orally and by the audience for whom it is intended, if the audience is the class group. Choral reading, and its many variations, in which a small group or the class group reads in unison after adequate preparation can increase learners' comprehension of the selections used.

Oral reading can be used to assess or diagnose the types of difficulties a learner may be having in reading comprehension. Lack of fluency, improper phrasing, poor intonation, hesitancies, lack of expression, and even some mispronunciations of words can provide evidence of problems in comprehension.

Oral reading often becomes a part of "guided" reading activities, especially during the primary grades. Through an individual's ability to locate and read orally passages containing answers to questions, comprehension can be detected and also guided.

Comprehension by an individual can be determined through his or her use of several skills required for effective oral reading. Some of these skills are those required for:
1. Recognition and pronunciation of words with speed and accuracy
2. Grouping words into meaningful phrases
3. Interpreting marks of punctuation
4. Interpreting meanings expressed by an author
5. Interpreting feelings expressed by an author
6. Verifying answers to questions
7. Interpreting characterizations
8. Interpreting the mood implied in a selection

---

[28] Henry A. Bamman, Mildred A. Dawson, and James J. McGovern, *Fundamentals of Reading Instruction* (N. Y.: David McKay Co., 1973), p. 191.

Guided Reading Activities

The term "guided reading" is often used to refer to a specified and unified group of instructional procedures designed to guide an individual or a group of learners in reading a selection or story. Steps in the guided reading procedure are indicated in manuals accompanying instructional materials used in many schools. These steps generally consist of (1) building background experiences for reading the selection or story; (2) setting purposes for reading; (3) encouraging silent or oral reading to achieve specified purposes; (4) discussion of the content or ideas; (5) development of pertinent skills; and (6) extended reading.

Procedures or activities involved in each step of guided reading are those largely evident from the label given the step. Building background experiences, for example, consists generally of helping learners become acquainted with a topic and its relationship to their needs and interests before engaging in actual reading. Activities at this stage generally are focused on development of concepts, new vocabulary, interests, and attitudes believed to be essential in developing comprehension of the selection.

Purposes set for guided reading should be related to the content of the selection and also to the needs and abilities of the learners. These purposes usually relate to one or several comprehension skills required for reading at an appropriate level of comprehension. The purposes set for a lesson in reading are generally kept immediately in the minds of learners either by questions asked by the teacher or by presentation in written or printed form.

Step three of the guided reading procedure requires silent or oral reading, depending on the learners. Step four, discussion, often is accompanied by rereading parts of the story or selection.

Skill development, as indicated in step five, may take several forms. Sometimes workbook exercises related to the particular reading selection are utilized to provide additional practice comprehension skills introduced during the guided reading activity. At other times, the teacher devises practice exercises tailored to the particular needs of the individuals.

Various techniques—such as dramatizations, creative writing, illustrating the story or parts of the story, and the like—often serve as extended activities during step six. Independent reading in related selections or stories is particularly desirable as an extended reading activity.

Using the term, "directed reading–thinking activity," Stauffer has offered a more refined and technical approach to development of comprehension skills than that generally claimed for guided reading. Major steps in Stauffer's approach include (1) identification of purposes for reading; (2) guiding adjustment of rate to purposes and materials; (3) observing the reading; (4) developing comprehension; and (5) conducting fundamental skill-training activities.[29]

As can be seen from the labels given the steps, there are many similarities in actual implementation of the guided reading procedure and the directed reading–thinking activity as described by Stauffer. Steps in either of these approaches can

---

[29] Russell G. Stauffer, *Teaching Reading as a Thinking Process* (N. Y.: Harper and Row, 1969), pp. 20–21.

be applied in reading instruction focused on helping learners read narrative-type materials or materials in the content areas.

Questioning Strategies

The purpose or purposes set for reading are influential on the level of comprehension learners are led to achieve. Questions asked by the teacher in the attempt to guide reading by learners help to establish real or contrived purposes for reading. Different types of questions have been found to encourage different levels of comprehension.[30] Several principles underlying the effective use of questions for development of reading comprehension have resulted from the findings of several studies.

1. *Questions should represent various levels of thinking.* In a study of the types of questions teachers ask, Guszak[31] recorded over two thousand questions in classrooms at second-grade, fourth-grade, and sixth-grade levels and ascertained the number answered correctly by learners. After categorizing questioning strategies, sequence of questions, and remarks used by teachers, Guszak found that the majority of questions focused on recall. Questions requiring recall, however, were more predominant in the lower grades. Questions ostensibly requiring thought at the level of evaluation often were found to be superficial.

2. *Questions designed to set purposes for reading should be as realistic as possible.* Questions should be related to the needs, interests, and abilities of the learners under consideration.

3. *Possibilities for asking questions which learners can relate to are increased when materials used for instruction are relevant to the learners of a particular age and in a particular situation.*

4. *Good questions require thinking on the teacher's part.* Seldom can the desired quality of questions be achieved by the teacher when adequate preparation has been neglected. Although some significant questions may become evident incidentally, teachers should plan basic questions to be asked during reading instruction. Perusal of the content to be read coupled with consideration of the nature of the particular learners should precede the use of instructional procedures for development of reading comprehension. Questions should be selective in terms of the skills to be developed. Generally, it is not essential to question learners regarding all details of the content read.

Not only should teachers take the time necessary to prepare good questions to facilitate the level of comprehension desired, but they should permit learners adequate time for responses. Teachers should allow learners time for response to high-order questions. According to Hunkins, ". . . it is possible to ask higher-level questions on one day and not expect a response until the end of the week. We need to get away from the practice of expecting an answer to all our questions three minutes or less after we ask them."[32]

---

[30] Frank J. Guszak, "Teachers' Questions and Levels of Reading Comprehension" in *The Evaluation of Children's Reading Achievement*, Thomas C. Barrett, editor (Newark, Del.: International Reading Association, 1967), pp. 227–34.

P. I. Bartolome, "Teachers' Objectives and Questions in Primary Reading," *The Reading Teacher*, 23 (October, 1969), pp. 27–33.

[31] Guszak, "Teachers' Questions and Levels of Reading Comprehenion" in *The Evaluation of Children's Reading Achievement*, pp. 227–34.

[32] F. P. Hunkins, *Questioning Strategies and Techniques* (Boston: Allyn and Bacon, 1972), pp. 66–67.

5. *Relationships between the use of questions and comprehension should be clarified for learners.* The reason for asking meaningful questions as guides for development of comprehension skills is not exhausted solely through teachers' uses. Learners should be taught to use questioning strategies on their own in order to elicit for themselves the best possible comprehension of any selection read.

Skills Indirectly Influential on Reading Comprehension

Although they differ from the basic and higher thinking skills involved directly, skills generally categorized as study skills and as skills of location contribute indirectly to the effectiveness of reading comprehension.

Competence in use of study skills and in use of location skills serve to increase the efficiency with which an individual can select, organize, evaluate, retain and communicate ideas, or with which he can locate pertinent information.[33] Skills categorized as study skills are closely related to many of the skills essential in achieving literal or higher levels of comprehension. Location skills are essential in making available to the reader the materials and ideas he needs for effective comprehension. Most of the skills in these two categories are vital in achievement of comprehension in reading in the content areas of the curriculum particularly. Many contribute, as well, to improvement of comprehension of narrative or story-type materials.

Specific Study Skills

Grouped in the general category of study skills are those specific skills essential for selecting, organizing, evaluating, retaining, and— if necessary—communicating ideas gained through reading. Basic to each skill are numerous subskills essential to effective use of the skill. The following are only a few specific study skills.

1. *Setting a purpose for reading.* As indicated earlier in this chapter, awareness of a purpose for reading improves comprehension of what is read. Purpose provides a reader with a focus for concentration on aspects of the selection that are significant.
2. *Selecting pertinent ideas.* Ideas encountered in a selection achieve importance in relationship to the purpose established for reading. An important study skill enables a reader to separate nonessential ideas from those essential for achieving his or her purposes.
3. *Organizing ideas.* Again, purpose establishes a basis for organizing important ideas gained as a result of reading. Skills such as outlining, skimming, scanning, note-taking, and summarizing can be used to organize ideas. The purpose for reading helps to determine the nature of organization needed for ideas encountered. Skills essential for organization of materials or ideas require specific planning and instruction in the reading program.

---

[33] Robert Kranyik and Florence V. Shankman, *How to Teach Study Skills* (Englewood Cliffs, N. J.: Teachers' Practical Press, 1963), p. 5.

4. *Retaining pertinent information.* Several techniques can be used to aid in memorization of ideas, specific facts, or general information sought as a result of reading. Techniques such as (1) reading for a specific purpose, (2) relating new material to previous experience, (3) associating ideas and information with vivid sensory experiences, (4) placing new information into a framework of major relationships, (5) overlearning important information, (6) reviewing important information in systematic and regular ways, and (7) applying new information and ideas wherever possible, all contribute to improved retention of what is read. Instructional practices in reading should be focused on helping learners develop all of these skills and other pertinent ones useful in improving memory and retention.

5. *Reading illustrative materials.* Reading material frequently is enhanced by inclusion of various types of illustrative or graphic materials designed to emphasize or clarify important information or ideas. Illustrative materials may consist of verbalized descriptions or examples to which basic and higher skills in comprehension apply. Often illustrative materials consist of charts, maps, graphs, diagrams, cartoons, and the like. Appropriate instruction related to development of study skills will pay attention to development of skills needed for comprehension of illustrative materials.

Skills Essential in Locating
Information and Materials

In order to deal effectively with many ideas encountered in or stimulated by reading, it is often essential to explore other sources of information. Efficient and effective use of textbooks and reference materials requires use of location skills. Several skills contribute to improved comprehension through increasing the reader's ability to locate information or materials.

Location skills essential for achieving the most effective use of texts and other reference materials found in the typical classroom situation include:
1. Following directions
2. Understanding various parts of a book
3. Use of the table of contents
4. Use of the index
5. Use of the dictionary
6. Use of encyclopedias
7. Use of maps, globes, charts, and other graphic materials

Location skills needed for use of the library include those listed above, as well as additional ones such as the following:
1. Use of the card catalog
2. Knowledge of the location of various types of materials in the library
3. Use of various sources of information found in the library

Development of Study and Location Skills

Principles underlying instructional procedures essential in helping learners develop study skills and skills of location are the same as those pertinent in development of other important reading behaviors. Generally, the following principles apply:
1. Learners' needs should be considered in determination of the nature of instruction required for development of study skills and skills of location.

2. Development of each of the skills should be started during the primary levels of elementary education and continued throughout the school years.
3. Instruction related to development of study skills and skills of location should be planned, regular, and consistent.
4. Subskills supportive of major skills must be developed if the skills are to be used effectively.
5. Major skills needed for studying and locating information and materials should be developed functionally.

Competencies Required of Teachers

Among competencies required for helping learners develop skills of reading comprehension are the types of competencies indicated in preceding chapters of this book. Competencies related, specifically, to development of skills of comprehension include:

1. Knowledge of the nature of comprehension.
2. Knowledge of factors influential in development of comprehension ability.
3. Ability to use instructional strategies that emphasize relationships between development of skills of word recognition and skills of comprehension.
4. Ability to use instructional strategies that emphasize relationships between the skills of comprehension and thinking skills.
5. Ability to implement guided reading activities as needed for helping learners develop comprehension abilities.
6. Ability to implement oral reading activities to help learners improve skills of comprehension.
7. Ability to use questioning strategies that require learners to use basic and higher skills of comprehension.
8. Ability to determine levels of comprehension appropriate for reading various types of materials.
9. Ability to implement instructional procedures that require learners to achieve comprehension at levels appropriate to the materials being read.
10. Ability to recognize structure of each content area in order to determine unique skills that should be developed by individuals.
11. Ability to help learners develop vocabulary related to technical terms used in mathematics, science, and the social studies.
12. Ability to help learners develop specialized skills required to gather and use various types of information.
13. Ability to help learners adjust reading rates to purposes and types of materials read.
14. Ability to help learners develop skills needed for organization of ideas and materials.

SUMMARY

Helping learners develop skills and abilities in reading comprehension is the major aim of reading instruction. All procedures used in reading instruction assume importance in proportion to the degree that learners achieve effective reading comprehension. Accountability in reading instruction depends, in the final analysis, on whether learners achieve reading comprehension according to their unique potentialities.

The precise meaning of the term, "reading comprehension," is not unanimously agreed upon by those involved in reading research, instruction, or test-making. Lack of agreement stems from the influence of several factors, including semantic differences associated with the term, the internal nature of reading comprehension, and the variety of responses that can be used as evidence of comprehension. Frequently, reading comprehension is equated with thinking, although even the precise nature of thinking is not unanimously agreed upon.

Authoritative definitions of reading comprehension are useful in clarifying the general nature of reading comprehension. Yet, for instructional purposes and in the interest of accountability, each teacher must arrive at a definition of reading comprehension that is operational in his or her particular instructional situation.

Recognition of factors influential in development of comprehension abilities and skills and their categorization helps to highlight those amenable to influence by the teacher.

Reading comprehension can be achieved at various levels. Each level depends on development of several specific skills. Evidence of the level of an individual's reading comprehension can be gathered on the basis of his responses to questions, and in other planned and incidental situations.

Skills of reading comprehension required for reading narrative and content materials are, to an extent, highly similar. Learners must be instructed, however, in the use of skills that may be uniquely required for reading materials in a particular content area.

Instructional procedures essential in helping learners develop reading comprehension include those involving the use of (1) oral reading, (2) guided reading, and (3) questioning strategies.

Skills categorized as study skills and skills of location influence development of basic comprehension skills in indirect ways. The use of study skills and skills of location increase efficiency and effectiveness of reading comprehension, particularly in the content areas.

Review Questions

1. Reading comprehension is defined variously by different writers, researchers, and test makers. What specific characteristics of reading comprehension account for the different ways in which it is often perceived? **(1.1)** *

2. State definitions given for reading comprehension by different writers. What similarities and differences are apparent in these definitions? **(1.2)**

3. How would you define reading comprehension so that your definition can be implemented in your instructional practices? **(1.3)**

4. Why is it essential for a teacher to arrive at an operational definition of reading comprehension when accountability for reading instruction is at stake? **(1.3)**

---

*Boldface numbers in parentheses refer to the numbered behavioral objectives at the beginning of the chapter.

5. How do the skills required in reading comprehension relate to those believed to be essential in thinking? What major differences between these two types of skills can be determined? **(1.4)**

6. List factors related to reading comprehension that pertain to (1) the individual, (2) the environment in which reading occurs, and (3) the materials being read by the individual. **(2.1) (2.2) (2.3) (2.4)**

7. What factors related to comprehension may be influenced by the teacher? Select specific factors and explain the nature of the teacher's influence. **(2.5)**

8. Describe the nature of each of the following levels of comprehension: (1) literal, (2) interpretive, (3) applied. **(3.1)**

9. What relationships can be described between the various levels of comprehension? **(3.2)**

10. State several specific procedures that may be used by a teacher in order to help learners acquire literal comprehension of a selection. **(3.3)** Do the same for the interpretive and applied levels of comprehension. **(3.3)**

11. Make a list of specific skills of comprehension that should constitute a focus for instruction of learners at the particular elementary level of your choice. **(4.1)**

12. Categorize skills in your list according to those essential in achieving comprehension at the literal level, the interpretive level, and the applied level. **(4.2)**

13. What types of evidence might be gathered to show learners' development of specific skills of reading comprehension? **(4.3)**

14. Make a list of comprehension skills essential in reading narrative type materials. Compare the skills included in this list with a list of those you deem essential in reading materials related to a content area. What similarities and differences can be noted in the skills included in the lists? **(4.4)**

15. Compare silent and oral reading practices according to the potential each has for development of comprehension skills and abilities. **(5.1)**

16. List the steps involved in "guided reading." Describe instructional procedures essential at each step. **(5.2)**

17. Prepare a plan for a "guided reading lesson." Include the questions you would use to guide learners' thinking. **(5.2)**

18. Explain the role of questions in helping learners improve comprehension of reading. **(5.3)**

19. Select a passage (either of a narrative type or related to a particular content area) and list the questions you might use to help learners achieve (1) literal comprehension, (2) interpretive comprehension, and (3) application of ideas or information acquired. **(5.3)**

20. Make a list of skills that can be termed "study skills." How do these relate to basic comprehension skills and abilities? **(6.1) (6.3)**

21. List skills that fit the description of location skills. Are these significantly different from those labeled study skills? **(6.2)**

22. What relationships do you see between skills of location and skills of comprehension? **(6.4)**

23. What competencies are important for teachers in the development of learners' comprehension skills and abilities? Can competencies required for helping learners develop comprehension skills and abilities be separated, discretely, from those generally required for effective instruction in reading? **(7.0)**

Selected References

1. Bamman, Henry A., Mildred A. Dawson, and James J. McGovern, *Fundamentals of Basic Reading Instruction*, Third edition. N. Y.: David McKay Co., 1973.
2. Barbe, Walter B., *Educator's Guide to Personalized Reading Instruction*. Englewood Cliffs, N. J.: Prentice-Hall, 1961.
3. Bartolome, P. I., "Teachers' Objectives and Questions in Primary Reading," *Reading Teacher*, 23 (October, 1969), 27–33.
4. Cleland, Donald L., editor, *Reading and Thinking*, Report of the Seventeenth Annual Reading Conference, Pittsburgh: University of Pittsburgh Press, 1961.
5. Cleland, Donald L., "A Construct of Comprehension in Reading and Inquiry," *Conference Proceedings*, 10. Newark, Del.: International Reading Association, 1965, 59–64.
6. Davidson, H. H., and G. Lang, "Children's Perceptions of Their Teachers' Feelings Toward Them Related to Self-Perception, School Achievement, and Behavior" in *The Self in Growth, Teaching and Learning*, Don E. Hamerchek, editor. Englewood Cliffs, N. J.: Prentice-Hall, 1965, 424–39.
7. Davidson, Roscoe, "Teacher Influence and Children's Levels of Thinking," *Reading Teacher*, 22 (May, 1969), 702–704.
8. Davis, Frederick B., "Psychometric Research on Comprehension in Reading," *Reading Research Quarterly*, 7 (Summer, 1972), 628–78.
9. Davis, Frederick B., "Research in Comprehension in Reading," *Reading Research Quarterly*, 3 (Summer, 1968), 499–545.
10. DeBoer, John J., and Martha Dallmann, *The Teaching of Reading*, Third edition. N. Y.: Holt, Rinehart and Winston, 1970.
11. Durkin, Dolores, *Teaching Them to Read*, Second edition. Boston: Allyn and Bacon, 1974.
12. Gall, Meredith D., "The Use of Questions in Teaching," *Review of Educational Research*, 40 (December, 1970), 707–21.
13. Guilford, J. P., "Frontiers in Thinking that Teachers Should Know About," *The Reading Teacher*, 13 (February, 1960), 176–82.
14. Goodman, Kenneth S., "Strategies for Increasing Comprehension in Reading," monograph. Glenview, Ill.: Scott-Foresman, 1973.
15. Goodman, Kenneth S., "Dialect Barriers to Reading Comprehension" in *Reading and Inquiry, Conference Proceedings*, 10 (1965), 240–42. Newark, Del.: International Reading Association, 1965.
16. Guszak, Frank J., "Teachers' Questions and Levels of Reading Comprehension" in *The Evaluation of Children's Reading Achievement*, Thomas C. Barrett, editor. Newark, Del.: International Reading Association, 1967.
17. Hafner, Lawrence E., and Hayden B. Jolly, *Patterns of Teaching Reading in the Elementary School*. N. Y.: Macmillan, 1972.
18. Harris, Albert J., and Edward R. Sipay, *Effective Teaching of Reading*, Second edition. N. Y.: David McKay Co., 1971.
19. Harris, Larry A., and Carl B. Smith, *Reading Instruction Through Diagnostic Teaching*. N. Y.: Holt, Rinehart and Winston, 1972.
20. Heilman, Arthur W., *Principles and Practices of Teaching Reading*, Third edition. Columbus, Ohio: Charles E. Merrill, 1972.
21. Herber, Harold L., *Teaching Reading in Content Areas*. Englewood Cliffs, N. J.: Prentice-Hall, 1970.

22. Hunkins, F. P., *Questioning Strategies and Techniques*. Boston: Allyn and Bacon, 1972.

23. King, Martha L., Bernice D. Ellinger, and Willavene Wolf, editors, *Critical Reading*. Philadelphia: J. B. Lippincott, 1967.

24. Sanders, N. M., *Classroom Questions: What Kinds?* N. Y.: Harper and Row, 1966.

25. Smith, Nila B., "The Many Faces of Reading Comprehension," *Reading Teacher*, 23 (December, 1969), 249–59.

26. Spache, George D., and Evelyn B. Spache, *Reading in the Elementary School*. Boston: Allyn and Bacon, 1973.

27. Stauffer, Russell G., *Directing Reading Maturity as a Cognitive Process*. N. Y.: Harper and Row, Publishers, 1969.

28. Stauffer, Russell G., *Teaching Reading as a Thinking Process*. N. Y.: Harper and Row, 1969.

Appendixes

Appendix A

Glossary

Terms and definitions selected for inclusion in this glossary are restricted in two important ways. First, only some of those terms related to educational accountability pertinent to teachers' classroom performances are included. The list, therefore, is representative (not exhaustive) of all important terms used in discussions of accountability. Second, most of the terms included can be defined in various ways, depending on the perspective from which they are viewed. Definitions presented here, however, are concise and restricted — in many cases — to one perspective. The purpose of the glossary should be kept in mind: it is intended as an introduction to the meaning of each selected term, not as a source that presents a full description of all aspects of each concept.

Achievement	Behavioral changes acquired by a learner or learners as a result of instruction oriented toward specified objectives.
Achievement test	A means by which a learner's achievement can be measured on the basis of the nature of his or her responses. Generally, questions sample pertinent content. Responses can be oral or written.
Achievement test scores	Numerical results from performance on an achievement test.
Competency	A specific skill or ability for performing a particular task. (*Teacher competencies:* Skills and abilities for helping learners achieve defined learning behaviors.)
Competitive bidding	Competing by offering a more attractive price than others for the privilege of doing a particular job.

Comprehensive evaluation	An evaluation program based on objectives sufficiently broad to include attention to all important elements in an instructional program.
Computer-Assisted Instruction (CAI)	An instructional technological procedure developed under Title III of the ESEA that utilizes computerization to provide independent learning particularly in mathematics and reading. (An example: Through an on-line computer program based at Stanford University, practice in reading and mathematics is provided for children in Kentucky and Mississippi.)
Contingency management	Management of a class based on the assumption that if the classroom environment contains appropriate rewards for desirable behavior, undesirable behavior will tend to disappear.
Continuous evaluation	Accompanying every stage of the instructional process with appropriate evaluation.
Contract	A legal agreement usually between a company involved in commercially producing and distributing educational materials and a school district. For most of these types of contracts, payment by the school district to the company depends on the success achieved by students in the pertinent schools during the period in which the company agreed to raise levels of achievement.
Contract teaching	A form of packaged learning for individualizing instruction in which the learner agrees to meet requirements through fulfillment of the terms of a contract. A contract generally contains the following components: (1) title, (2) rationale or purpose, (3) instructional or behavioral objectives, (4) pretest (5) resources or activities (usually representing a multimedia approach to learning), (6) self-test, and/or posttest, and (7) optional activities for achieving objectives. Each student proceeds through the steps of a contract according to his own rate and ability. There is no pressure to keep up and no reason for failure.
Cooperative evaluation	Involvement of all persons affected by the results of an evaluation in the process of evaluation.
Cost-effectiveness	Units of achievement balanced effectively with costs of the units.
Criterion	A standard by which performance on a test may be judged. Sometimes used to indicate an objective toward which instruction is focused.
Criterion measure	A procedure or technique of measurement or observation to determine the degree to which a criterion (objective) has been mastered.
Criterion-referenced tests	Tests of mastery designed to assess behavior specifically related to defined criteria (objectives) for determining, directly and exactly, what an individual can or cannot do.

Educational accountability	The concept that, in part, means that some person or persons will be held responsible for producing identifiable, measurable results of instruction.
Educational auditor	An individual responsible for determining the appropriateness of the design, operation, and results of the evaluation process used to determine the results of instruction.
Equivalent-test forms	Forms of a test constructed independently, but according to the same set of test specifications — including types of test items, distribution of difficulty values, nature of content, and types of scores yielded. Equivalence of the forms is determined statistically.
Feedback	Reports of facts and other information related to educational efforts.
Goal	Ultimate aim, purpose, or mission toward which educational efforts are focused, or oriented.
Grade-equivalent score	A score interpreted as being equivalent to a particular grade level in the schools: usually interpreted to show whether a learner is at, above, or below a specified grade level in a particular area of the curriculum.
Group test	A test that can be administered to a group of learners all at once; usually requires use of paper and pencils.
Humanistic education	Educational experiences designed to help each individual realize his fullest potential as a human being; particularly focused on influencing positive changes in learners' affective behaviors.
Incentive	Usually an extrinsic reward offered learners for learning. Dolls, hamburgers, green stamps, and books are among incentives that have been offered as rewards for learning. Other incentives have been praise, attractive environments, and the like. *(Teacher Incentive:* Term used to refer to agreements between school districts and teachers which offer teachers opportunities to receive salary increments or merit pay increases for learners' improved achievement as revealed in results of standardized tests.)
Individualized instruction	Any plan designed to accommodate individual differences in the classroom. Also, an approach to classroom management.
Individually prescribed instruction	A method of designing instruction to fit the diagnosed needs and abilities of an individual learner. Term can be applied generally to any instructional efforts designed to meet specific known needs of a learner.
Individual test	A test administrable to one individual at a time.
Instructional system	Planned approach to instruction characterized by formal procedures for defining goals and objectives, for identifying tasks essential for achieving goals and objectives, for organizing to accomplish the tasks, for evaluating the

degree to which goals and objectives are achieved, and for revising the entire process as experience indicates. Also, sets of prescribed instructional procedures, accompanied by sets of organized, specific, and related materials deemed essential for helping learners achieve specified objectives.

Learning center
Arrangement of sets of materials designed to enable an individual learner to proceed independently toward achievement of specified objectives. (2) A designated area or room where instructional and learning materials usually representing a variety of types of media are housed. (3) Name frequently given to classrooms where emphasis is on individualized, independent learning oriented toward achievement of specified objectives.

Learning director
Term sometimes used to refer to a teacher who, by design, injects his influence on an individual's learning only when that influence is required or needed, as opposed to the teacher who guides every aspect of the learning process for learners in a classroom.

Learning sequence
A particular order of steps or stages designed to help learners acquire a behavior or set of behaviors.

Management system
Application of program designs and management techniques developed in business and industry to education. Among these systems are:
PERT: Progam Evaluation and Review Techniques
CPM: Critical Path Method
PPBS: Planning, Programming, and Budgeting System
MBO: Management by Objectives

Modular learning
A type of planned "package" for independent learning by individuals in which each person proceeds through all steps provided in the plan at his own rate and ability. Generally, a module contains the following parts: (1) objectives, (2) rationale, (3) pretest, (4) learning tasks, (5) alternative learning tasks, and (6) posttest.

Need
The discrepancy between what a learner can do and what he should be able to do.

Need assessment
Application of procedures and techniques to compare the present status of a learner to the status he should have attained.

Norm-referenced test
A test whose results can show an individual's relative performance as compared with persons in a specified norm group.

Norms
Scores representing typical performance of persons in clearly defined reference groups.

Objective
Statement of the precise, observable behavior a learner is expected to show as a result of instruction; often referred to as "instructional objective," "behavioral objective."

Option
An alternative way in which an objective may be achieved.

Paraprofessional	An instructional aide, usually a local parent who performs auxiliary services in the classroom; also referred to as assistant learning directors or, more simply, aides.
Performance contract	A type of legal agreement by which the contractor is paid on the basis of how much learners learn. The first performance contract was between the schools of Texarkana on the Texas-Arkansas border and the Dorsett Educational Systems. The contract stipulated that Dorsett would be paid a certain amount for each child in grades six through eight whose performance in mathematics and English was raised by one grade level.
Performance objective	An objective that specifies the performance expected, the level and direction of the performance, units of performance measurement, means of measurement to be used, and the conditions under which the performance is to be manifest.
Prescriptive learning	Learning activities prescribed for an individual on the basis of his diagnosed strengths and abilities.
Product of education	Student learning; actual behavioral changes; results accomplished by instruction.
Programmed instruction	Prepared materials or activities designed to permit a learner to proceed step by step through a predetermined learning sequence until an objective is achieved. Provisions are made for appropriate feedback at every step.
System	A goal-oriented enterprise characterized by formal procedures for defining goals and objectives, for identification of tasks essential for evaluation of the total process.
Token	An item given as a reward for desirable behavior. (*Token-Exchange Program:* A system by which learners can exchange tokens earned for desirable behavior for premiums such as candy, books, privileges, etc.)
Turnkey	Term used in the building trades when a contractor accepts full responsibility for construction of a building and turns the keys over to the new owner at completion. In education, the term refers to an educational contractor who assumes full responsibility for a project for a period of time at the end of which the project is turned over to the school system.
Voucher	An amount paid to parents to cover costs of educating children at the school of their choice; plan proposed by the Office of Economic Opportunity.

Selected References

1. Banathy, Bela, *Instructional Systems.* Palo Alto, Ca.: Fearon Publishers, 1968.
2. Betts, Emmett Albert, "What is Individualized Reading?" *The Reading Teacher,* 26, No. 7 (April, 1973), 678–79.

3. Cunningham, Luvern L., "On Accountability Problems," *Theory Into Practice*, 8 (October, 1969), 285–92.

4. Farr, Roger, *Reading: What Can be Measured?* Newark, Del.: International Reading Association Fund, 1969.

5. House, Ernest R., Wendell Rivers, and Daniel L. Stufflebeam, "An Assessment of the Michigan Accountability System," *Phi Delta Kappan*, 55, No. 10 (June 1974), 663–69.

6. Karlin, Robert, *Teaching Elementary Reading*. N. Y.: Harcourt Brace Jovanovich, 1971.

7. Kearney, C. Philip, David L. Donovan, and Thomas H. Fisher, "In Defense of Michigan's Accountability Program," *Phi Delta Kappan*, 56, No. 1 (September, 1974), 14–19.

8. Mecklenberger, James A., and John A. Wilson, "Learning C. O.D.: Can the Schools Buy Success?" *Saturday Review* (September 18, 1971), 62–65; 76–79.

9. Mehrens, William A., and Irvin J. Lehmann, *Standardized Tests in Education*. N. Y.: Holt, Rinehart, and Winston, 1969.

10. Vernon, Walter M., *Motivating Children*. N. Y.: Holt, Rinehart and Winston, 1972.

11. Wilder, Amos, "Client Criticism of Urban Schools: How Valid?"*Phi Delta Kappan*, 51 (November, 1969), 129–30.

Appendix B

Instructional Units: Objectives and Related Evaluation Procedures

Contents

Unit	Page
Initial Reading Skills	238
Comprehension Skills	243
Developing Reading Skills—Primary Level Comprehension Skills	245
Development of Ability to Use Compound Words in Word Recognition— Development of Comprehension Ability	249
Developing Word-Recognition and Comprehension Skills (Primary Level)	255
Improving Listening Ability (Upper Primary Level)	261
Reading Readiness: Visual Discrimination	263
Developing Skills in the Use of the Dictionary (Intermediate Grades)	271

Units of instruction selected for inclusion in Appendix B represent samples of accountability procedures teachers can devise for themselves. Each unit demonstrates typical general and specific objectives that can be sought during an instructional period or, as the case may be, during a series of instructional periods. Each list of objectives is followed by a measure or measures typical of those that can be used to evaluate learners' achievement of the behaviors sought. Teaching strategies or materials of instruction used to help learners achieve the objectives are not included in the plans.

Initial Reading Skills

Behavioral Objectives

1.0 Recognizes words by sight
    1.1 Identifies words selected from Dolch Word List
    1.2 Identifies words selected from primer
2.0 Applies basic rules related to word recognition
    2.1 Identifies single initial consonant sounds
    2.2 Pronounces single initial consonant sounds
    2.3 Identifies single initial consonant sounds in the final position
    2.4 Pronounces single consonant sounds in final position
    2.5 Pronounces sounds of consonant blends: bl, wh, st, fl, pl, and cl
3.0 Recognizes elements of word structure
    3.1 Identifies word endings: ed as in wanted, ed as in liked, and ed as in laughed
    3.2 Identifies compound words
    3.3 Develops common word families: all, at, it, etc.
4.0 Recognizes various clues to word recognition
    4.1 Differentiates between upper- and lower-case letters
    4.2 Discriminates between different lengths of words
    4.3 Detects double letters in words
5.0 Demonstrates comprehension skills
    5.1 Concludes that printed symbols represent ideas, actions, or objects
    5.2 Follows printed directions
    5.3 Verifies a statement
    5.4 Expresses a conclusion drawn from given facts
    5.5 Retells what has been read orally
    5.6 Places events into proper sequence
    5.7 Finds answers to specific questions
6.0 Applies skills in oral and in silent reading
    6.1 Articulates speech sounds correctly
    6.2 Pronounces phrases correctly
    6.3 Uses voice intonation to give proper meaning
    6.4 Displays a good posture while reading
    6.5 Observes simple punctuation (. , ? !)
    6.6 Reads silently without vocalization
    6.7 Reads silently without head movement

Checklist For
Selected Reading Behaviors

Child's Name _____ Date _____

Behavior	*Yes*	*No*
1. Pronounces the following words: all, am, big, down, look, play, was, of, saw, etc. **(1.1)**		
2. Reads selection from pre-primer **(1.2)**		
3. Pronounces sounds represented by single consonants in initial position: boy, sing, hear, see, was, father, etc. **(2.1)**		

4. Pronounces sounds represented by single consonants in final position: bat, said, took, up, etc. **(2.4)**
5. Pronounces word endings: ed, s, ing: wanted, laughed, boys, saying, etc. **(3.1)**
6. Differentiates between length of words: farm, farmer; bring, bringing, etc. **(4.2)**
7. Articulates speech sounds correctly **(6.1)**
8. Reads by phrases **(6.2)**
9. Uses voice intonation to express meaning **(6.3)**
10. Displays good posture **(6.4)**
11. Observes punctuation **(6.5)**

Several objectives can be evaluated by child's responses to paper and pencil tests.

4.1   Directions: *Circle the right answer.*
1. Jane, jane.
2. Spot lives in a (Doghouse, doghouse).
3. I live in a (Town, town).

3.3   Directions: *In each list, circle the word that does not belong in the family.*

all	ten	sit	or
ball	men	bite	far
call	bin	bit	for
car	wren	hit	

3.2   Directions: *Place a check mark beside each compound word.*

farmyard	schoolyard	mother
grandmother	classroom	chalkboard
bringing	hearing	morning
seeing	teacher	month

2.6   Directions: *Circle the consonant blend in each word.*

blue	float
what	plane
stop	clear

4.3   Directions: *Circle the double letters in each word.*

free	better	little
bubble	letter	narrow

2.5   Directions: *Circle the letter that makes the short vowel sound in each word.*

sat   met   got   kitten   pup   had   sing   was   sad

2.1   Directions: *Circle the beginning consonant in each word.*

tea   nose   cake   like   bike   dish   boy   girl

2.3   Directions: *Circle the consonant at the end of each word.*

bird   chair   salt   run   said   took   this

5.1   Directions: *Draw a line from the picture to the word that matches the picture.*

cat   clock   ball   girl

5.6   Directions: *Circle the sentence that tells what Sue did first.*

Sue went to the blackboard.

Sue wrote her name on the blackboard.

Sue got up from her desk.

Sue picked up the chalk.

4.1   Directions: *Circle the uppercase letters.*

a   A   k   K

Johnny   Z   z

5.4   Directions: *Circle what you think happened.*

It is summer and Johnny is wearing his bathing suit. What is Johnny going to do?

Johnny is going to build a snowman.

Johnny is going to the beach.

Mary just woke up. It is morning. Mary is going to eat. What meal will Mary have?

breakfast   lunch   dinner

Initial Reading Skills

Behavioral Objectives: The Child

1.0   Interprets auditory stimuli
  1.1   Follows oral directions
  1.2   Repeats rhythmic patterns
  1.3   Differentiates between like and unlike sounds
  1.4   Identifies beginning sounds
2.0   Uses visual skills
  2.1   Points to like and unlike objects
  2.2   Matches like letter symbols
  2.3   Matches like word symbols
  2.4   Classifies objects according to size
  2.5   Classifies objects according to shape
  2.6   Classifies objects according to color
  2.7   Uses left-right direction while classifying
3.0   Recognizes symbols
  3.1   Locates own name in print
  3.2   Identifies names of letters
  3.3   Identifies numerals
  3.4   Matches upper- and lower-case letters
4.0   Understands meanings of words
  4.1   Matches words with pictures
  4.2   Discusses ideas
  4.3   Describes pictures
  4.4   Draws pictures of selected objects
5.0   Understands meaning of the story
  5.1   Identifies characters by names
  5.2   Identifies roles of characters

    5.3   Chooses the main idea
    5.4   Describes the conclusion of the story
    5.5   Retells the story
6.0   Demonstrates fundamentals of oral expression
    6.1   Relates experiences spontaneously
    6.2   Speaks in complete sentences
    6.3   Uses clear speaking voice

Test One

Directions: The teacher plays a note on the piano after instructing the child to listen very carefully to determine whether the note is high or low. (Teacher plays middle C and then plays the C an octave higher. When the child hears a high note, he stretches his arms above head. When the note is low, the child squats. Eventually, the teacher hits the same note twice. **(1.1, 1.3)** The teacher marks the number of times the child answered correctly.

Number of times problems were presented to the child _____
Number of like sounds identified _____
Number of unlike sounds identified _____

Directions: The teacher instructs the child to listen to the rhythm played on the piano. After the child has heard the rhythm, he uses a pencil to tap out the same rhythm. **(1.2)**

Test Two

Directions: The teacher pronounces several series of words, each series beginning with the same sound: day, dog, do, does, etc. The child states another word or several words that begin with the same sound. **(1.4)**

            boy, by, buy, bought, being
            cat, come, carry, call, coat
            name, need, no, neck, never

Test Three

Directions: The teacher assembles several items—such as small balls, paper clips, pencils, chalk, crayons, etc. Include pairs of several of the items. Ask the child to select items that are the same or those that are different. **(2.1)**

Test Four

1. Prepare a worksheet similar to the following. Have the child make a crossmark (X) above each word that begins with the same letter as that of the first word in the line. **(2.2)**

find	feel	took	few	sing	she
go	get	goat	gone	boy	boat
see	sit	say	try	bee	sound

2. Draw a line from the word in the first column that is the same as the word in the second column. **(2.3)**

I	II
bring	here
today	bring
here	hear
hear	today
take	take

3. Assemble several items of varying sizes ranging from small to large. Provide the child with two boxes and ask him to place the small objects in one of the boxes and the large ones in the other. **(2.4)**

4. Provide the child with several pictures of round and rectangular-shaped objects. Ask him to place pictures of round objects on one half of a sheet of paper, and rectangular ones on the other half. **(2.5)**

5. Provide the child with a sheet of paper upon which are uncolored items that are either worn or eaten. Instruct the child to use one color for all items that can be worn and another color for those that can be eaten. **(2.6)**

6. Observe the child as he works the preceding task to determine whether he uses left-to-right direction in completing it. **(2.7)**

7. Provide child with an oaktag strip upon which his name is printed. Ask child to select his name from among his and two other names (Use the chalkboard or a chart). **(3.1)**

8. Use an alphabet chart and have child identify the indicated symbol by name. **(3.2)**

9. Distribute cards containing a numeral between one and ten. As each numeral is called, have the child that holds that particular card bring the card to the front of the room. **(3.3)**

10. Using mimeographed sheets, have the child locate the letter in the row that matches the first one in the row. **(3.4)**

A	C	A	Y	D	F
M	K	L	N	P	M

11. Using mimeographed sheets, have the child locate the lower-case letter in the row that matches the upper-case letter that begins the row. **(3.5)**

A	c	a	y	d	f
M	k	l	n	p	m

12. Prepare exercises that require the child to identify the picture named by a particular word. **(4.1)**

13. Instruct the child to draw a picture of a familiar object. **(4.4)**

Checklist For Evaluation of Objectives 4.2 - 6.3

Name_____   *Yes*   *No*

Expresses ideas   **4.2**
Describes selected pictures   **4.3**
Identifies characters of a story   **5.1**
Describes roles played by selected
   characters   **5.2**
Selects the main idea in the story   **5.3**
Retells the story   **5.5**
Volunteers personal experiences related
   to story   **6.1**
Speaks in complete sentences   **6.2**
Uses clear speaking voice   **6.3**

Comprehension Skills
(Based on *The Hungry Thing*) *

Behavioral Objectives

1.0   Knows facts of the story
   1.1   Lists events in order
   1.2   Describes main characters
   1.3   Matches characters and their traits
2.0   Understands the story content
   2.1   Distinguishes between fact and fantasy
   2.2   Predicts the outcome of the story
   2.3   Summarizes the story
3.0   Interprets meaning of story content
   3.1   Dramatizes the story
   3.2   Depicts a major event or a favorite character
   3.3   Relates events in the story to personal experiences
4.0   Recalls details of the story
   4.1   Discriminates between major ideas and minor details
   4.2   Identifies the setting of the story
   4.3   Describes the mood of the story
5.0   Thinks critically about the story
   5.1   Choose an original title for the story
   5.2   Explains why the existing title is appropriate

Reading Comprehension Test

1. Number the events in order from 1 to 5.   **(1.1)**
   _____The "Hungry Thing" asked for shmancakes.
   _____The "Hungry Thing" turned his sign around to say "Thank you."

*Jan Slepian and Ann Seider, *The Hungry Thing* (N. Y.: Scholastic Book Services, Scholastic Magazines, 1971).

_____The little boy offered the Hungry Thing some foodles.
_____The Hungry Thing came to town.
_____The Hungry Thing asked for feetloaf.

2. *Directions:* Draw a line from the character to his description.   (**1.3**)

The Hungry Thing   always gave the wrong answer for what the
                          Hungry Thing wanted

The little boy   ran away from the townspeople

The wiseman   wore a sign that said "Feed me"

                          always knew what the Hungry Thing wanted

3. Directions: Put an X in the space before each statement that is true. Put an O in the space before each statement that is false.   (**2.1**)
_____The Hungry Thing was a little boy.
_____Smello means soup.
_____The Hungry Thing wore a sign that said "Feed me."
_____The Hungry Thing tried to eat the townspeople.
_____The Hungry Thing was friendly towards the people.

4. Directions: Choose the correct word from the following list and write it in the blank. (**4.1** and **4.3**)

"Thank you"	ate	unhappy
townspeople	"Feed me"	soup
all	little boy	

a. The Hungry Thing wore a sign that said _____.
b. The _____ knew how to change the letters around to get the right food for the Hungry Thing.
c. The _____ gave food to the Hungry Thing.
d. The Hungry Thing _____ all the food given to him.
e. On the other side of the sign was written _____.
e. "Boop the smacker" was "_____ with cracker."
g. The townspeople fed the Hungry Thing _____ day.
h. The townspeople were _____ when the Hungry Thing sat down to be fed again.

5. Directions: Choose the correct answer and circle its number.   (**5.3**)
a. As the Hungry Thing asked for shmancakes the townspeople
   (1) walked away
   (2) cried
   (3) gave the Hungry Thing pancakes
b. When the townspeople gave the Hungry Thing some cookies he
   (1) ate the cookies and smiled
   (2) ate the plate
   (3) walked away angrily
c. The little boy gave the Hungry Thing some noodles and said,
   (1) "Have some foodles"
   (2) "Go away"
   (3) "Have some smello"
d. When the Hungry Thing ate all the food, he
   (1) fell asleep
   (2) ate the cook
   (3) smiled and turned the sign around

e. Write why you think the title, "The Hungry Thing," fits the story.   **(5.2)**
f. Directions: Draw a picture of your favorite scene or character.   **(3.2)**
g. Objectives **4.1, 4.2, 3.3** will be evaluated through oral discussion with the children.

Key to Selected Answers

1. 2, 5, 4, 1, 3
3. O, O, X, O, X
4. a. "Feed me"
   b. little boy
   c. townspeople
   d. ate
   e. "Thank you"
   f. soup
   g. all
   h. unhappy

Developing Reading Skills — Primary Level Comprehension Skills*

Behavioral Objectives

1.0 Knows basic terms
   1.1 Uses new vocabulary correctly in oral expression
   1.2 Uses new vocabulary correctly in written work
   1.3 Applies word-recognition skills to unfamiliar words
   1.4 Matches terms that have the same meanings
   1.5 Selects the term that best fits a particular definition
2.0 Understands the story
   2.1 Describes the plot of the story
   2.2 Arranges details of the story into proper sequence
   2.3 Identifies characters in the story
   2.4 Gives a reason for a particular action by a character
   2.5 Creates a story using the new vocabulary
3.0 Applies information effectively
   3.1 Distinguishes between a proper and an improper ending for the story
   3.2 Follows directions
   3.3 Answers oral questions correctly
   3.4 Answers written questions correctly
4.0 Appreciates good literature
   4.1 Voluntarily selects good literature during free reading time
   4.2 Gives reasons for liking or disliking the story
   4.3 Cooperates in making a mural based on the story

---

*Based on Lee Lothrop, "The Strange Present" in *Star Bright* (Shepard Company, 1969), pp. 44–55.

5.0 Demonstrates psychomotor skills
    5.1 Draws original pictures related to the story
    5.2 Constructs puppets depicting characters of the story
    5.3 Dramatizes actions of characters in the story
    5.4 Writes a "thank you" letter

Test

1. Fill in the blank spaces with words from the following list that fit the description given. **(1.2–1.5)**

mountain   present   envelope   wheels

morning   pillows   secret   clock

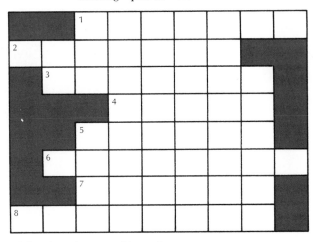

    (1) A word that describes something soft to rest on.
    (2) This word can mean that you are here or it can mean a gift.
    (3) The sun rises at this time of day.
    (4) Substitute "cl" for "bl" in block and you have this.
    (5) It starts like "when" and rhymes with "steel."
    (6) This is a word that tells the name of a container for a letter.
    (7) This is between two people. No one else must know.
    (8) Climbers often like to explore this.

2. Directions: Underline the word in parenthesis that best completes the sentence. **(1.2)**
    a. Julie gave me a birthday (present, envelope).
    b. There was a (strange, wagon) in our car.
    c. Someone (knocked, noise) on our door.
    d. We put new (wheels, pillows) on the bed.

3. Select the word that begins the same as the first word in each line. **(1.3)**
    a. present — chair, prove, floor
    b. strange — picture, window, stripe
    c. mountain — maybe, paint, tan
    d. knocked — count, kitchen, knows
    e. secret — sand, cave, noise
    f. panda — wagon, top, pillows
    g. clock — city, cave, clown

h. hammered — have, envelope, nailed
i. wrong — won, wagon, write
j. wonderful — win, train, world

4. Underline the correct word. (**1.3**)
   a. Which word ends with the first sound in mountain?
      town, cap, ham
   b. Which word ends with the first sound of tight?
      lamp, light, not
   c. Which word starts like the first sound in wheels?
      when, only, flowers
   d. Which word ends with the same sound as the first sound in pillows?
      whip, tractor, pig
   e. Which word rhymes with clock?
      knock, can, still

5. Draw a circle around the root word in each of the following words: (**1.3**)
   a. knocked
   b. hammered
   c. wheels
   d. going
   e. secrets

6. Underline the word in column 2 that means the same as the word in column 1.
   (**1.4**)

1	2
automobile	car, tent, truck
present	bear, clown, gift
noise	fan, sound, noon
wheels	glasses, tires, car
clock	television, watch, morning

7. Draw a circle around the word in column 2 that includes the same sound as that
   underlined in the word in column 1. (**1.3**)

1	2
envelope	knives, fun, cow
pillows	king, book, some
automobile	lot, hot, hope
hammered	pan, tape, wait
television	light, kind, hit

8. Read the description. Write the name of the character described in the blank following the description. (**5.2** and **2.3**) (Note: Instead of a written test, each description can be pantomimed by a child and the children can guess who the character is).
   a. This bear delivered the letter to Mama and Papa Panda. He is a brown bear.
      He told the Pandas the kind of noise their present made. This bear's name is

      _____.
   b. This bear read the letter to his family. He is a black and white bear. He helped
      to put the automobile together. He got a rope to try to keep the present from
      running away. This bear's name is _____.
   c. This bear made cookies for the present in case it was hungry. She took two green
      pillows that came with the present and used them for the two big chairs. She is a
      black and white bear. This bear's name is _____.

d. This brown bear delivered the present to the Pandas. He wore a cap on his head, and had a handkerchief sticking out of his back pocket. This bear's name is

_____.

e. This bear wore his good clothes. He wore a bow tie and a top hat. He gave the present to the Pandas. He helped Papa Panda put the automobile together. His name is _____.

9. Put the happenings of the story in the correct order by placing numbers in the blanks at the left. **(2.2)**

_____ Mama Panda made cookies for the present.

_____ Willie delivered the letter.

_____ Mr. Brown delivered the present.

_____ Uncle Panda came to see if the Pandas liked the present.

_____ Sing, Sang, and Sung made toys out of the parts of the present.

_____ Willie showed the family the type of noise the present made.

_____ Papa and Uncle Panda put the present together.

_____ They all drove off down the mountain.

_____ Papa Panda got the rope.

10. Draw a circle around the best answer for each question.

a. After the bears opened the present, they

(1) could not figure out what it was and gave it away

(2) put it together and made a washing machine

(3) tried to put it together but they came out with a funny looking thing **(2.4)**

b. Once the bears put the present together they went

(1) shopping

(2) on a picnic

(3) to visit friends **(3.2)**

c. Which ending best fits this story?

(1) The Pandas were happy with their presents

(2) Uncle Panda came and put the present together

(3) They gave the present to the garbage collector **(3.2)**

11. Children can participate in a dramatization of this story. They have probably experienced the excitement and appreciation of receiving a present. They can write a "thank you" note to Uncle Panda for the automobile. Some of the vocabulary encountered in the story can be used in the note. This provides opportunity for the teacher to test children's understanding and application of the words. This activity provides for self-expression and for experience in writing. **(2.5 and 5.4)**

12. Draw separate pictures of events that occurred in the story on cards. Have the child arrange these pictures to illustrate the sequence of events in the story. Through this activity an evaluation can be made of how well the child understands and recalls events of the story. **(2.2)**

13. Have children construct puppets representing the characters in the story. Materials to be used include paper bags for the head and body of each puppet and construction paper glued onto the bags for different body parts. (Other materials can be used, depending on their availability.) Ideas for details on the puppets can be gained through pictures presented for motivational purposes before reading the story, the pictures accompanying the story, and research in other books about bears. This activity provides for self-expression and an exciting experience related to the story. **(5.2)**

14. Children use the puppets not only for acting out the events of the story but also for extending the experiences and adventures of the characters. This includes studying the character personalities from the context of the story, identifying with the characters, and becoming involved in the adventure. **(5.3)**

15. Through oral activities, children will discuss reasons for liking or disliking the story. Each child must give reasons for his opinion. This exercise provides the child with an opportunity to communicate with others, to listen, and to incorporate the ideas expressed by others into his own. The teacher can determine how well the child is progressing in the ability to validate his judgment and in his appreciation for literature. **(4.2)**

16. Each child will be asked to draw his own idea of the automobile as described in the story. This will give the child the opportunity to analyze, select, and organize the details and show his interpretation of the story through an art activity. The child's understanding and interpretation of this aspect of the story can then be determined. **(5.1)**

17. All children interested in participating will become engaged in producing a mural. The child's appreciation of the story will be indicated through his enthusiasm and involvement in the activity. The teacher will be able to determine how well the child works in a group situation in which cooperation is essential. This mural will serve as a culminating exeperience. **(4.3)**

Several objectives will be evaluated through use of the following checklist.

Checklist For Evaluation of Objectives

Name _____

Objectives	Satisfactory Progress	Needs Help
Is expressive in retelling story **(2.1)**		
Enunciates clearly **(3.4)**		
Is at ease during activities **(2.2)**		
Shows interest **(5.3)**		
Follows directions **(3.2)**		
Volunteers participation **(5.4)**		

Development of Ability to Use Compound Words in Word Recognition

Development of Comprehension Ability*

Behavioral Objectives

1.0 Knows new vocabulary words
  1.1 Identifies compound words
  1.2 Pronounces new vocabulary words correctly

---

*Based on John Steptoe, *Stevie* (N. Y.: Scholastic Book Services, 1969).

1.3 Matches parts of compound words
1.4 Labels pictures with correct words
1.5 Completes selected compound words
1.6 Chooses the correct word when the meaning of the word is given
2.0 Recalls facts included in the story
    2.1 Lists given parts of the story in the correct sequence
    2.2 Identifies specific characters
    2.3 Describes events in the story
3.0 Understands the main theme of the story
    3.1 Differentiates between main and subordinate ideas
    3.2 Selects the most appropriate title for the story
    3.3 Associates appropriate details with the main ideas these represent
4.0 Draws interferences from the story
    4.1 Describes feelings of the characters
    4.2 Identifies motives of the characters
    4.3 Explains a basis for inferences drawn from the story
    4.4 Differentiates between how a character really feels and what he says
    4.5 Participates in dramatizations
5.0 Interprets dialect spoken by the characters
    5.1 Compares own dialect with that of the character (Robert) in the story
    5.2 Explains meaning of words used in dialect
    5.3 Explains significance of the use of dialect in the story
6.0 Shows sensitivity to human needs and social problems
    6.1 Demonstrates cooperativeness with fellow classmates
    6.2 Expresses consideration for property of others

Test

1. Draw a line from a word in the first column to a word in the second column to make a compound word. **(1.1)** **(1.3)** **(1.5)**

	I	II
a.	up	box
	bread	baby
	foot	prints
		one
		stairs
b.	door	boy
	some	bell
	cow	more
		one
		prints
c.	every	where
	any	baby
	cry	boy
		more
		bell

2. Match the words in the first column with the words in the second column that mean the same thing. Write the letter of your answer in the space provided. **(5.2)**

I	II
_____ (1) somma that	a. got to take
_____ (2) gimme this	b. listening

_____ (3) gotta take	c. got to take
_____ (4) y' all	d. doing
_____ (5) listenin'	e. some of that
_____ (6) makin'	f. kind of
_____ (7) doin'	g. some of that
_____ (8) playin'	h. you all
_____ (9) thinkin'	i. playing
_____ (10) kinda	j. give me this
	k. making
	l. you always
	m. thinking

3. Draw a line from the picture to the compound word it represents. **(1.3) (1.4)**

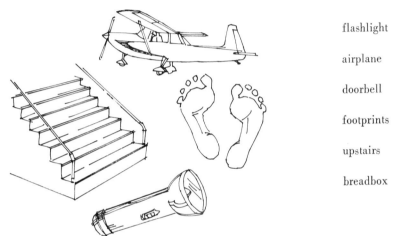

flashlight

airplane

doorbell

footprints

upstairs

breadbox

4. Complete the compound words. Select your answer from the choices given and write the complete word in the space provided. **(1.6)**

(1) _____ boy
   a. man
   b. baby
   c. cow

(2) home _____
   a. shoe
   b. work
   c. tray

(3) _____ time
   a. some
   b. watch
   c. cow

5. In each group, number the sentences (1), (2), and (3) in the order that they happened. **(2.1)**

   Group 1 _____a. Mrs. Mack brought Stevie to Robert's house.
   _____b. Momma told Robert that he would have a little friend to stay with him.
   _____c. Robert found out that Stevie always had to have his own way.

   Group 2 _____a. Bobby was called a baby-sitter.
   _____b. Stevie said, "I'm sorry Robert."
   _____c. Bobby's friends wanted to know if Stevie was Bobby's cousin.

   Group 3 _____a. Stevie's mother and father picked Stevie up and said that they were moving.

_____b. Bobby remembered that Stevie wasn't there.

_____c. Bobby made two bowls of corn flakes.

6. Read each question carefully. Select the best answer and place its number in the space provided.

_____a. Another name for the book *Stevie* might be   (**3.2**)

    (1) *The Crybaby*

    (2) *A Bad Boy*

    (3) *A Visitor*

    (4) *Little Brother*

_____b. While Stevie was at Robert's house, Robert thought that Stevie was   (**1.3**)

    (1) fun

    (2) a pest

    (3) mean

    (4) no trouble at all

_____c. When Robert called Stevie a crybaby, he meant that   (**4.4**)

    (1) Stevie always cried.

    (2) Stevie was a baby that always cried.

    (3) Stevie always had to have his own way.

_____d. After Stevie left, Robert thought that Stevie was   (**4.1**)

    (1) not so bad

    (2) stupid

    (3) mean

    (4) awful

_____e. Which sentence below best describes the main idea of the book *Stevie?*
(**3.1**)

    (1) Stevie was a crybaby who made trouble for Robert.

    (2) When Stevie was around, Robert complained about him, but when Stevie left, Robert missed him.

    (3) Stevie was a little boy who visited in Robert's house.

    (4) Robert was a baby-sitter for Stevie.

    (5) Robert did not like Stevie and he was happy that Stevie was never coming back.

7. Who did these things? Put the letter of your answer into the space provided.   (**2.2**)

a. Bobby

c. Stevie

c. Bobby and Stevie

_____(1) Who had a little boy stay with him?

_____(2) Who got footprints all over the bed?

_____(3) Who was like a little brother?

_____(4) Who played "boogie-man"?

_____(5) Who was called "baby-sitter" by his friends?

8. Answer each of the following questions in a complete sentence.   (**4.2**)

a. Why did Stevie have to stay with Robert and Robert's mother?

_____

_____

b. Why did Robert's mother make him play with Stevie?

_____

_____

9. Group discussion will be used to evaluate children's achievement of objectives **4.3** and **4.4.**

10. Achievement of objective **4.5** will be evaluated through various types of dramatic expression; role-playing, pantomime, etc.

11. Below are three main ideas found in the book *Stevie*. Listed under the ideas are some sentences. On the blank in front of each numbered sentence put the letter of the idea that goes with it.   (**3.3**)

a. Robert wanted Stevie to have his own toys to play with.

b. Robert didn't like to take Stevie outside to play.

c. Stevie wasn't coming back anymore. Robert decided that they used to have some good times together.

_____(1) Robert and Stevie used to play cowboys and indians on the stoop.

_____(2) Robert's friends teased him and called him "baby-sitter."

_____(3) Stevie broke Robert's toys.

_____(4) "Momma, can't you watch him and tell him to leave my stuff alone?"

_____(5) Robert and Stevie played in the park.

_____(6) "Come on Stevie. Why you gotta make all my friends laugh for?"

_____(7) They played "Boogie-man" and hid under the covers with Daddy's flashlight.

_____(8) Stevie always had to have his own way and he wanted everything he saw.

12. In the word puzzle, fill in the answer in the direction that the arrow indicates. (**1.6**)

(1) Stevie called Bobby's momma _____.

(2) What day of the week did Mrs. Mack always pick up Stevie?

(3) Stevie's real name was _____.

(4) How many brothers and sisters did Bobby have?

(5) Bobby and Stevie used to play Cowboys and _____.

(6) Stevie was _____ than Bobby.

horses
Monday
two
bigger
none
smaller
Steven
Saturday
Steve
Mother
four
one
Indians
Mommy

Key to Selected Answers

1. a. upstairs
      breadbox
      footprints
   b. doorbell
      someone
      cowboy
   c. everywhere
      anymore
      crybaby

2. (1) e
   (2) j
   (3) a
   (4) h
   (5) b
   (6) k
   (7) d
   (8) i
   (9) m
   (10) f

3. airplane
   upstairs
   flashlight
   footprints

4. *cow*boy
   home*work*
   *some*time

5. Group 1 a. 2
            b. 1
            c. 3
   Group 2 a. 2
            b. 3
            c. 1
   Group 3 a. 1
            b. 3
            c. 2

6. a. 4
   b. 2
   c. 3
   d. 2
   e. 2

7. (1) a
   (2) b
   (3) b
   (4) c
   (5) b

8. Any answer similar to the following:
   a. Stevie's mother works and he needs someone to take care of him.
   b. Stevie is Robert's guest so Robert should be nice to him.

11. (1) c
    (2) b
    (3) a
    (4) a
    (5) c
    (6) b
    (7) c
    (8) a

Who is Stevie (**6.1**)

1. Stevie's   coming   to   stay with me,   stay   with   me,   stay with   me,

Stevie's   coming   to   stay with me,   who   is   Stevie?

Other verses:
  2. Stevie's always following me around,
    That dumb Stevie.

  3. Stevie's going away from me,
    I'll miss Stevie.

Developing Word-Recognition and Comprehension Skills (Primary Level)*

Behavioral Objectives

1.0 Knows content of the story
    1.1 Lists events in sequence
    1.2 Retells the story
    1.3 Chooses the correct word or group of words to complete a sentence
    1.4 Identifies the main idea in the story
    1.5 Identifies details in the story
2.0 Knows new words found in the story
    2.1 Pronounces new words
    2.2 Spells new words
    2.3 Defines new words
    2.4 Writes synonyms and antonyms for new words
3.0 Uses phonics and structural-analysis skills

*Content based on "The City Woodchuck" in *Down Singing River*, Betts Basic Readers, Third edition (N. Y.: American Book, 1963), pp. 208–14.

3.1 Selects vowel sounds in words
3.2 Identifies accented syllables in two-syllable words
3.3 Identifies prefixes, suffixes, and root words
3.4 Selects appropriate definition for a word that has more than one meaning

4.0 Distinguishes between real and make-believe
    4.1 Differentiates between real and make-believe characters
    4.2 Differentiates between real and make-believe events
5.0 Participates in follow-up activities
    5.1 Writes a skit based on the story
    5.2 Rewrites the story ending
    5.3 Paints part of a mural
    5.4 Makes puppets to illustrate characters in the story
6.0 Appreciates reading
    6.1 Reads voluntarily
    6.2 Chooses his own books
    6.3 Writes his own story

Test

1. *Directions:* Number the events described below in the order in which they occurred in the story. **(1.1)**

_____The city woodchuck wished that he was back in the city.
_____The city woodchuck thought that Mr. Magic could help him.
_____The city woodchuck became Mr. Magic's helper.
_____The city woodchuck could not find anything to eat in the country.
_____The city woodchuck took a ride to the country.

2. *Directions:* In your own words, retell the story. **(1.2)**
(An ideal answer will include details such as the following.)

Once upon a time, there lived a woodchuck in the city. He was unhappy because he was the only woodchuck in the city. He wanted to go back to the country, but he did not know how to get there.

One day the woodchuck went to see Mr. Magic, who could fix anything. Mr. Magic sent the woodchuck to the country on a magic chair. When the woodchuck arrived in the country, he was cold and hungry. There was nothing to eat and nowhere to go.

The woodchuck wished that he was back in the city. Soon he went to sleep. When he woke up, he found himself in Mr. Magic's office. Mr. Magic offered the woodchuck a job. Now the woodchuck was happy. He was home again.

3. *Directions:* Complete each of the following statements with a word or phrase. **(1.3, 2.2, 2.3)**

a. The city woodchuck liked to eat at the Kingfish Eating Place where he could get nice warm _____.
b. The city woodchuck read the _____ and found Mr. Magic.
c. The city woodchuck rode in a _____ to get to the country.
d. When the city woodchuck arrived in the country, he found the country woodchucks finishing their _____ homes.
e. _____ suggested that the city woodchuck take an airplane to the country.
f. The first thing that the city woodchuck did after he wished he was back in the country was _____.

g. The first thing that the city woodchuck wanted after he arrived in the country was _____.

h. After the city woodchuck returned to the city, Mr. Magic suggested that he should go to _____.

4. *Directions:* Choose the correct answer to complete each statement. Place the number of your answer on the line before each statement.   (**1.3, 1.4**)

_____a. Woodchucks who live in the country eat during the
   (1) spring
   (2) summer
   (3) fall
   (4) winter

_____b. After the city woodchuck arrived in the country, he was
   (1) cold and hungry
   (2) cold and wet
   (3) warm and hungry
   (4) warm and dry

_____c. The woodchuck lived in the city because   (**4.1, 4.2**)
   (1) he moved away from the country
   (2) the city grew up around him
   (3) he did not like the country
   (4) the city is where all woodchucks live

_____d. Which one of the following events is the most important?   (**4.1, 4.2**)
   (1) Mr. Magic knew the talk of all the animals and birds
   (3) The city woodchuck could read and write
   (3) The city woodchuck thought he would be happier if he lived in the country.
   (4) Mr. Magic needed a helper in his office

5. *Directions:* Read each of the following statements. If a statement is true, circle the "T." If a statement is false, circle the "F."   (**4.1, 4.2**)

T   F   a. Mr. Magic knew the talk of all the animals and birds.
T   F   b. The woodchuck took an airplane back to the city
T   F   c. The city woodchuck had plenty to eat after he arrived in the country.
T   F   d. Mr. Magic asked for the woodchuck's help before the woodchuck went to the country.
T   F   e. There was one woodchuck living in the city.
T   F   f. Woodchucks can read and write.
T   F   g. Before he went to the country, the woodchuck did not feel safe in the city.
T   F   h. The woodchuck liked the crowded city before he went to the country.
T   F   i. Woodchucks can talk just as you and I can talk.

6. *Directions:* Briefly answer each of the following questions. Use complete sentences. (**2.3**)

1. Have you ever been into an elevator?

2. Describe an elevator.

3. State three ways in which the city differs from the country.

7. *Directions:* Draw a picture of your favorite part of the story.   (**2.3**)

8. *Directions:* If the word in the egg contains a short "e" sound, color the egg. If the word contains a long "e" sound, put an X on the word.   (**3.1**)

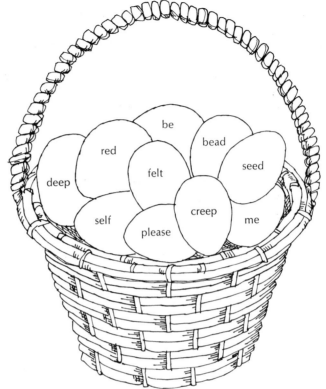

9. *Directions:* **If a word in an apple contains a short "a" sound, color the apple. If a word contains a long "a" sound, put an X on the apple.** **(3.1)**

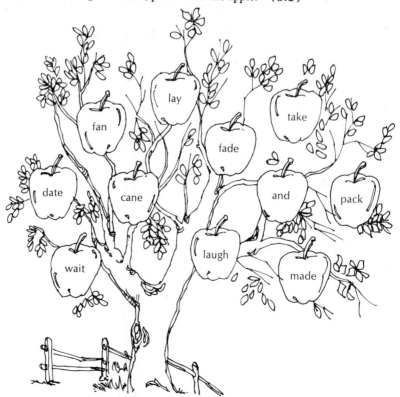

10. *Directions:* Write the name of the vowel sound in the space provided. **(3.1)**
   a. hot   short _____
            long _____
   b. ate   short _____
            long _____
   c. left   short _____
            long _____
   d. cup   short _____
            long _____
   e. right   short _____
            long _____
   f. home   short _____
            long _____

11. *Directions:* Write the name of the vowel in the accented syllable in the space provided. **(3.2)**
   a. city   short _____
            long _____
   b. surprise   short _____
              long _____
   c. clever   short _____
             long _____
   d. magic   short _____
            long _____

12. *Directions:* Draw one line under the root word. Draw two lines under the suffixes. **(3.3)**

        pleased   dressed   reading   smiled   building
        walked   holding   working   helper   crowded

   Directions: Draw one line under the root word. Draw two lines under the prefixes.
        untie   unhappy   repainted   displeased   replace

13. *Directions:* Write an antonym beside each of the following words. **(2.4)**
        happy   _____
        alone   _____
        clever   _____

   Directions: Write a synonym beside each of the following words. **(2.4)**
        surprise   _____
        pleased   _____
        happy   _____

14. *Directions:* On the line at the right, write the number of the best definition of the underlined word. **(3.4)**
   a. Just a <u>second</u> later, the child started to laugh. _____
   b. The <u>second</u> page is easy. _____
      (1) Short amount of time
      (2) The next after first
   c. "Take a <u>rest</u> before you eat," said Mother. _____
   d. The <u>rest</u> of the picture is blue. _____
      (1) The part that is left
      (2) A short sleep
   e. Can your dog <u>roll</u> over? _____
   f. Jerry had a <u>roll</u> and milk for breakfast. _____

g. Mom bought a <u>roll</u> of paper towels. _____
   (1) Something to eat
   (2) Something wound around a tube
   (3) Turn over

15. *Directions:* Draw a circle around the correct answer for each question   **(4.1, 4.2, 4.3)**
    a. Can woodchucks read and write?   Yes No
    b. Would you be surprised to see a wookchuck wearing a cap?   Yes No
    c. Do you think animals have ways of talking to each other?   Yes No
    d. Could you find a woodchuck living in the city?   Yes No
    e. Do wookchucks eat all summer and sleep all winter?   Yes No

16. Follow-up Activities Rating Scale   **(5.0)**

Rating S   Satisfactory
        U   Unsatisfactory

Child's Name: _____

	Partici-pates	*Shows creativity*	*Is cooper-ative*
Writes a skit			
Participates in a skit			
Rewrites the story ending			
Paints a mural			
Makes puppets			
Writes a puppet show			

Comments:

17. *Reading Appreciation Rating Scale*   **(6.0)**

Child's Name _____

S Satisfactory
U Unsatisfactory
P Progress shown

	S	*U*	*P*
Initiative (Reads voluntarily)			
Completes Assignments			
Selects a variety of types of books			
Writes original stories			

Comments:

Key to Selected Answers

1. 4, 1, 5, 3, 2
3. a. fishcakes
   b. newspaper
   c. magic chair
   d. winter
   e. Mr. Magic
   f. sleep
   g. something to eat
   h. work
4. a. (2)
   b. (1)
   c. (2)
   d. (3)

5. a. T   10. a. short 'o'   13. sad, crowded, dull
   b. F   b. long 'a'   startle, satisfied, glad
   c. F   c. short 'e'   14. a. (1)
   d. F   d. short 'u'   b. (2)
   e. T   e. long 'i'   c. (2)
   f. F   f. long 'o'   d. (1)
   g. T   11. a. short 'i'   e. (3)
   h. F   b. long 'i'   f. (1)
   i. F   c. short 'e'   g. (2)
                   d. short 'a'

Improving Listening Ability
(Upper Primary Level)

Behavioral Objectives

1.0 Applies basic listening skills as a story is read by the teacher
    1.1 Identifies details in the story
    1.2 Recalls sequence of events
    1.3 States inferences made in the story
    1.4 Retells the story
2.0 Recognizes sounds
    2.1 Identifies familiar sounds
    2.2 Locates sources of sounds
    2.3 Imitates animal sounds
3.0 Interprets emotion and mood in music
    3.1 Describes the mood of the music heard
    3.2 Identifies change in mood
    3.3 Explains how instruments affect mood
    3.4 Indicates that loudness or softness affects the mood in music
    3.5 Distinguishes various tempos as these change the mood in music
4.0 Displays good listening habits
    4.1 Listens without talking to neighbors
    4.2 Sits at ease while listening
    4.3 Looks at the speaker
    4.4 Prepares self for careful listening
    4.5 Follows speaker's message
5.0 Formulates opinions related to speaker's message (or to music)
    5.1 Shares personal experiences related to topic
    5.2 Reacts to new information
    5.3 Organizes thoughts during opening sequence
6.0 Participates in follow-up discussions
    6.1 Answers questions
    6.2 Summarizes speaker's message
    6.3 Compares own opinion and that of speaker

Test

The following is an objective test which deals with the story *Little Black Goes to the Circus.**

*Walter Farley, *Little Black Goes to the Circus* (N. Y.: Random House, 1963).

1. *Directions:* (Teacher)   Read the story to the class.
   (Class)   Read the questions and the phrases following each question. Circle the letter in front of the phrase that best completes the statement or answers the question.
   (**1.1**)
   a. Mr. Bruno, the circus man, did tricks with the animals, but he did not have
      (1) a monkey ride on a little bike
      (2) an elephant stand on a little box
      (3) a pony walk across the ring
      (4) a lion jump through a hoop
   b. Mr. Bruno had Little Black do several tricks, but he did not have Little Black
      (1) walk across a tall plank
      (2) jump over a little box
      (3) walk across a low plank
      (4) run back across a plank

2. Read the sentences below. Put a numeral 1 in the blank in front of the sentence that tells what happened first in the story. Put a 2 in the blank in front of the sentence that tells what happened second in the story. Put a 3 in the blank in front of the sentence that tells what happened third in the story. Put a 4 in the blank in front of the sentence that tells what happened las in the story. (**1.2**)
   _____a. Little Black ran away from the little boy to go back to the circus.
   _____b. Little Black tried to show Mr. Bruno that he could do tricks.
   _____c. Little Black decided to stay with the little boy.
   _____d. Little Black and the boy saw the circus come to town.

3. *Directions:* Read each sentence below. Circle "T" if the sentence is true. Circle "F" if the sentence is false.
   T   F   a. Little Black wanted to show Mr. Bruno that he could do tricks.   (**1.1**)
   T   F   b. Little Black did the trick for Mr. Bruno without falling down.   (**1.1**)
   T   F   c. Mr. Bruno did not think Little Black was a very smart pony.
   T   F   d. The little boy was proud of his pony.
   T   F   e. It was not a surprise to see the people run into the circus tent.   (**1.3**)
   T   F   f. The little boy wanted Little Black to walk across the high plank.   (**1.1**)
   T   F   g. Little Black was happy to be back with the little boy.   (**1.3**)

4. *Directions:* Read the questions. Answer each question in a few words. You will have to think back to what happened in the story.
   a. Why did Little Black walk away from the circus with his head down?   (**1.3**)
   b. What did the litle boy do to make Little Black happy?   (**1.4**)
   c. Why did the people in the circus want to be friends with Little Black?   (**1.3**)
   d. Why did Little Black leave the circus when he was the star of the show?   (**1.3**)
   e. Why did Little Black run away from the little boy?   (**1.4**)

5. *Directions:* Objectives **2.1**, **2.2**, and **2.3** can be evaluated by playing a tape upon which has been recorded several sounds made by animals, instruments, and different types of transportation. After the tape has been played, ask questions similar to the following.
   a. What animal makes this sound?
   b. Where would you find this animal?
   c. What sound does a cat make?
   d. What sound do sheep make?
   e. Name the instrument that makes this sound.
   f. Name the vehicle that makes this sound?

6. *Directions:* Play the record, "On a Bicycle Built for Joy."* Have the children read the following statements. Circle "T" if the statement is true; circle "F" if the statement is false.   (**3.4** and **3.5**)

T   F   a. Mood is something one feels.
T   F   b. A fast tempo moves quickly.
T   F   c. The same instruments are played throughout the music.
T   F   d. Instruments used in the music have nothing to do with the mood.
T   F   e. A slow tempo is softer than a fast tempo.
T   F   f. A fast tempo is loud and it makes you feel sleepy.
T   F   g. This record is a good one to show fast and slow tempo.

7. *Directions:* Circle the correct answer.   (**3.3**)
What instrument or instruments do you hear in Section A of the record?
a. Banjo
b. Harp
c. Guitar

8. *Directions:* Draw a picture of how you felt when the first part of the record was played.   (**3.1**)

9. *Directions:* Draw a picture of how you felt when the second part of the record was played.   (**3.1**)

10. Children use the following checklist to check up on their own listening habits.   (**4.0, 5.0, 6.0**)

> *Self-Check on My Listening Habits*   *Yes*   *No*

1. Do I get myself ready to listen?
2. Am I courteous toward the speaker?
3. Can I see and hear from my seat?
4. Are my eyes usually on the speaker?
5. Do I think about what the speaker is saying?
6. Do I find out right away what the speaker is talking about?
7. Can I tell the main idea?

Reading Readiness: Visual Discrimination

Behavioral Objectives

(Cognitive Domain)

1.0   Knows basic facts related to colors and shapes
    1.1   Identifies colors: red, yellow, orange, blue
    1.2   Identifies shapes: square, triangle, circle
    1.3   Recognizes relative sizes: large and small
    1.4   Identifies pattern sequences
2.0   Knows differences in colors and shapes
    2.1   Identifies differences between colors

---

*Burt Bacharach, "On a Bicycle Built for Joy," *Butch Cassidy and the Sundance Kid.* (Hollywood, California: AM Records, 20th Century-Fox Productions).

    2.2 Identifies differences between shapes

3.0 Applies basic concepts

    3.1 Reproduces shapes

    3.2 Discriminates between large and small shapes

    3.3 Reconstructs given pattern sequences

    3.4 Copies given pattern sequences

    3.5 Distinguishes various colors

(Affective Domain)

4.0 Participates in class discussions

    4.1 Answers questions

    4.2 Volunteers information

    4.3 Listens attentively

5.0 Cooperates in group activities

    5.1 Shares ideas with classmates

    5.2 Participates in group activity

    5.3 Helps others willingly

Table of Specifications: General Objectives

Cognitive Domain

Content	*Knows basic facts*	*Knows basic differences*	*Applies basic concepts*	
Colors	5	2	5	
Shapes	3	3	3	
Size	3		3	
Patterns			3	
Totals	11	5	14	30

Affective Domain

Content	*Participates in class discussions*	*Cooperates in group activities*
Colors		
Shapes	**Check the rating scale**	
Size		
Patterns		

Directions for Test of Visual Discrimination

PART I **(1.1)** and **(2.1)**

Section A

1. Give each child a packet of one-inch circles containing one of each of five colors: red, orange, blue, green, and yellow.
2. Supply paste for each child.
3. Give the following directions, allowing enough time for the child to complete work.
   a. Paste the red circle in box number 1.
   b. Paste the orange circle in box number 2.
   c. Paste the blue circle in box number 3.
   d. Paste the green circle in box number 4.
   e. Paste the yellow circle in box number 5.

Section B

In section B all the circles that are labeled a color will already be colored that particular color. The teacher instructs the children to place an X on one of the three circles that matches the circle in the box. Children use their crayons for this activity.

Section C

The children should each have five crayons, one of each color red, blue, yellow, orange, and green. Give the following directions:

a. Color the spoon blue.
b. Color the ball red.
c. Color the tub green.
d. Color the mitten orange.
e. Color the top yellow.

PART I

Section A   (**1.1, 2.1**)

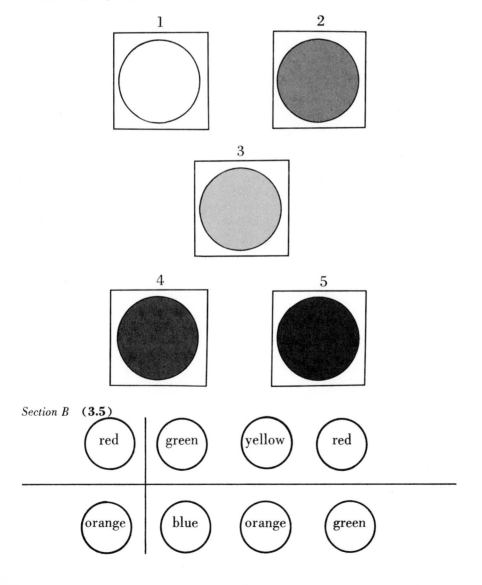

Section B   (**3.5**)

Section C   (**2.1, 3.5**)

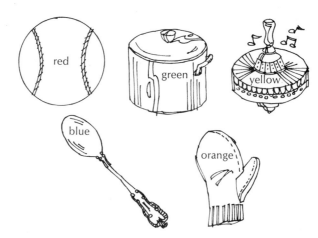

Directions (continued)

PART II

Section A   (**1.2**)

   Instruct the children as follows: Put your finger on the apple. Look at the first shape under it and find the one that looks like it under the grapes. Now take your crayon and draw a line from the shape under the apple to the one that looks like it under the grapes. (Do the same for the remaining shapes).

Section B   (**2.2**)

   Instruct the children: Put your finger on the candy cane and in that row find the shape that is different. Put an X on that shape with your crayon. (Do the same for the remaining rows).

Section C   (**3.1**)

   Instruct the children: (1) Draw a circle. (2) Draw a square. (3) Draw a triangle.

PART III

Section A   (**1.3, 3.2**)

1. Ask the children to put their names on the paper.
2. Ask, "What is in the first box?" (*Birds*)
   Then say, "Mark the LARGE bird with an X."
3. Use the same procedures for rows 2 and 3, alternating "small" and "large."

Section B   (**3.2**)

1. Ask the children to put their names on the paper.
2. Ask the children to look at the first box and name the object that is there. (Saw) "With your crayon, place an X on the saw in the row that is the same size as the one in the first box.
3. Use the same procedure for rows 5 and 6. (Repeat directions as needed)

PART IV

Section A   (**1.4, 3.3, 3.4**)

1. Demonstrate on the chalkboard the following visual patterns:

2. Have some children come to the board and continue the pattern.
3. Have children repeat the patterns on their paper.

PART II

Section A   (**1.2**)

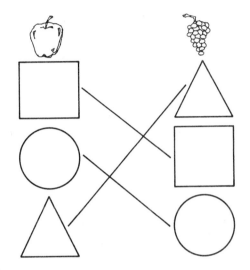

Section B   (**2.2**)

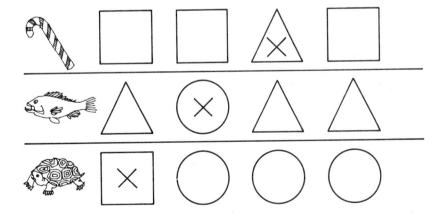

Section C   **(3.1)**

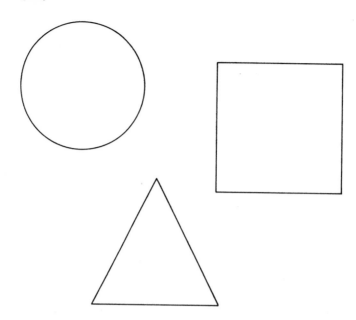

PART III
Section A   **(1.3, 3.2)**
Name _____

1.

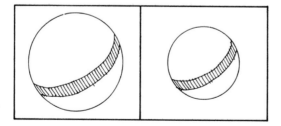

2.

3.

Section B   **(3.2)**

Name _____

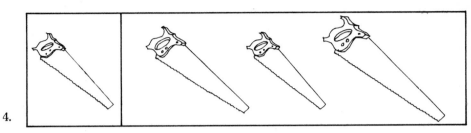

4.

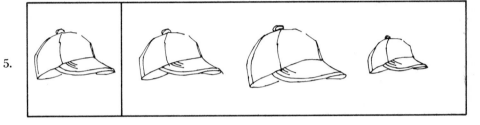

5.

6.

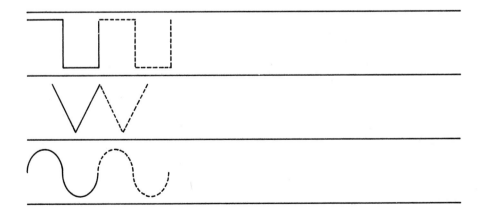

PART IV

Section A   **(1.4, 3.3, 3.4)**

Rating Scale for Evaluation of Group Activities

Name of Child _____

Objectives	Number of Observations	Scale
		1 2 3 4 5

(Affective Domain)
Answers questions (**4.1**)
Volunteers information (**4.2**)
Listen attentively (**4.3**)
Shares ideas with classmates (**5.1**)
Participates in group activities (**5.2**)
Helps others willingly (**5.3**)

Directions: Indicate the degree to which the child shows progress in achievement of each objective by recording the appropriate number. Numbers represent the following values: 5—outstanding, 4—above average, 3—average, 2—below average, and 1—unsatisfactory.

Additional Activities

1. Arrange on the floor several, varied shapes (triangles, squares, circles) representing the colors red, yellow, blue, and orange. Ask the children to follow various directions such as: (1) walk on the red triangle, (2) sit on the yellow square, (3) pick up the blue circle, etc. (**1.1**)

2. Use a blank filmstrip and arrange various shapes and colors in various sequences on the strip. Use several shapes and colors in various combinations. Ask the children to identify color, shape, and sequence. (**1.1, 1.2, 1.4**)

3. Use the basic idea of the game "Dominoes" and have the children match colors and shapes rather than dots. (**1.1, 1.2**)

4. Hold up a color and ask the children to identify those in the class who are wearing the color. (**1.1**)

5. Give each child a set of five colors. Play Simon Says—"Simon Says hold up your red color," etc. (**1.1**)

6. The teacher names a color. The children locate objects in the room that are that color. (**1.1**)

7. Using the different food groups, have children identify the colors of selected foods. (**1.1**)

8. Give each child one color or shape card. Give directions such as: "Red cards stand up, turn around, etc." (**1.1, 1.2**)

9. Play the fishing game. Cut large fish out of different colored construction paper. Place a steel paper clip on each fish and place in a container. Hook a magnet to the end of a "fishing pole" made out ofa small stick and string and let the children take turns fishing for a colored fish. When a child hooks a fish, he must identify its color. (**1.0**)

Instructional Aids Helpful in Achieving Objectives Related To This Unit
"*Fun and Felt*"

A flannel board toy which comes complete with a 16″ × 20″ flannelboard and more than 125 assorted felt cut-outs, including numbers, letters, birds, and assorted geometric shapes helps children learn about colors and shapes. Illustrated suggestion sheet is included.   (Instructo Educational Toys)

The "Hook 'N' Loop" Board
The Ohio Flock-Cote Company
5713 Euclid Avenue, Cleveland, Ohio 44103

Charles Mayer Studios, Inc.
776 Commins Street, Akron, Ohio 44307

Plastic "Take-Apart" Figures
   Walt Disney's Snap--eeze by Marx. Walt Disney Productions, Louis Marx and Company, Inc.

Instructional Books for Use by the Teacher
1. Ellis, Mary J., *Manipulative Language Arts*   (All Grades)   Includes suggestions for nonreading activities at the lower levels, guidance in development of reading readiness, concept enrichment, language activities, games, sequential thinking, motor activities, left-to-right direction, and work habits. Available from Teachers Publishing Corporation, Darien, Connecticut   06820.
2. Long, Paul E., *Teaching With the Flannelboard.* Available from Instructo Products Co., 1653 North 55th Street, Philadelphia, Pennsylvania.
3. Scott, Louis Binder, *Stories that Stick on the Flannelboard.* The Instructor Handbook Series available from F. A. Owen Publishing Co., Dansville, New York.

Selected References

1. Gronlund, Norman E., *Stating Behavioral Objectives for Class-Room Instruction* (N. Y.: Macmillan, 1970).
2. Shaw, Jules Harold, "Vision and Seeing Skills of Pre-School Children," *The Reading Teacher*, 18, No. 1 (October, 1964), pp. 35–36.
3. South Euclid-Lyndhurst City Schools, "A Guide for Perceptual-Motor Training— Activities in Kindergarten." (Department of Pupil Services, 1250 Professor Road, Cleveland, Ohio 44124).

Developing Skills in the Use of the Dictionary (Intermediate Grades)

Introduction:
Dictionary skills generally are not new to children at the intermediate levels of the elementary schools. Development of the skills into a more refined operation is usually correlated with practical experiences children gain from making reports and the like. At this point, the dictionary is important not only as a means of learning the pronunciation and meanings of words, but also as a tool for research. Evaluation of skills related to the use of the dictionary is the major focus of this unit, but the most important evaluation is an ongoing process from day to day where each individual applies the skills as the need arises.

Behavioral Objectives

1.0 Knows basic terms
    1.1 Identifies guide words
    1.2 Differentiates between synonyms, antonyms, and homonyms
    1.3 Differentiates between prefixes and suffixes
    1.4 Describes purpose of the pronunciation key
2.0 Understands use of the dictionary
    2.1 Aphabetizes lists of words
    2.2 Determines sections of the dictionary in which selected words are found
    2.3 Matches words and their abbreviations
    2.4 Selects appropriate definitions by context
    2.5 Locates entry words
    2.6 Pronounces new words according to diacritical markings
    2.7 Hyphenates words correctly
    2.8 Identifies part of speech of a word in context.
    2.9 Constructs sentences using words with respect to the appropriate definition
3.0 Appreciates use of the dictionary
    3.1 Answers questions voluntarily
    3.2 Asks pertinent questions
    3.3 Completes assigned work
    3.4 Relates comments to topic under discussion
    3.5 Cooperates in group work
    3.6 Explains value of the dictionary
    3.7 Identifies origin of specified English words

General Outline of Content

  I. Locations of words in the dictionary
    A Alphabetical order
    B. Guide words
    C. Entry words
    D. Parts of the dictionary
      1. A–H front
      2. I–P middle
      3. Q–Z back
  II. Aids in pronunciation
    A. Pronunciation key
    B. Diacritical markings
    C. Hyphenation
    D. Variant pronunciation
  III. Word meanings in the dictionary
    A. Multiple meanings
      1. Order of definitions
    B. Abbreviations
    C. Parts of speech
    D. Affixes
    E. Antonyms, homonyms, and synonyms
  IV. History
    A. Origins of words

Test on Dictionary Skills

1. Circle the guide words under which you would find the words on the left   (**1.1**)

    ghost   garden–gentle
    give–gossip
    gem–giraffe

    television   tea–teeth
    team–tonight
    trouble–twist

    smile   snap–soap
    slip–smash
    smell–smoke

2. Circle the words in each group that you would find on a page with the guide words at the top of each column.   (**1.1**)

    plane–plastic   *read–riding*

    play   rest
    plant   rock
    plate   reply
    planet   reach
    plank   really

3. Circle the (S) if the two words are synonyms. Circle the (A) if they are antonyms. Circle the (H) if they are homonyms.   (**1.2**)

    S A H   blue–blew
    S A H   courageous–brave
    S A H   sweet–sour
    S A H   explode–burst

4. Match the words in column A with the antonyms in column B.   (**1.2**)

Column A	*Column B*
＿＿ 1. cold	a. light
＿＿ 2. dark	b. happy
＿＿ 3. hard	c. hot
＿＿ 4. big	d. soft
＿＿ 5. sad	e. little
	f. huge

5. Match the words in column A with the synonyms in column B.   (**1.2**)

Column A	*Column B*
＿＿ 1. little	a. cheerful
＿＿ 2. bad	b. large
＿＿ 3. happy	c. wicked
＿＿ 4. big	d. small
	e. good

6. Draw one line under each prefix and two lines under each suffix in the following words: (**1.3**)

    jumping   manageable
    unfold   dependable
    impossible   enable
    uncover   lowest
    cheerful

7. Arrange the following words into alphabetical order by placing numbers from 1 to 5 in the blanks at the left. **(2.1)**

_____ a. munch

_____ b. mumps

_____ c. municipal

_____ d. mumble

_____ e. mummy

8. Indicate the part of the dictionary in which the following words are found. Use "F" for front, "M" for middle, and "B" for back. **(2.2)**

a. paste

b. baptize

c. knight

d. understand

9. Match the abbreviations in column A with the words they stand for in column B.

A	B
_____ 1. qt.	a. Rural Free Delivery
_____ 2. P. O.	b. quart
_____ 3. R. F. D.	c. Post Office
_____ 4. lb.	d. ounce
_____ 5. oz.	e. pound

10. Read each sentence below and notice the word in bold. Find that word among the entry words at the right. Write the number of the definition that has the same meaning as the **boldface** word on the left.   **(2.4)** **(2.5)**

_____ a. My mother attended the meeting of her sewing **club.**

_____ b. We fished from the **bank.**

_____ c. John hurt his **foot.**

_____ d. The noise seemed to **grate** on me.

bank (bangk),   1. ground bordering a river, lake, etc.   2. sloping an airplane to one side when making a turn.

club (klub),   1. a stick or bat used to hit a ball in some games; golf clubs. 2. A group of people joined together for a purpose: tennis club.

foot (fu̇t),   1. end part of a leg.   2. the lowest part, the base, the foot of a column, the foot of a hill.

grate (grāt),   1. have an unpleasant or annoying effect.   2. wear down or grind off in small pieces.

11. On the line at the left of column A, write the letter from column B that identifies the correct pronunciation for the words in column A. **(2.6)**

A	B
_____ 1. children	a. chīl′ dish
_____ 2. chilling	b. chick′ n
_____ 3. chicken	c. chil′ ē
	d. chil′ ing
	e. ski kān
	f. chil′ dren

12. Write each of the following words to show how it may be divided in writing.   **(2.7)**

a. character   _____

b. kangaroo   _____

c. satellite   _____

d. explanation   _____
e. however   _____
f. frontier   _____
g. receptive   _____

13. Write the part of speech of each boldface word.   (**2.8**)

_____ 1.   **Mary** went to the store for her mother.
_____ 2.   We saw three **yellow** birds.
_____ 3.   **We** will try to finish the job.
_____ 4.   John and Samuel **played** ball.

14. On the line following each definition, write a sentence using the word defined. (**2.9**)

a. *remedy:* something that cures a disease or disorder.

_____

b. *responsibility:* an assigned job or duty.

_____

c. *collide:* to come together with force.

_____

d. *offend:* to irritate or cause displeasure.

_____

e. *lag:* to move slowly; fall behind.

_____

f. *antic:* a silly trick or prank.

_____

g. *scour:* to clean or policy by rubbing.

_____

h. *envy:* desire for some advantage possessed by another.

_____

Rating Scale for Evaluation of Learner-Participation   (3.0)

(Indirect evaluation of appreciation)

Directions: Rate each individual on the following characteristics by placing an X where appropriate along the horizontal line.

1. To what extent does the individual answer questions voluntarily?   (**3.1**)

never   as often as   more than
                     most others in   others in
                     the group   the group

Comment:

2. To what extent does the individual ask questions? (**3.2**)

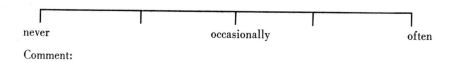

never   occasionally   often

Comment:

3. To what extent are the individual's questions related to the topic being discussed?
(**3.2**)

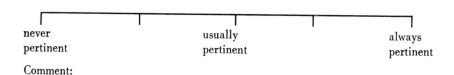

never   usually   always
pertinent   pertinent   pertinent

Comment:

4. To what extent does the individual complete assigned work? (**3.3**)

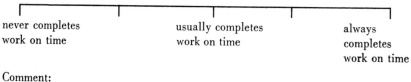

never completes   usually completes   always
work on time   work on time   completes
                                                    work on time

Comment:

5. To what extent does the individual cooperate in group activities? (**3.5**)

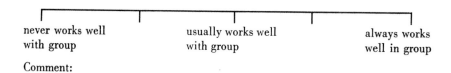

never works well   usually works well   always works
with group   with group   well in group

Comment:

INDEX

Accountability, educational, 231; as an attitude, 3, 4; as cost effectiveness, 4, 5; basic tenets of, 1; constraints facing teachers, 8; factors influencing, 5; implications for the teacher, 6; limitations, 6; linked with a system approach, 4; nature of, 3; of teachers, 10

Achievement, 3, 229

Achievement test, 28, 299

Affective behavior: informal assessment, 42; objectives, 11

Allen, James E., Jr., 88

Allophone: meaning, 197

Anderson, Paul S., 171

Anderson, Robert H., 92

Anecdotal record, 151

Approaches to initial reading instruction, 184

Attitudes and interests, reading: components of humanistic education, 13; teachers' influence on development, 128; improving attitudes toward reading, 174

Auckerman, Robert C., 88

Auditory: blending, 183; discrimination, 172, 176

Austin, Mary C., 86, 92

Baker, Eva L., 65

Balow, Irving H., 83

Bamman, Henry A., 218

Bank Street Readers, 109

Barbe, Walter B., 86, 87, 205, 214

Barnhart, Clarence, 195

Barr, Donald, 6

Bartolome, P. I., 220

Basal Reader: approaches, 104; test characteristics, 147

Benne, Kenneth O., 117

Betts, E. A., 26

Bills, Robert E., 60

Bishop, Lloyd K., 91

Blaine, Nelson Lee, 71

Bloom, Benjamin S., 206

Bloomfield, Leonard, 195

Bloom's Taxonomy of Educational Objectives, 72

Bond, Guy L., 217

Botel Reading Inventory, 41

Building Reading Power Programs, 99

279

Buros Mental Measurements
   Yearbooks, 149
Burr, Marvin Y., 91

California Achievement Tests, 36
California Reading Tests, 38
Carillo, L. W., 209
Challenger Books, 109
Checklists, 153
Children's reading interests, 119
Clasen, Robert Earl, 25
Classroom Reading Inventory (CRI), 40
Cleland, Donald P., 207
Cloze Procedure: description, 46; uses, 46
Cohen, Arthur M., 66
Combs, Arthur W., 11, 12, 66, 115, 117
Competencies required for teachers: for
   determining objectives of reading
   instruction, 75; for individualizing
   reading instruction, 109; for need
   assessment, 49; for fostering
   development of affective behaviors, 132;
   for evaluation of reading achievement,
   157; for developing skills and abilities
   in word recognition, 197; for developing
   skills of comprehension, 223
Competency, 229
Comprehension, reading: definitions, 204,
   205; evidence of, 215; factors in, 207;
   instructional procedures, 217; levels,
   212; relationships among levels, 213;
   relationships between reading
   comprehension and thinking skills, 206;
   specific skills, 214, 243, 255; teacher's
   role in development, 213
Configuration, 186
Context: as a word-recognition skill, 194;
   contextual clues, 183
Contract teaching, 230
Cook, Walter W., 83
Cost effectiveness, 4, 230
Cottrell, Donald P., 10
Criterion, 230
Criterion-referenced measures, 148, 230
Croft and Hess, *An Activities Handbook
   for Teachers of Young Children,* 63
Crosby, Muriel, 118

Curtin, James, 83

Dallmann, Martha, 212
Davidson, H. H., 211
Dawson, Mildred, 206, 218
DeBoer, John, 212
Decode: meaning, 196
Dewey, John, 117, 119
Dictionary Skills, 271
Dolch, Edward W., 104
Durkin, Dolores, 170, 205, 214
Durrell Analysis of Reading Difficulty, 39

"Early to Read" I/T/A Program, 63
E. D. L.: Listen and Read Programs, 100;
   Study Skills Library, 100
Emans, Robert, 121
Empathy, role in reading, 129
Enthusiasm, role in reading, 129
Evaluation in reading instruction:
   meaning, 138; as a process, 139; function
   of objectives, 139; principles, 140
Experiential background of learners, 176

Farr, Roger, 147
Figurel, J. A., 209
Fitzgerald, James A., 167
Fitzgerald, Patricia, 167
Formal measures of reading abilities, 38
Frazier, Alexander, 89
Fries, Charles C., 196
Frostig Test of Visual Perception, 34

Gates-MacGinitie Reading Tests, 32, 37
Gates-McKillop Reading Diagnostic Tests,
   39
Gilmore Oral Reading Test, 41
Goldberg, Lynn, 197
Goodlad, John I., 92
Gottmann, John Mordechai, 25
Grade-equivalent score, 145, 231
Gray Oral Reading Test, 42
Gray, William S., 166
Gronlund, Norman E., 59, 64, 141

Grouping within classrooms, 92
Guided reading, 219
Guilford, J. P., 207
Guszak, Frank J., 220

Hafner, Lawrence E., 64
Hamerchek, Don E., 211
Harris, Albert J., 167, 205
Harris, Dale B., 119
Harris, Larry A., 28, 166, 205, 208, 212
Harrison-Stroud Reading Readiness Profiles, 32
Harvey, Lois F., 93
Heilman, Arthur W., 89, 171
Henderson, E. H., 209
Henderson, Judith P., 25
Herber, Harold L., 216
Highet, Gilbert, 14, 15
Hildreth, Gertrude, 29, 167
Hilgard, Ernest P., 56
Holmes, Darrell, 93
Homework assignments, 128
Humanistic education, 231; attitudes and interests in reading, 13; concerns in reading instruction, 117; focus, 11
Hunkins, F. P., 220
Huus, Helen, 120

Illich, Ivan, 6
Independent reading, 127
Individual differences: in abilities and achievement, 83; in experiential and cultural backgrounds, 84; in favored learning modality, 85. Also, see *Similarities among learners*.
Individualized instruction, 231
Individualized reading instruction: arranging instructional materials, 94; arranging learning spaces, 95; conventional approaches, 90; effective teaching as a means of, 92; importance in educational accountability, 8; meaning, 86; necessity for, 82; planning, 93; principles, 88; problems, 87; strategies and materials, 97; teachers' accountability for, 13; using approaches

to reading instruction, 104
Informal assessment: of affective behaviors, 42; of skills and abilities in reading, 43
Informal reading inventory, 44; materials, 45; procedures, 46; teacher-constructed, 46
Initial reading instruction, 184
Initial reading skills, 238, 240
Instructional Objectives Exchange, 65
Intellectual climate of classroom, 124
Interests and attitudes: development of readiness, 121; specific activities and techniques for development, 130
Interests, nature of, 119
Interviews, 156
Iowa Every-Pupil Tests of Basic Skills, 36

Jefferson, Benjamin F., 120
Jersild, Arthur T., 118
Johns, Jerry L., 121
Johnson, Margaret Seddon, 44, 45
Jolly, Hayden B., 64
Jones, Daisy M., 93
Joyce, Bruce R., 214
Justman, Joseph, 83

Kaplan, Sandra Nina, 103
Karlin, Robert, 127, 166, 217
Kellogg, Ralph E., 171
Kerfoot, J. F., 206
King, Ethal M., 120
Kranyik, Robert, 127, 221
Krathwohl's Taxonomy of Educational Objectives, 73
Kress, Roy A., 44, 45

Lang, G., 211
Language development, 172, 175
Language-experience approach, 105
Lanier, Perry E., 25
Lasnik, Len, 171
Learners: needs, 12; concepts of reading, 170, 174
Learning center, 232

Learning stations, 103
Lee-Clark Reading Readiness Test, 32
Lee-Clark Reading Test, 38
Lee, Dorris M., 88
Lessinger, Leon, 3
Lessons for Self-Instruction in Basic Skills, 99
Levels of reading performance, 45; criteria for determining, 45
Linguistics: influences, 195; approaches to reading, 197
Listening ability, 171, 261
Location skills, 222

Mager, Robert F., 57
Marks, James R., 10
McCullough, Constance, 26, 195
McDonald, A. S., 209
McGovern, James J., 218
McNemar, Quinn, 83
Measurement: in accountability, 141; characteristics of measurement techniques, 141; types of results obtainable, 143
Merrill, M. David, 71
Metropolitan Achievement Tests, 37
Metropolitan Readiness Tests, 33
Modular learning, 232
Modules, 101
Morrison, Coleman, 86, 92
Muntyan, Bozidar, 117
Murphy-Durrell Reading Readiness Analysis, 33
Mussen, Paul H., 56

National Assessment of Educational Progress, 5
Need: definition, 25
Need assessment: application in reading instruction, 7; basis for individualizing instruction, 24; determinant of instructional procedures, 24; importance in educational accountability, 7; importance in reading instruction, 23; in the classroom, 27; meaning, 25; planning for, 28; problems, 48; procedures and materials, 26, 34;

relation to diagnosis and evaluation, 47, 48
Norm-referenced tests, 149, 232
Norvell, G. W., 120

Objectives, behavioral, 1: affective objectives, 11; in affective domain, 71; determination, 13; general and specific, 58; how to state, 68; influence on scope of instruction, 66; tangible and measurable, 7
Objectives for reading instruction, 54: criteria for selecting or deriving, 65; determination, 65; how to state, 68; nature of, 56; roles in instruction, 59; sources of, 61; stated and unstated, 59
Observational techniques, 43, 151
Observing and recording information, 43
Olson, Willard C., 86
Oral reading: and comprehension, 217; in audience situations, 218; for diagnosis, 218; as part of guided reading, 218
Oral reading tests, 41

Peabody Rebus Reading Program, 99
Phoneme, 196
Phonetics, 187
Phonic elements and patterns, 181; techniques for introducing to learners, 182
Phonics instruction: guidelines, 191
Phonics skills, 187, 188, 189
Planning, 28
Pratt, Edward, 208
Professional journals, 150
Programmed instructional materials, 98

Questioning Strategies, 220
Questionnaires, 157

Rankin, E. F., 209
Rating scales, 154
Reading: authorities' definitions, 165; nature, 165; skills, primary level, 245; in content areas, 126; developmental nature, 185
Reading Behaviors Checklist, 155

Reading Readiness: activities used in development, 174; assessing needs related to, 29; developmental, 179; development of, 168; factors influencing, 29, 170; for initial reading instruction, 168

Reading Readiness Tests: characteristics, 31; skills and abilities measured, 31

Reading survey tests, 38; limitations, 38

Reasoner, Charles F., 216

Rasmussen, Donald, 197

Rinsland, Henry, 104

Robinson, Helen M., 212

Ruddell, R. B., 208

Schatz, Esther E., 89

School-wide grouping plans, 90

Sequential Tests of Educational Progress (STEP), 36

Shankman, Florence V., 127, 221

Sharing periods and reading, 126

Shaw, Phillip, 212

Sheldon, W. D., 209

Sight vocabulary, 178: continuous development, 178; basic concern during initial reading instruction, 180; techniques of development, 180, 181

Silberman, Charles E., 6

Silvaroli, Nicholas J., 40

Similarities among learners, 85

Sipay, Edward R., 205

Slingerland Screening Tests, 34

Smith, Carl B., 28, 166, 205, 208, 212

Smith, Helen K., 209

Social climate of classroom, 124

Spache, Evelyn B., 29, 205, 214

Spache, George D., 29, 205, 214

Standardized tests: administration, 35; advantages and limitations, 147; characteristics, 144; criteria for selection, 35, 145

Stanford Diagnostic Reading Test, 39

Stauffer, Russell G., 219

Stoops, Emery, 10

Strang, Ruth, 166, 208

Structural Analysis Skills: in beginning reading, 184; meaning, 192; specific content, 192, 193; sequence for development, 194; skills, 192

Study skills, 221, 222

Survey tests, 37

Swenson, Esther J., 15

Syllabication, 189

Tanner, Daniel, 67

Tasch, Ruth J., 118

Test information, 149

Test Publishers' Catalogs, 150

Thorndike, Edward L., 118

Tinker, Miles A., 26

Townsend, Agatha, 216

Travers, John F., 60

Travers, M. W., 56

Traxler, Arthur E., 216

Turner, Harold E., 117

Unruh, Adolph, 117

Utterback, Roberta, 89

Veatch, Jeannette, 86

Visual discrimination, 263; developing skills in, 175

Visual Symbol Environment Program, 101

Wagner, Eva Bond, 217

Wallen, Carl J., 64, 167

Wepman Auditory Discrimination Test, 33

Willsberg, Mary E., 89

Wilson, Robert M., 28

Wolfson, Bernice J., 120

Word-recognition Skills, 255: application of phonics skills, 187; basic skills involved, 186; initial development, 179